The Courthouse Square in Texas

Number Two
Clifton and Shirley Caldwell Texas Heritage Series

The Courthouse Square in Texas

ROBERT E. VESELKA

Edited by Kenneth E. Foote

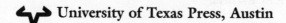 University of Texas Press, Austin

Publication of this work was made possible in part by support
from Clifton and Shirley Caldwell and a challenge grant from
the National Endowment for the Humanities.

First edition, 2000

Requests for permission to reproduce material from this work
should be sent to Permissions, University of Texas Press,
Box 7819, Austin, TX 78713-7819.

∞ The paper used in this book meets the minimum
requirements of ANSI/NISO Z39.48-1992 (R1997)
(Permanence of Paper).

LIBRARY OF CONGRESS
CATALOGING-IN-PUBLICATION DATA

Veselka, Robert E.
The courthouse square in Texas / Robert E. Veselka ;
edited by Kenneth E. Foote.— 1st ed.
p.   cm.
Includes bibliographical references and index.

ISBN 978-0-292-78736-0

1. Courthouses—Texas—History.   2. Plazas—Texas—
History.   3. Texas—History, Local.   4. Texas—Historical
geography.   5. Texas—Social life and customs.   6. City and
town life—Texas—History.   7. Courthouses—Texas—
Design and construction—History.   8. Plazas—Texas—
Design and construction—History.   9. City planning—
Texas—History.   10. Human geography— Texas.
1. Foote, Kenneth E., 1955-   11. Title.
F387 .V47   2000
976.4—dc21   99-050684

Contents

Contents

Figures

Figures

Tables

Tables

Foreword

This book is based on the doctoral dissertation of Dr. Robert E. Veselka. Robert completed the manuscript in August 1993 and had begun to prepare it for publication when he died in Austin in January 1994. Shortly before his death, I assured Robert that I would continue his work and see the manuscript into print. I think he would be pleased with the result and to know that he will be remembered for this fine contribution to Texas scholarship.

I can think of few scholars better suited to their subject than Robert was to the topic of the courthouse square in Texas. He was a native Texan with a deep and abiding love for the state's architecture, landscape, and history. His education at the University of Texas at Austin in anthropology (B.A.), architecture (M.A.), and geography (Ph.D.) was perfectly matched by his interest in the social and cultural roles of architecture and urban design. And, for twenty years, Robert maintained his own highly successful building firm specializing in architectural restoration and renovation. Robert brought all of these interests and experiences to bear on his study of Texas courthouse squares with the same care and thoughtfulness he applied to all of his endeavors.

Robert will be remembered as a gifted, gentle, and compassionate man, but also for his generosity. One of Robert's bequests was to endow a travel scholarship for geography and architecture students at the University of Texas. It has been a tremendous honor for me to help award these scholarships over the past several years. I know how much Robert valued travel and fieldwork, and it is wonderful to see the difference these funds have made to the work of so many students in my department. The bequest was particularly poignant for me because my friendship with Robert began not in Austin but in Oxford in 1985, when he enrolled in a summer program I was leading on English landscape history. I shall always remember the many hours that Robert and I spent comparing notes on travel, on architecture, and on the landscapes of Texas and the world.

Robert's death was a tremendous loss to his family and all of us who were his friends. While we grieve at Robert's passing, we are glad to have known him, and we can take comfort and pride in what he has left behind.

I am indebted to Karl Butzer, Kirsten Connelly, Shannon Crum, Shannon Davies, Richard Francaviglia, Terry Jordan-Bychkov, Damon Scott, and Isobel Stevenson for their help in preparing this book for publication.

Kenneth E. Foote
Austin, Texas

The Courthouse Square in Texas

Chapter One

The Courthouse Square in Texas

The county seat exemplifies one of the more self-conscious expressions of American urban design, both spatially and symbolically. The courthouse square was designed explicitly to express community values and to serve as a focal point of community life. Through time, the square often assumed even greater importance as a symbol of a town's social, political, and economic prosperity. For these reasons, the courthouse square offers an interesting window on American town planning traditions and the relationships between these traditions and the social meaning of civic space. Town planning, land use, social activity, and architectural symbolism are interwoven at the square in ways matched by few other elements of American urban design (Figure 1).

Texas, perhaps more than any other state, offers unparalleled opportunities for considering these relationships. The state is divided into 254 counties that range across diverse cultural and physical landscapes (Appendix 1). As the second most populous state in the nation, Texas provides an urban landscape ranging from small towns to major metropolitan areas. Due to its size and period of settlement, Texas reflects many of the same forces that shaped the American urban landscape at large, including a variety of competing town planning traditions, different notions of local government, and complex interactions among diverse cultural groups. As a result of this diverse settlement history, Texas is the only state that employs all major survey and land tenure systems found in the United States, including long-lots, metes and bounds, its own township-and-range system, and irregular rectangular surveys (Arbingast

1

Figure 1 Aerial view of Denton, Denton County, in 1925. This photo illustrates a central courthouse square that serves as the community's main focus. Note the grid pattern, concentration of commerce at the square, and dominance of the townscape by the courthouse.

et al. 1976). In addition, Texas is also the only state in the union to have retained ownership of its vast public lands, a significant factor in the state's settlement and later development (McKitrick 1918, 7).

During Texas' primary period of settlement in the nineteenth and early twentieth centuries, rapid expansion in population and town building led to the increasing importance of county government. Many counties erected elegant and symbolic buildings on their squares. Since many Texas towns were planned and settled during a period of widespread urbanization in America, they provide valuable insight into urbanization and planning processes in a broader national context. In the use of open plazas, some county seats still bear the stamp of early Hispanic influence or the mark of Central European settlers. Others reflect the dominance of Anglo-American planning traditions that favored a central courthouse square. This legacy of diverse cultural elements during a formative period of expanding settlement and the concomitant planning and building of numerous county seats makes the Texas courthouse square so valuable for investigation.

To explore these issues, this study begins by describing the urban morphology of the state's 254 county seats in terms of block patterns and town planning traditions. Then it examines explicit linkages between built form and social meaning by considering land uses, symbolic features, and social activities concentrated at the courthouse square. These lines of analysis lead to a broader appreciation of the role of the courthouse square in community life, one stressing the centripetal power of the square to attract specific land uses, activities, and civic functions. Just as important, however, are centrifugal factors such as changing economic conditions and population growth that have altered or diminished the square's influence through time. This study benefits from previous research on the courthouse square and, in return, offers the first complete classification of Texas' courthouse squares, including the description of patterns never before discussed in the literature. It departs from previous studies in both scale and focus as well as in its desire to call attention to important connections between civic space and a community's sense of identity. After all, the courthouse square offers an unparalleled opportunity to study how early decisions about urban design shape landscapes and human activity for generations. To set the context for interpretation, it is useful to consider previous studies of courthouse squares and town planning traditions and the settlement history, cultural landscape, urban development, and land policy of Texas.

PERSPECTIVES

Albert Demangeon once wrote, "It is permissible to say that the entire history of civilization is reflected in present forms of human establishments" (Demangeon 1962, 506). The geographical perspective adopted in this research subscribes to this view as it has come to be expressed in four interrelated themes in the geographic literature: (1) study of urban morphology and planning; (2) fascination with the landscape as offering clues to the diffusion of cultural groups; (3) concern for the symbolic or social meaning of urban landscapes; and (4) interest in the courthouse square as a uniquely American landscape form. All four themes are addressed in this study, but it is the last that serves as its starting point.

Scholars have long been interested in the architectural and historical significance of the courthouses of individual states (Radoff 1960; Brasseaux, Conrad, and Robinson 1977; Johnson and Andrist 1977; Pare 1978; Santos 1979; Whisenhunt 1979; Jackson 1980; Jordan and Puster 1984; Peet, Keller, and Brink 1984; Perry 1984; Peveto 1984; Hines 1986). Other studies have focused on the courthouse as an important American building type (Handler 1983) and on the competition that took place among towns vying for county seats (Schellenberg 1987). A number of studies have combined architectural analysis of the courthouse proper with concern for the square's physical form (Robinson 1972; Burns 1978). Noting the importance of this relationship, one research team concluded that "the physical prominence and visibility of the courthouse site is crucial in endowing the courthouse itself with significance" (Burns 1978, 84). Studies in Texas have varied greatly in scope and subject, including collections of county histories, photographic essays on courthouses, studies of squares, histories of architectural styles, and analyses of how county seats were selected (Carroll 1943; Coursey 1962; Anderson 1968; Price 1968; Goeldner 1971; Chipley 1985; Jackson 1996).

Of those studies that have focused specifically on the square itself, it is fair to say that their primary interest has been in what has been termed the "central courthouse square" (Pillsbury 1968; Price 1968; Francaviglia 1973; Ohman 1982). This was an idea developed by E. T. Price (1968) in his influential study of the spread of the courthouse square from Pennsylvania to Texas. Central squares were characterized by a prominent courthouse set in a parklike central block created by streets converging on the square and surrounded by a town's major business district (Price 1968, 29). Price was one of the first to attempt a classification scheme for major prototypes, and his terminology is still used by researchers today.

Two interesting studies that included Texas county seats were based on Price's original classification of central courthouse squares. One interdisciplinary project analyzed squares in Kansas, Oklahoma, Texas, Missouri, and Arkansas. That study surveyed 137 county seats in Texas and identified 73 central courthouse squares (Aikins et al. 1971). In addition, the researchers conducted interviews with local residents that allowed them to identify over one hundred features that influence a square's use and role. The depth of information collected was impressive, but only ten Texas squares were studied in detail. The results of this research suggested clear connections between courthouse architecture, urban morphology, and a central focus on the square. T. G. Jordan (Arbingast et al. 1976, 42) conducted a far more extensive survey of Texas courthouse squares that concentrated exclusively on central squares. Jordan's work considerably expanded the available information for Texas. His study located 136 "traditional" squares, so-called because they were based on known prototypes of central courthouse squares. He found another 64 county seats to be "lacking a true courthouse square"—that is, they did not fit the traditional patterns identified by Price. A group of 54 county seats was listed as "undetermined" due to lack of data, and a further 19 were described as "uncertain" (Arbingast et al. 1976, 42).

Together these studies resulted in the classification of roughly half of the state's county seats. As many as 137 sites remained unclassified or unconfirmed. Because these previous studies targeted traditional central courthouse squares, very little attention focused on squares derived from other planning traditions. The present work serves to redress this situation by studying all 254 Texas county seats. Archival research and site visits to 139 county seats were used to collect data on town plans as well as to gather information on courthouse architecture and on social activities, monuments, and memorials located at the square.

This book employs the nomenclature of earlier courthouse square studies where possible, but develops new terms to identify previously undescribed patterns found in Texas. It also diverges from previous studies that used the courthouse squares primarily as an index of cultural diffusion. Although the main objective of the present study is to classify the state's county seats, it cannot overlook the centripetal role played by the square in civic life as well as its social and symbolic significance. Many squares remain the central focus of their communities, while the importance of others has eroded through time. The question of how and why this has occurred lies at the heart of this book. As case studies of how urban design is used to represent, reinforce, and sustain the ideals and identity of a community, courthouse squares offer insight into the past, present, and future of the Texas landscape. To begin, it is useful to set the courthouse square in the context of the overall settlement history of Texas and the emergence of the state's cultural and urban landscape.

SETTLEMENT HISTORY

The first European settlers in Texas were the Spanish, who occupied towns beginning in the 1730s; but these settlements remained small and few. Texas in 1803 contained only three active civil settlements: San Antonio (Béxar) with a population of 2,500; Nacogdoches with 770 people; and Goliad (Bahía) with 618 inhabitants (Hatcher 1927, 67). By 1820 these numbers had declined to around 800 persons each in Béxar and Bahía. Nacogdoches was all but abandoned, with only ten families reported in the area (Hatcher 1927, 355–356).

The number of towns increased under Mexico's *empresario* program, but by the time of Texas independence in 1836 there were only about a dozen communities. The vast majority of Texans lived in rural settings, so town populations remained small. Estimates of Texas' population in 1820 placed the number around 4,000, which climbed to 25,000 by 1836 (Wheeler 1968, 16).

After independence in 1836, settlers encouraged by land grants and new opportunities migrated in increasing numbers. Most of these were Anglos. However, Hispanics and African-Americans also inhabited the Republic, along with groups of Europeans. Following statehood the total population in 1850 was 215,700: 57 percent Anglo-Americans, 6.5 percent Hispanics, 27 percent African-Americans, and 7.5 percent Europeans (Jordan 1986, 418).

In terms of growth rates, Texas witnessed dramatic change as soon as it was opened to settlement by Mexico in 1821. From that year to annexation in 1845, the population exploded by almost 2,000 percent (Harris 1972, 2). As a state, Texas saw its greatest increase between 1850 and 1860, when the population increased by 184.2 percent, from 212,592 to 604,215 (Harris 1972, 54).

Another large percentage gain occurred from 1870 to 1880, when the population went from 818,579 to 1,591,749, an increase of 94.5 percent (Harris 1972, 54). In 1887 Texas' population exceeded 2 million, of which 64 percent were Anglo-American, 4 percent Hispanic, 20 percent African-American, and 11 percent European (Jordan 1986, 418). These figures indicated strengthening Anglo-American and European presence at the expense of Hispanics and African-Americans during the years 1850 to 1887. The proportion of Hispanics to African-Americans increased drastically in the twentieth century, reversing the trend of the previous century.

The primary source of population increase in Texas during these periods was migration (Table 1). The decades with the greatest immigration include 1870 to 1880, when more than 308,500 entered the state, and 1920 to 1930, when 243,500 immigrated. Figures of that magnitude were not surpassed until the 1970s and 1980s (Davies 1986, 522). There have been only two periods of net loss in migration: 1930 to 1940 and 1955 to 1960 (Davies 1986, 521).

The average rate of increase for the twelve decades from 1860 to 1980 has been 31.5 percent for each census period (Harris 1972, 54; Davies 1986, 498; see Table 2). In 1990 the population of Texas was almost 17,000,000. In that same census year the Hispanic population stood at 26 percent of the state's total, while African-Americans constituted only 12 percent. In addition, British-descended Anglo-Americans lost their majority status, dropping to 45 percent in 1980 (Jordan 1986, 418). Interestingly, the European proportion of 12 percent in 1980 nearly echoed the 11 percent of 1887 (Jordan 1986, 418). In absolute terms, growth in the current century has been significant, especially with respect to urban development. Yet it was nineteenth-century settlement that formed many of the patterns of the cultural and urban landscape in Texas.

Table 1. Net Migration to Texas, 1870–1985

PERIOD	MIGRATION
1870–1880	308,500
1880–1890	151,200
1890–1900	147,700
1900–1910	131,100
1910–1920	114,300
1920–1930	243,500
1930–1940	-72,800
1940–1950	132,900
1950–1960	172,500
1960–1970	198,400
1970–1980	1,428,800
1980–1985	1,107,400

Source: Davies 1986, 522.

The Courthouse Square in Texas

Table 2. Texas Population; 1850–1990
(Showing Change in Total Population and Urban Population)

YEAR	POPULATION	INCREASE	%	URBAN	%
1850	212,592			7,665	3.6
1860	604,215	391,623	184.2	26,615	4.4
1870	818,579	214,364	35.5	54,521	6.7
1880	1,591,749	773,170	94.5	146,795	9.2
1890	2,235,527	643,778	40.4	349,511	15.6
1900	3,048,710	813,183	36.4	520,759	17.1
1910	3,896,542	847,832	27.8	938,104	24.1
1920	4,663,228	766,686	19.7	1,512,689	32.4
1930	5,824,715	1,161,487	24.9	2,389,348	41.0
1940	6,414,824	590,109	10.1	2,911,389	45.4
1950	7,711,194	1,296,370	20.2	4,838,060	62.7
1960	9,579,677	1,868,483	24.2	7,187,470	75.0
1970	11,196,730	1,617,053	16.9	8,920,946	79.7
1980	14,229,191*	3,032,461*	27.1*	11,383,360**	80.0**
1990	16,986,510*	2,757,319*	19.4*	13,860,992*	81.6*

*Figures from 1992–1993 *Texas Almanac.*
**Figures from other sources are approximated.
  Source: Harris 1972, 54.

THE CULTURAL LANDSCAPE

The cultural landscape of Texas is one of diversity and change, yet persistent patterns reveal linkages between material culture, social custom, and urban form. Two cultural geographers, in separate but related studies, traced the cultural imprint of various Anglo-American groups along with Hispanics and Germans. Both D. W. Meinig (1969) and T. G. Jordan (1967) have published maps describing these culture areas in Texas (Figure 2).

Jordan's study was based upon patterns of nineteenth-century rural material culture as well as mid-twentieth-century town plans. He determined the influence of six subcultures: Midwestern, Lower Southern, Upper Southern, Spanish-Mexican, German, and Mixed.

Jordan characterized the Lower Southern subculture, located in east Texas and along the upper Gulf coast, in terms of three subgroups. A plantation culture in east Texas was composed mainly of an Anglo aristocracy transported from Alabama, Georgia, and Mississippi and a large African-American population. A more concentrated area was made up of "poor whites" and a few African-Americans. A third region occupied the coastal plains. It, too, was based upon a plantation economy, but in this case derived from the Louisiana area.

The Upper Southern subculture was also divided into three subgroups. The northeastern part of the state consisted of an area of middle-class Anglo-Americans who came to Texas from Tennessee, Missouri, Kentucky, Arkansas, and southern Illinois. More centrally located was an area populated by "poor whites" from Appalachia and the

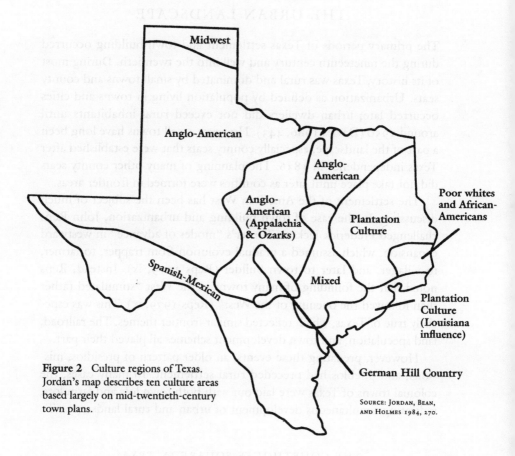

Figure 2 Culture regions of Texas. Jordan's map describes ten culture areas based largely on mid-twentieth-century town plans.

9

Ozarks. In west Texas an area of farming and ranching was composed of Anglos who originally inhabited the eastern part of the state.

In southwestern Texas Jordan found a large borderland of underlying Spanish-Mexican influence. He also noted a small area of Midwestern influence in the extreme north of the Panhandle and a small area of persistent German culture in the Hill Country. A final area located in central Texas was characterized by a mix of Europeans, including Germans, Czechs, Scandinavians, Wends, and Poles (Jordan, Bean, and Holmes 1984, 270).

These patterns have proven to be somewhat durable in terms of reported ancestry as recently as 1980 (Jordan 1986, 391). The customs practiced by these groups contributed directly to the urban landscape and built form of Texas towns and county seats.

THE URBAN LANDSCAPE

The primary periods of Texas settlement and town building occurred during the nineteenth century and well into the twentieth. During most of its history, Texas was rural and dominated by small towns and county seats. Urbanization as defined by population living in towns and cities occurred late; urban dwellers did not exceed rural inhabitants until around 1950 (Davies 1986, 443). However, small towns have long been a part of the landscape, especially county seats that were established after Texas independence in 1836. The planning of many other county seats did not take place until later as counties were formed in frontier areas.

The settlement of the American West has been the subject of much discussion. In the case of town building and urbanization, John Reps challenged Frederick Jackson Turner's "modes of advance" in westward expansion, which assumed a gradual evolution from trapper, to farmer, to villager, and later to town builder (Reps 1979, ix). Instead, Reps noted that the founding of many towns in the West "stimulated rather than followed the opening of the West" (Reps 1979, ix). This was especially true of Texas, which reflected similar frontier themes. The railroad, land speculation, and town development schemes all played their part.

However, predating these events, an older pattern of presidios, missions, and pueblos had preceded rural settlement. In many cases, the colonial towns of Texas were laid out with both town lots and farm lots, indicating simultaneous development of urban and rural landscapes. To be sure, towns did follow farming or ranching interests, such as Laredo and other towns along the Rio Grande that were founded by local ranchers and land owners; but many Texas towns were newly etched lines in the frontier landscape. Reps reiterated this point and quoted an observer of Texas in 1837:

> a mania for towns is characteristic of all new countries and is especially so here. Many enterprising men have gone to Texas to seize upon the advantages which a new country affords to acquire wealth, and many of these have some city in prospect as the speediest means to effect their object. Should they all succeed, they will no doubt at someday make Texas as famous for her cities as Thebes was for her hundred gates. (Reps 1979, 134)

Unlike Turner's basic premise of evolving phases of settlement, urban development in Texas was characterized by "episodic" changes rather than gradual growth (Davies 1986, 450). Such episodes would reflect periods of great immigration as well as developments in economies, transportation, and land policies. During the nineteenth century, large-scale immigration and widespread town building were concomitant factors in the settlement of Texas. "Texas' urban history," one scholar noted, "is the history of small towns" (Davies 1986, 484).

Spanish and Mexican land grants resulted in a tenuous urban landscape. These included the Spanish-founded towns at San Antonio, Goliad, and Nacogdoches. Another dozen or so small towns were established under Mexico's rule, such as Gonzales and San Felipe de Austin. However, most of the urban landscape in Texas resulted from rapid Anglo-American immigration following independence and statehood. Reps described the period:

> It was an era of massive change in the pattern of town location, planning, and development. Uniform laws governing town design were eliminated; individual town site promoters now decided these matters. Some of the older towns, badly damaged during the Texas revolution, either vanished or lost their initial impetus for growth. (Reps 1979, 127)

Indeed, towns such as San Felipe de Austin, Harrisburg, and Gonzales had been destroyed during battles with Mexico. Places like Gonzales would recover; the other two would not. In all of this the county seat played an important role, both in recording the impress of diverse cultural groups and in creating a distinctive signature on the Texas cultural and urban landscapes.

Chapter Two

From Land Policy to County Seats
and Squares

The role of the county seat and courthouse square in Texas is deeply en-twined with the history of and laws governing the formation of counties and the establishment of county seats. From colonial times to its days as a Republic and eventual annexation as a state of the union, Texas fol-lowed a remarkable course of events with regard to its use of public lands. In the case of land policy, Texas is indebted to both Spanish and Mexican practices, as well as Anglo-American traditions that were de-rived from English common law. Perhaps equally reflective of Anglo-American influence was development of the land through the founding of towns and creation of counties and county seats. Underlying all of these is one fundamental fact—the land.

Myths notwithstanding, the abundance of land, public land in partic-ular, shaped both reality and fiction in Texas. When Texas entered the union, it was the only state to do so retaining its public lands. This fact, when coupled with the magnitude of that endowment, accounts for many of the state's land policies and development strategies. The story of Texas settlement is bound up with the distribution, development, and administration of these lands, both public and private. Texas land policy encouraged land ownership, established a rectangular geometry in the landscape, helped develop a system of railroads, and led to the formation of counties and county seats. Today Texas contains 254 counties spread over 169,356,000 acres of land.

Just as in the case of national land policy, the transfer of vast portions of public land to private use was a recurrent theme in the settlement of

Texas. Such transfers occurred under Spanish, Mexican, Republic, and state laws. Land tenure policy in Texas derives from all of these sources. However, most of the Texas system was patterned on U.S. practices, which arose in response to dissatisfaction with English law and the need to settle an ever-expanding frontier. The land tenure and survey system adopted in the United States was established early by the Continental Congress. An observer and official of federal land policy, Marshall Harris, remarked upon America's departure from European practice:

> The land system that emerged in 1787 was quite different from the one brought to America by the early settlers, and it was in sharp contrast with the feudal tenures forced upon rural England . . . The [American] land system today is essentially the same as outlined in the 1785 and 1787 ordinances. (Harris 1953, 394)

A major feature of the land ordinance was use of the rectangular grid. This system, known as township and range, was based upon units six miles square with thirty-six subunits of one square mile each (Carter 1983, 120). Although it is often credited to Thomas Jefferson, an advocate and architect of the ordinance, "a fundamental part of the Northwest Land Ordinance was derived from colonial experience" (Harris 1953, 399). The influence of this system on the American landscape can not be overemphasized.

Almost half of the Texas landscape was subdivided using a modified rectangular system that was prescribed later by state laws. These were based largely on the U.S. Ordinances of 1785 and 1787. However, use of the section and rectangular survey system was predated in Texas by several forms of land tenure including metes and bounds, long-lots, and irregular surveys (Figure 3).

Much of the state employed an irregular rectangular survey, which combined Anglo-American practices of metes and bounds with rectangular surveys (Arbingast et al. 1976, 41). This was a natural consequence of the fact that most Texans were Anglo-American and were accustomed to such systems of survey. In addition, settlement under Mexican law had required systematic surveys for townships.

Another feature of Mexican law that influenced Texas was a provision in the Constitution of 1824 granting Mexican states all rights to public lands (McKitrick 1918, 29). This legal precedent would prove crucial to Texas history. During the days of the Republic, Texas law also extended

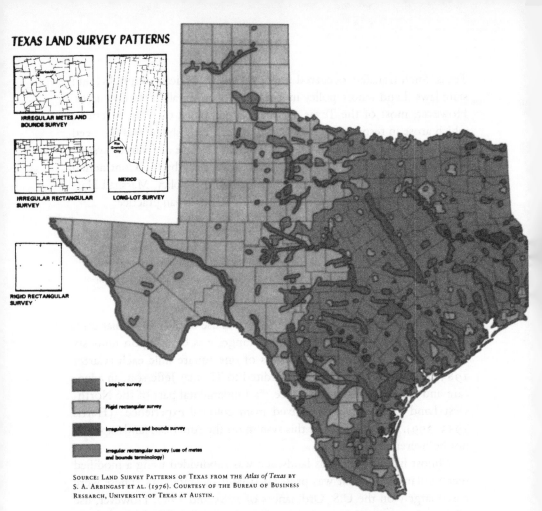

TEXAS LAND SURVEY PATTERNS

IRREGULAR METES AND
BOUNDS SURVEY

IRREGULAR RECTANGULAR
SURVEY

LONG-LOT SURVEY

RIGID RECTANGULAR
SURVEY

Rio
Grande
City

MEXICO

Long-lot survey

Rigid rectangular survey

Irregular metes and bounds survey

Irregular rectangular survey (use of metes
and bounds terminology)

SOURCE: LAND SURVEY PATTERNS OF TEXAS FROM THE *Atlas of Texas* BY
S. A. ARBINGAST ET AL. (1976). COURTESY OF THE BUREAU OF BUSINESS
RESEARCH, UNIVERSITY OF TEXAS AT AUSTIN.

Figure 3 Land survey patterns in Texas. The patterns recorded by Jordan using
General Land Office maps include a modified system of township and range, metes and
bounds, long-lots, and irregular rectangular surveys. While the majority of the state used
rectangular survey systems based on Anglo-American experience, other patterns were
derived from Spanish and Mexican practices.

most of the Colonization Laws of Mexico except when contradicted by
new laws, which were not long in coming.

   Grappling with an unstable independence, large war debts, and an
abundance of public land, Texas quickly enacted its own land policies.
The first Texas Constitution, adopted in September 1836, established a
generous land program to encourage settlement. The amount of acreage
disposed through land grants in Texas history was staggering (Table 3).
Gradually, this land was divided into counties.

Table 3. Public Lands in Texas (Estimated Disposition by 1910)

DESCRIPTION OR PURPOSE OF LAND	ACREAGE
Titled by Spain and Mexico	26,280, 000
Titled by Republic of Texas, headright grants and certificates	36, 876,492
Titled by Republic of Texas, *empresario* grants	4,494,806
Preemption claims and homestead donations	4,847,136
Grants to railways	32,400,000
Grants to companies for internal improvements	4,061,000
Capitol building	3,050,000
County school fund	4,229,166
State school fund	45,000,000
University fund	2,289,225
Other institutions	400,000
Veterans of Texas Revolution	1,169,382
Veterans of Confederacy	1,979,852
Sold to pay public debt	1,660,936
Ceded to United States in Compromise of 1850	67,000,000
Total	235,737,995
Total excluding amount ceded to United States in 1850	168,737,995*

*Represents estimates made in 1918. Compare the total figure to the current acreage of 169,356,000 acres reported by the General Land Office of Texas. This excludes submerged acreage, territorial waters, and excess acreage, which amount to another 6,900,000 acres.

Source: McKitrick 1918, 158.

COUNTY FORMATION

The county in Texas is the product of both Hispanic and Anglo-American practices of self-government. Seymour V. Connor, a scholar of county formation, concluded that Texas counties and county seats owe much of their form to the Mexican *municipio* (municipality) and to "elements of the three basic patterns of American local government: the New England town system, the midwestern and middle Atlantic town-county system, and the county system of the south Atlantic and southern states" (Connor 1951, 199). Discussion of these influences can be limited to the period 1836 to 1845 and to those provisions in the Constitution that refer specifically to counties and county seats. Most counties were formed after 1845, but the basic laws remained unchanged after this date and guided all subsequent development.

The first forms of local government derived from the Mexican municipality system, which dated from a Spanish royal decree of August 27, 1776, and had the effect of transplanting elements of governance from Castilian towns to the northern provinces of New Spain, including Texas (Cruz 1988, 5). The *cabildo* or *ayuntamiento,* which had ancient precedents in Spain, was the local administrative structure of the municipality (Cruz 1988, 5). These town councils included a number of specific offices such as *alcaldes* (mayors), *regidores* (council members), *alguaciles* (constables), and *escribanos* (scribes) (Cruz 1988, 6). This legal institution was long-lived and introduced to the frontier "municipal law and order, patterns of local government, a rough democracy, and the concept of justice based on law" (Cruz 1988, 165).

In Texas the municipal system remained operational from Spanish rule through Mexico's *empresario* program, which saw the introduction of several Anglo-American colonies and communities. When Texas colonists first met at San Felipe de Austin during the Consultation of 1835 to discuss independence and governance, they came as delegates from their respective municipalities. The twelve jurisdictions represented were Austin, Bevil, Columbia, Gonzales, Harrisburg, Liberty, Matagorda, Mina, Nacogdoches, San Augustine, Viesca, and Washington.

At that time Texas was subdivided into three departments (Béxar, Brazos, and Nacogdoches), which had been established by Mexican law. These departments were quickly abolished, leaving the municipality as the only organized unit of representation. During the months before the Convention of 1836, the number of municipalities seeking participation increased from twelve to twenty-three. These included the six additional municipalities of Béxar, Goliad, Refugio, San Patricio, Teneha, and Victoria (Fulmore 1915, 278). Another five municipalities were created by the Consultation and Provisional Government (Connor 1951, 180): Colorado, Jackson, Jefferson, Red River, and Sabine. Representatives from all twenty-three municipalities met in 1836 at the Constitutional Convention and established a new Republic.

Although the Constitution did not explicitly state that existing municipalities were to become counties, it did list the twenty-three former municipalities by name as new counties. Thus, the basic form of Texas government took shape as a "centralized republican government, and the principal subordinate unit was the county" (Connor 1951, 170). The Constitution established numerous laws relating to the formation, size, and administration of counties. It also specified the functions of county government. These were amended from time to time, but many of the original articles referring to counties and county seats have remained viable.

Early in its history the Texas Congress was given explicit power to form new counties. The process required a petition of one hundred free male residents from an area of at least nine hundred square miles (Connor 1951, 181). The county seat was to be selected by Congress, by the county commissioners, or by an election. The Constitution also provided that new counties would observe U.S. land ordinances and assume the same administrative functions as the original counties (Connor 1951, 181). Additional constitutional provisions established a system of county courts and county officers. These positions reflected both Hispanic and Anglo-American traditions. Those officials who had constituted the Mexican *ayuntamiento* became county officials, "as alcaldes became justices of the peace or county judges, secretaries turned clerks or recorders, and alguaciles, sheriffs" (Connor 1951, 172). The requirement that counties provide accurate descriptions of their boundaries and land titles led to the appointment of another officer, the county surveyor. This office has been eliminated in many counties, although elimination still requires a statewide vote.

Other provisions that were contained in Article 9, Section 1, of the Constitution of 1876 stipulated that all new counties contain no less than "900 square miles in a square form, unless prevented by pre-existing boundaries," or 700 square miles if created from an existing county. Also, counties could only be created by a two-thirds vote of both houses of the legislature. Another requirement was that no new county could place its boundaries within twelve miles of the seat of the county from which it was created.

Section 2 of Article 9 specifically referred to the siting of county seats and emphasized the need for a central location (Francaviglia 1973; Jackson 1996). Indeed, any county seat within five miles of the geographic center of the county could not be changed without the agreement of two-thirds of the county's voters. Only a simple majority was required to remove a seat that was further than five miles off-center to a new site that was within five miles of the geographic center. With these laws in place, the Republic's twenty-three counties grew to thirty-six by 1845. Fannin, Fayette, Fort Bend, Houston, Montgomery, and Robertson Counties were created in 1837. Galveston County was added in 1838; Harrison County in 1839; Bowie, Lamar, and Travis Counties in 1840; Brazos County in 1841; and Rusk County in 1843. After statehood, the pattern of county formation spread from east to west. By 1930, as the last counties were formed in far west Texas, final boundaries were established for all 254 counties (Appendix 1).

Once a county was established and a county seat selected, plans were laid for the erection of a courthouse to house the offices of the principal officials. In many cases, county seats were new towns established just before or after the county itself, so the courthouse could be set in a prominent location in the new town plan. When a previously established town was selected as a county seat, the courthouse had to be sited within the existing urban pattern. As would be expected, variations in settlement history led to tremendous differences in the siting of courthouses among county seats. These plans can be divided into two broad categories: (1) those derived from English colonial and Anglo-American planning traditions that were intended specifically for the siting of a central courthouse square; and (2) those derived from other planning traditions that originally did not include a courthouse, but were adapted to meet the need. This second category includes Hispanic and Central European plaza designs and towns platted by railroad engineers and Works Progress Administration (WPA) designers. In most cases, the Anglo-American central squares were planned from the beginning as county seats, while many towns of the second type became county seats sometime after they were platted. Railroad towns proved an exception to this trend and were planned and surveyed in anticipation of becoming county seats.

THE ANGLO-AMERICAN CENTRAL COURTHOUSE SQUARE

Most studies of Texas counties have focused on the central courthouse square associated with Anglo-American settlement (Zelinsky 1951; Price 1968; Aikins et al. 1971; Arbingast et al. 1976; Jordan, Bean, and Holmes 1984). These squares have received much attention by reason of their

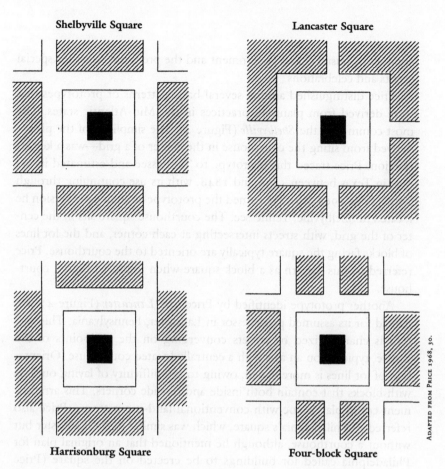

ADAPTED FROM PRICE 1968, 30.

Figure 4   Four prototypes of central courthouse squares in the United States.

prevalence, but also because they were designed specifically to make room for a courthouse in the town plan. Price's (1968) original system of classification remains useful because it focuses on elements of urban design that serve to reinforce the centrality of the courthouse and square. Price defined the central courthouse square as

> a rectangular block surrounded by streets, with the courthouse, often the grandest and most ornate building in the county, standing alone in the middle of the square and the town's leading business houses enclosing the square symmetrically on all four sides. (Price 1968, 29)

Described in these terms, the central courthouse square assumes both economic and symbolic significance. The square is the focus for the daily conduct of business and government and the preferred scene for special events and celebrations.

Price distinguished among several basic patterns or prototypes that were derived from planning practices in the Mid-Atlantic states. The most common is the *Shelbyville* (Figure 4). The simplicity of the plan—derived from siting the courthouse in the center of a grid—was a key attraction. Price traced this prototype to Tennessee and estimated its arrival in Texas between 1836 and 1848, with its use continuing through 1900 (Price 1968, 49). He named the prototype after an early version he located in Shelbyville, Tennessee. The courthouse square sits in the center of the grid, with streets intersecting at each corner, and the lot lines of blocks facing the square typically are oriented to the courthouse. Price referred to this pattern as a block square when found without a courthouse.

Another prototype identified by Price, the *Lancaster* (Figure 4), was named for its assumed predecessor in Lancaster, Pennsylvania. This pattern is characterized by streets converging on the midpoints of the square, typically on an axis with a centrally located courthouse. Orientation of lot lines is more varied, owing to the difficulty of laying out lots with blocks that contain both inside and outside corners. This arrangement could play havoc with conventional land-use patterns. Price also referred to Philadelphia's square, which was similar to the Lancaster but without a courthouse, although he mentioned that an original plan for Philadelphia called for buildings to be erected on the square (Price 1968, 39).

Price's *Harrisonburg* prototype (Figure 4) combined certain elements of the Shelbyville and Lancaster. This prototype is defined by two streets that meet at the midpoint of the square and two streets that converge on the corners. This pattern is formed most typically by altering the regular block arrangement of the grid. Here, too, the lot lines front the square.

Price's fourth prototype, the *four-block* square (Figure 4), places the courthouse in the midst of what would otherwise be four city blocks. Other researchers noted two additional prototypes in Texas: *two-block* and *six-block* patterns (Figure 5). Some confusion has arisen in the literature between the six-block type described by D. B. Aikins' group and the two-block observed by T. G. Jordan. In most cases, these researchers appear to be describing the same pattern. Close examination of the six-block square reveals that Aikins' team misinterpreted several two-block schemes and a Harrisonburg square by defining them as six-blocks. The two-block designation makes more sense in keeping with Price's original description for the four-block, and that term has been adopted for this classification.

COURTHOUSE SQUARES DERIVED FROM OTHER TRADITIONS AND PRECEDENTS

Most Texas towns were platted without the expectation of becoming county seats. If towns were selected later, planners had to adapt or devise suitable schemes for positioning the courthouse in the preexisting urban pattern. Careful examination of the evidence reveals that these adaptations fall into several groups: plaza squares, railroad-influenced squares, half- and quarter-block squares, and irregular-block squares (Figure 6). A few of these patterns represent incompletely developed courthouse squares. Price used the term "incomplete square" to refer to those county seats where the courthouse "occupies only part of a block, or the courthouse has no square at all" (Price 1968, 34). The present study instead applies this term more precisely to a number of different subgroups defined by more specific morphological features. This is because there are few county seats in Texas where planners did not at least attempt to strive for the appearance of a complete square even if partially thwarted by preexisting town plans.

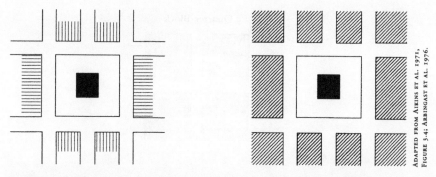

ADAPTED FROM AIKINS ET AL. 1971, FIGURE 3-4; ARBINGAST ET AL. 1976.

Figure 5 Two-block and six-block squares. The figure on the left was identified by Aikins' research as a six-block square. However, as the figure on the right from Jordan's classification indicates, it is best described as a two-block.

From Land Policy to County Seats and Squares

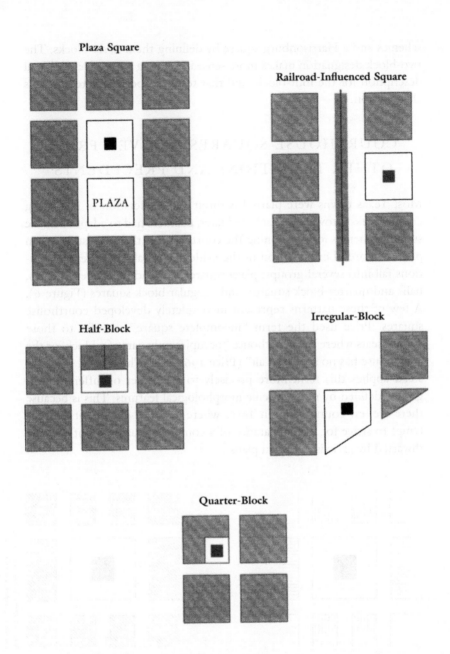

Figure 6 Types of nontraditional courthouse squares. These newly defined prototypes are described in this study as plaza squares, railroad-influenced squares, half- and quarter-blocks, and irregular blocks.

The most important prototypes of this group are county seats with courthouses placed adjacent to an open public space or plaza. These *plaza* courthouses constitute a fairly heterogeneous group that derives from a wide range of influences, including Hispanic, Central European, and later Anglo-American planning traditions. Many plaza courthouses maintain prominent positions, but a few do not. Some of these plazas have been obscured or used for other public purposes and are no longer open. Taken as a whole, this group combines elements of a number of town planning traditions.

The *half-block* and *quarter-block* prototypes approximate the appearance of an Anglo-American central square, but do not occupy the same extensive block plan. *Irregular-block* prototypes include courthouses situated on irregularly shaped blocks created by anomalies in the street grid such as those resulting from attempts to accommodate competing street patterns or diagonal street intersections.

Because of the significant influence of railroads on certain county seats, these are placed in their own subgroup. Many Texas towns were connected by rail, and several were founded by rail companies or their agents. However, only those county seats where the courthouse was placed near the tracks or where the form of the square was determined by the railroad's layout are classified here as *railroad* squares.

CLASSIFICATION OF TEXAS COURTHOUSE SQUARES

Classification of all Texas counties and county seats (Table 4) makes two points clear: the importance of Anglo-American planning traditions and the enduring influence of other cultures and planning practices. Both have left distinct signatures on the landscape. The most frequently found pattern in Texas is the Shelbyville. This is to be expected, as it is the most common central courthouse square in the United States and the easiest to plat. Its Tennessee origin relates nicely to the importance of that state in the peopling of Texas. This pattern alone accounts for 62 percent of Texas squares. Many of these were modified over time; yet no other plan matches its endurance. Of those squares documented by site visits, 23 percent (eighteen of seventy-eight) retain the hallmark features described by Price for the prototypical Shelbyville.

Table 4. Texas Courthouse Squares Classified by Block Pattern

COURTHOUSE SQUARE BLOCK PATTERN	NUMBER	%
		Traditional Courthouse Patterns
Shelbyvilles and variants	157	62.0
Two-Block and variants	15	6.0
Harrisonburgs and variants	14	5.5
Lancasters and variants	4	1.5
Four-Block	3	1.0
Total traditional patterns	193	76.0
		Nontraditional Courthouse Patterns
Plaza and variants	33	13.0
Railroad and variants	18	7.0
Irregular-Block	5	2.0
Half-Block	3	1.0
Quarter-Block	2	1.0
Total nontraditional patterns	61	24.0
Total of all block patterns	254	100

The next most frequent are plaza patterns, with thirty-three (13 percent) of the state's county seats. These are more varied in form and suggest diverse origins. Many of these predate the coming of county courthouses, such as those towns platted during Spanish and Mexican rule. A number of plazas found in association with courthouses today are the result of twentieth-century urban planning preferences.

Following the plaza patterns, railroad patterns are the most prevalent. There are eighteen county seats in this category, although that figure underrepresents the total number of towns founded or platted by railroads. This is because only those courthouse squares directly influenced by the railroad are tallied in this category, which accounts for 7 percent of the state's county seats.

County seats with two-block squares constitute the next group in terms of numbers, with fifteen or 6 percent of the total. These are followed by the Harrisonburg patterns, which account for fourteen or 5.5

percent of the state's total. The four-block square requires a great deal of space, which may account for its scarcity, with only three examples. The space afforded by these squares has made them vulnerable to intrusion by parking lots or other public buildings.

However, the two most frugal patterns with respect to land use, the half-block and quarter-block, are also few, with three and two examples, respectively. Perhaps a threshold exists: more than a single block is considered excessive and less than a whole block insufficient for the square's status and space requirements.

The most elaborate central courthouse square, the Lancaster, is little seen in Texas, most likely because of its complicated grid and the diffi-

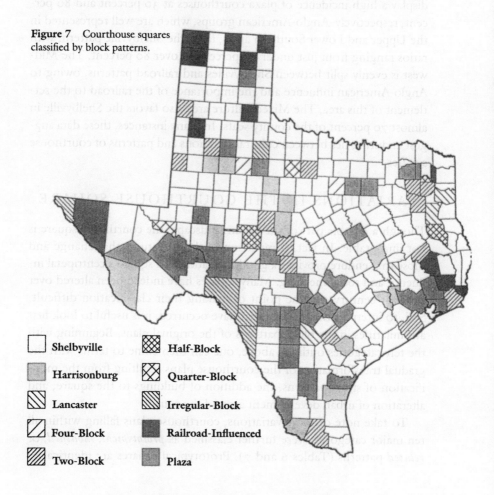

Figure 7 Courthouse squares classified by block patterns.

☐ Shelbyville	▨ Half-Block
▨ Harrisonburg	▨ Quarter-Block
◪ Lancaster	◪ Irregular-Block
◪ Four-Block	■ Railroad-Influenced
▨ Two-Block	▨ Plaza

From Land Policy to County Seats and Squares

culty in providing for conventional land use at the square. Only four county seats display this pattern.

The areal distribution (Figure 7) of these ten block patterns illustrates the dominance of Anglo-American prototypes, particularly the Shelbyville. Close examination of the spatial arrangement of the various prototypes also suggests some degree of correspondence between those patterns and certain cultural groups. Comparison of the distribution of block patterns noted above with the culture areas reported by Jordan (Jordan, Bean, and Holmes 1984) reveals several interesting trends (Table 5).

In broad terms, the Spanish-Mexican and German Hill Country areas display a high incidence of plaza courthouses at 30 percent and 80 percent, respectively. Anglo-American groups, which are well represented in the Upper and Lower Southern areas, favor the Shelbyville pattern, with ratios ranging from just under 43 percent to over 80 percent. The Midwest is evenly split between Shelbyvilles and railroad patterns, owing to Anglo-American influence and the importance of the railroad to the settlement of this area. The Mixed culture area also favors the Shelbyville in almost 70 percent of the county seats. In many instances, these data suggest enduring ties between cultural traditions and patterns of courthouse squares.

VARIATIONS IN THE COURTHOUSE SQUARE

Though a durable part of the urban landscape, the courthouse square is not immutable. In fact, comparison of those features that change and those that endure provides a good indication of a square's centripetal influence and social meaning. Many squares have indeed been altered over the past century—to the point of making their classification difficult. Still, to interpret the changes that have occurred, it is useful to look first at similarities in the block patterns of the original plans. Beginning with the ten categories outlined above, one can then come to terms with the gradual transformation of the courthouse plans resulting from the modification of street patterns, the addition of buildings to the square, and alteration of urban development around the square.

To take note of these variations, courthouse plans falling within all ten major categories were further classified as *prototypical, modified,* or *related* patterns (Tables 6 and 7). Prototypical squares are identical to

Table 5. Texas Courthouse Squares by Culture Areas

CULTURE AREA	PATTERNS	NUMBER	%
Upper South—1 (25):	Shelbyville	20 of 25	80.0
	Plaza	4 of 25	16.0
	Railroad-Influenced	1 of 25	04.0
Upper South—2 (36):	Shelbyville	29 of 36	80.5
	Two-Block	3 of 36	08.3
	Harrisonburg	2 of 36	05.5
	Plaza	1 of 36	02.7
	Four-Block	1 of 36	02.7
Upper South—3 (76):	Shelbyville	51 of 76	67.1
	Plaza	6 of 76	07.9
	Harrisonburg	5 of 76	06.5
	Railroad-Influenced	5 of 76	06.5
	Two-Block	3 of 76	03.9
	Four-Block	2 of 76	02.6
	Quarter-Block	2 of 76	02.6
	Half-Block	1 of 76	01.3
	Irregular-Block	1 of 76	01.3
Midwest (6):	Shelbyville	3 of 6	50.0
	Railroad-Influenced	3 of 6	50.0
German Hill Country (5):	Plaza	4 of 5	80.0
	Two-Block	1 of 5	20.0
Lower South—1 (33):	Shelbyville	19 of 33	57.5
	Two-Block	4 of 33	12.1
	Lancaster	3 of 33	09.1
	Railroad-Influenced	3 of 33	09.1
	Harrisonburg	2 of 33	06.1
	Half-Block	2 of 33	06.1
Lower South—2 (4):	Shelbyville	3 of 4	75.0
	Railroad-Influenced	1 of 4	25.0

CULTURE AREA	PATTERNS	NUMBER	%
Lower South—3 (14):	Shelbyville	6 of 14	42.8
	Plaza	4 of 14	28.5
	Railroad-Influenced	2 of 14	14.3
	Two-Block	2 of 14	14.3
Spanish-Mexican (33):	Shelbyville	11 of 33	33.3
	Plaza	10 of 33	30.3
	Irregular-Block	4 of 33	12.1
	Railroad-Influenced	3 of 33	09.1
	Harrisonburg	3 of 33	09.1
	Lancaster	1 of 33	03.0
	Two-Block	1 of 33	03.0
Mixed (22):	Shelbyville	15 of 22	68.2
	Plaza	4 of 22	18.2
	Harrisonburg	2 of 22	09.1
	Two-Block	1 of 22	04.5

Note: Culture areas after T. G. Jordan (Arbingast et al. 1976, 42).

the basic pattern, without any variation whatsoever. Modified squares are those that deviate from a basic plan but can still be easily recognized. Related squares have been substantially changed, but can be viewed as hybrids of one of the ten basic types. Although these subcategories have not been employed by previous researchers, their use here permits a better understanding of the evolution and influence of the square in Texas.

Some of the earliest changes involved transformation of Hispanic or European open plazas to variations of central courthouse squares favored by Anglo-Americans. Some courthouse precincts have been so rearranged as to change from one classification to another, such as those altered by railroads and WPA planners or transformed by urban growth. The most significant alterations were additional buildings on the square, incomplete or inconsistent development around the square, and modifications to street or block patterns. Such changes were usually consequences of growth, stagnation, decline, or renewed development. A commonplace change involved the construction of an annex or addition

Table 6. Texas Traditional Courthouse Squares by Subtypes and Sources

CATEGORY	SITE VISIT	HISTORICAL DATA ONLY	OTHER	SUBTOTALS ($n=254$)
Shelbyvilles				
Prototypical	17	31	5	53
Modified	57	29	2	88
Related	1	15	0	16
	75	75	7	157 (62.0%)
Two-blocks				
Prototypical	0	2	0	2
Modified	7	0	0	7
Related	4	2	0	6
	11	4	0	15 (6.0%)
Harrisonburgs				
Prototypical	0	2	0	2
Modified	7	1	0	8
Related	1	3	0	4
	8	6	0	14 (5.5%)
Lancasters				
Prototypical	0	0	0	0
Modified	2	0	0	2
Related	0	2	0	2
	2	2	0	4 (1.5%)
Four-blocks				
Prototypical	0	1	0	1
Modified	2	0	0	2
Related	0	0	0	0
	2	1	0	3 (1.0%)
Total	98	88	7	193 (76.0%)

Table 7. Texas Nontraditional Courthouse Squares
by Subtypes and Sources

CATEGORY	SITE VISIT	HISTORICAL DATA ONLY	OTHER	SUBTOTALS (n=254)
Plaza				
Prototypical	1	1	0	2
Modified	13	3	0	16
Related	14	1	0	15
	28	5	0	33 (13.0%)
Railroad				
Prototypical	0	1	0	1
Modified	6	2	0	8
Related	4	5	0	9
	10	8	0	18 (7.0%)
Irregular-Block				
Prototypical	0	2	0	2
Modified	0	3	0	3
Related	0	0	0	0
	0	5	0	5 (2.0%)
Half-Block				
Prototypical	0	0	0	0
Modified	2	1	0	3
Related	0	0	0	0
	2	1	0	3 (1.0%)
Quarter-Block				
Prototypical	0	1	0	1
Modified	1	0	0	1
Related	0	0	0	0
	1	1	0	2 (1.0%)
Total	41	20	0	61 (24.0%)

to the courthouse. Many county seats have seen a series of courthouses erected on their squares to replace those destroyed by mishap, dilapidation, or intentional demolition. Fires were a frequent threat, including arson to destroy court records. Rebuilding with a new scale and design often challenged the integrity of the original plan.

Some rural county seats never matched the ambitions of their planners and exhibit incomplete or inconsistent development of the central business district (CBD) adjacent to the courthouse square. In other cases, the central business district grew away from the square or developed elsewhere. Additional changes include closing a street at the square, changing land use around the square, and obscuring formerly open plazas. In larger cities urban growth has altered the character of the courthouse square.

Taken as a whole, the patterns and variants that constitute this morphological classification depict an urban landscape dominated by familiar forms, particularly the Shelbyville. Anglo-American courthouse prototypes account for 193 squares, or 76 percent of the state's county seats, with other planning traditions accounting for the remainder. However, it is these 24 percent—described in this study in detail for the first time—that highlight the diversity to be found in the Texas landscape.

Chapter Three

Anglo-American Courthouse Squares

SHELBYVILLE SQUARES

The Shelbyville square is the most prevalent pattern in Texas. Many factors explain its widespread adoption: it was familiar to many settlers and easy to plat, caused no disruption of the grid plan and adjacent patterns of land use, and provided a central focus for the community. These characteristics are shared in varying degree with other Anglo-American courthouse squares, but none offers as straightforward a solution as the Shelbyville.

This block pattern and its variants (Figure 8) are found in 157 Texas county seats. Of these, 53 sites reflect the prototype described by Price, 88 indicate some degree of modification, and 16 exhibit closely related or more elaborate block patterns. On-site inspection of 75 of these county seats revealed detailed information: 39 of those inspected (52 percent) had additional structures on the square; 50 (67 percent) had limited commercial development at the square; and 22 (29 percent) had altered lot lines, streets, or alleyways. In many cases, these changes did not significantly reduce the central focus on the square, which in part accounts for the success of the Shelbyville in terms of its civic role within the community.

The Shelbyville's introduction into Texas accompanied Anglo-American settlement in the state. One of the first Shelbyvilles was laid out by 1833 in the northeast Texas town of Clarksville. Another early Anglo town, San Augustine, also adopted an early Shelbyville square, as indicated by county maps dated 1839. The last county seat to use this plan, in 1923, was Morton in Cochran County in west Texas. Most Shel-

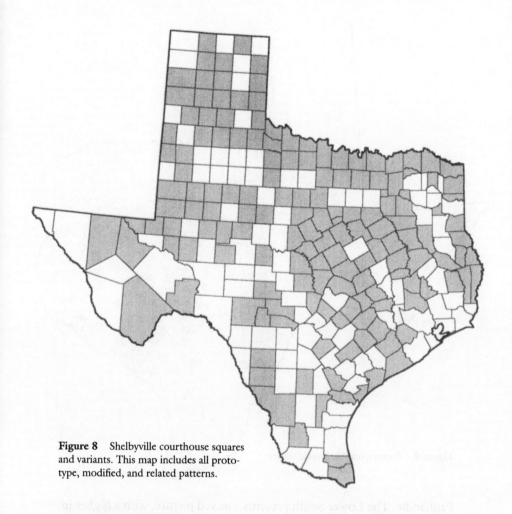

Figure 8 Shelbyville courthouse squares
and variants. This map includes all prototype, modified, and related patterns.

byvilles were laid out between 1840 and 1890, a period of active settlement and town building.

The distribution of Shelbyvilles followed settlement of the state from
east to west. Closely associated with Anglo-American culture, particularly that derived from the Mid-Atlantic states, the Shelbyville dominated
Texas' urban landscape. This association is partly revealed by comparing
the spread of the Shelbyville with specific culture areas (Table 5). As
might be expected, the square is prevalent in all three Upper South areas,
with ratios ranging from 67 to 80 percent. The Shelbyville also dominates (68 percent) the area of Mixed cultural groups. The ratio drops to
50 percent in the few counties associated with Midwest influence in the

Anglo-American Courthouse Squares

33

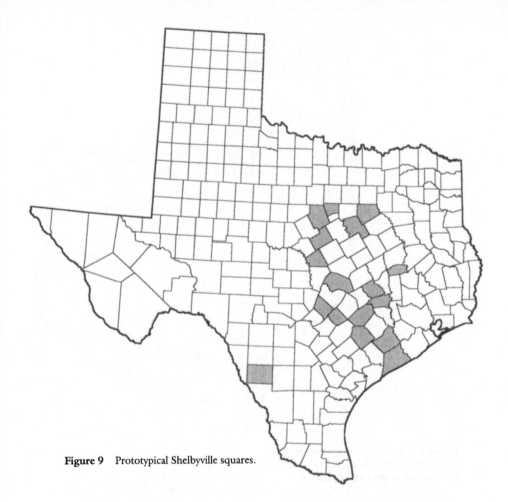

Figure 9 Prototypical Shelbyville squares.

Panhandle. The Lower South presents a mixed picture, with a higher incidence of Shelbyville squares in all but those counties along the Gulf Coast, where the ratio drops to around 43 percent. This may reflect French and early Hispanic influence along the coast. The lowest frequencies occur in the Spanish-Mexican area (33 percent) and the five counties that constitute the German Hill Country, where no Shelbyvilles are found.

Prototypical Shelbyville Squares

Owing to their simplicity and stability, many prototypical Shelbyville squares remain in the Texas landscape (Figure 9). Archival research and site visits indicate that fifty-three county seats retain the prototypical pattern (Table 8). Most of these are found in small towns, since urban growth often led to changes at the square. Prototypical squares are characterized by a prominent courthouse sited on a central square in a park-like setting of shade trees, walks, and monuments, surrounded by the town's major commercial establishments. The courthouse is typically the only building centered on the square and dominates the townscape.

Table 8. Shelbyville Squares Retaining Prototypical Patterns

COUNTY SEAT / COUNTY

Athens / Henderson	Henrietta / Clay
Bay City* / Matagorda	Hillsboro* / Hill
Big Spring / Howard	La Grange* / Fayette
Breckenridge / Stephens	Lamesa / Dawson
Brenham* / Washington	Lampasas* / Lampasas
Brownfield / Terry	Linden** / Cass
Caldwell* / Burleson	Lockhart* / Caldwell
Cameron / Milam	Madisonville* / Madison
Carrizo Springs* / Dimmit	Marlin / Falls
Childress / Childress	McKinney / Collin
Clarendon / Donley	Meridian / Bosque
Clarksville / Red River	Montague** / Montague
Comanche / Comanche	Odessa / Ector
Cooper / Delta	Paducah / Cottle
Crockett / Houston	Pecos / Reeves
Decatur / Wise	Rockwall / Rockwall
Dimmitt** / Castro	Rusk / Cherokee
Dumas / Moore	San Marcos* / Hays
Emory** / Rains	San Saba / San Saba
Gainesville / Cooke	Sherman / Grayson
Gatesville / Coryell	Stephenville* / Erath
Georgetown* / Williamson	Sweetwater / Nolan
Glen Rose** / Somervell	Vernon / Wilbarger
Goldthwaite / Mills	Waxahachie* / Ellis
Granbury* / Hood	Wellington / Collingsworth
Hallettsville* / Lavaca	Wharton* / Wharton
Hamilton* / Hamilton	

*Confirmed by site visit. (Others confirmed by historical data only.)
**Confirmed by other researchers only, not verified in this study.

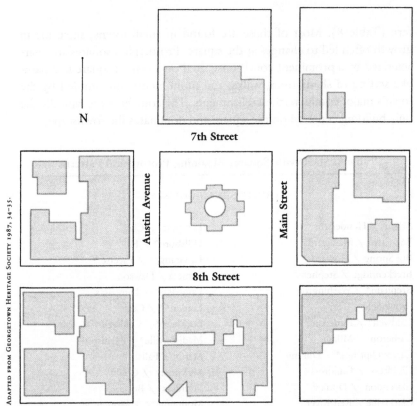

ADAPTED FROM GEORGETOWN HERITAGE SOCIETY 1987, 34–35.

7th Street

Austin Avenue

Main Street

8th Street

Figure 10 Plan of Williamson County's courthouse square in Georgetown. The town's major businesses surround the square in a fashion typical of nineteenth-century urban landscapes and characteristic of prototypical Shelbyville squares.

A good example of this prototype is Georgetown (Figure 10), which was founded in 1848 as the county seat for Williamson County. Georgetown's first permanent courthouse was completed on the square in 1857. The present neoclassical structure (Figure 11), built in 1910, is the fifth official courthouse and still stands on the square. Recent recognition of the square's importance to the community came in the 1980s with the town's participation in the Main Street Program. This program of public and private restoration of the square's traditional townscape reversed a trend of decline that began in the 1960s. Many county seats suffered the effects of decentralization or modernization. However, not all modifications to the prototypical pattern resulted in the square's loss of focus or influence.

THE COURTHOUSE SQUARE IN TEXAS

Figure 11 Williamson County Courthouse in Georgetown. This courthouse square has recently been restored and revitalized, retaining many of the main elements indicative of the prototypical Shelbyville square, including the prominent courthouse building.

Modified Shelbyville Squares

This research recorded eighty-eight county seats with modified Shelbyville patterns (Figure 12). On-site investigation included fifty-seven of these squares, (Table 9). Modified Shelbyville squares are typified by a number of deviations from the prototypical pattern. Most deviations involve an incomplete or underdeveloped square. These are often associated with small rural towns that never fully developed the blocks around the square. Other modified squares are residential in character or lack commercial development. Some modifications involve modest changes in street patterns or the location of the courthouse or the addition of buildings to the square.

Despite these deviations from their prototypical pattern, many modified Shelbyville squares maintain a central role in the community. Some retain their dominant place in the townscape precisely because of the paucity of development and lack of competition from other structures.

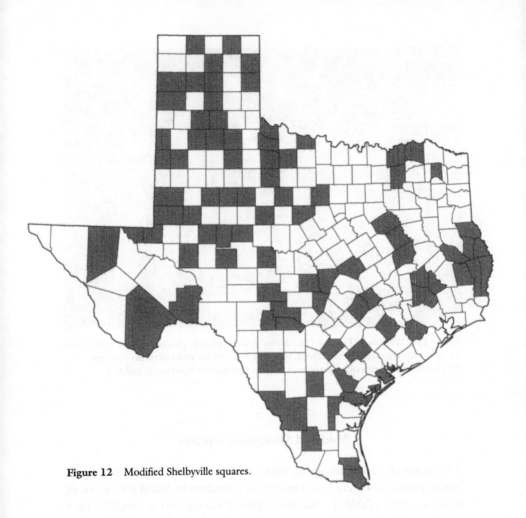

Figure 12 Modified Shelbyville squares.

Table 9. Shelbyville Squares Exhibiting Modified Patterns

COUNTY SEAT / COUNTY

Abilene / Taylor
Albany** / Shackelford
Alice* / Jim Wells
Alpine* / Brewster
Amarillo* / Potter
Andrews* / Andrews
Bandera* / Bandera

Bastrop* / Bastrop
Beeville* / Bee
Belton* / Bell
Benjamin* / Knox
Bonham / Fannin
Brownsville/ Cameron
Burnet / Burnet

Canadian / Hemphill

Center / Shelby

Centerville* / Leon

Claude* / Armstrong

Coldspring* / San Jacinto

Columbus* / Colorado

Conroe* / Montgomery

Corsicana* / Navarro

Crowell / Foard

Crystal City* / Zavala

Cuero* / DeWitt

Dickens* / Dickens

Eastland / Eastland

Fairfield* / Freestone

Floresville* / Wilson

Floydada* / Floyd

Gail / Borden

Garden City* / Glasscock

Giddings* / Lee

Greenville / Hunt

Haskell / Haskell

Hebbronville / Jim Hogg

Hemphill* / Sabine

Hereford* / Deaf Smith

Huntsville* / Walker

Jasper * / Jasper

Johnson City* / Blanco

Junction* / Kimble

Kermit / Winkler

Kerrville* / Kerr

Laredo* / Webb

Leakey* / Real

Levelland / Hockley

Llano* / Llano

Lufkin* / Angelina

Matador / Motley

Mentone / Loving

Mertzon* / Irion

Morton* / Cochran

Mt. Pleasant / Titus

Muleshoe* / Bailey

Newton* / Newton

Paint Rock* / Concho

Palo Pinto / Palo Pinto

Panhandle* / Carson

Paris / Lamar

Perryton / Ochiltree

Plainview / Hale

Port Lavaca* / Calhoun

Quanah / Hardeman

Rankin* / Upton

Raymondville* / Willacy

Richmond* / Fort Bend

Robert Lee* / Coke

Roby/ Fisher

Rockport* / Aransas

San Augustine* / San Augustine

Sanderson / Terrell

Seminole* / Gaines

Seymour* / Baylor

Silverton* / Briscoe

Sinton* / San Patricio

Snyder / Scurry

Stanton / Martin

Sterling City* / Sterling

Stinnett* / Hutchinson

Stratford* / Sherman

Tilden* / McMullen

Tulia/ Swisher

Van Horn / Culberson

Vega* / Oldham

Wheeler** / Wheeler

Wichita Falls / Wichita

Woodville* / Tyler

*Confirmed by site visit. (Others confirmed by historical data only.)
**Confirmed by other researchers only, not verified in this study.

Anglo-American Courthouse Squares

The courthouses at many modified squares also remain the most prominent buildings and dominate their townscapes. Often the lawns of these squares serve as the town's "front yard," with a community Christmas tree or a hand-lettered sign boosting the local football team. These are common scenes at many active courthouse squares, including some with modified patterns.

Typical of many modified Shelbyville squares is the rural town of Claude (Figure 13) in Armstrong County, which exhibits land use inconsistent with the prototype pattern. This courthouse square remains central to its ranching community, which serves a large hinterland. At the time of the survey, land use at Claude's square included a feed store, an auto parts store, two gas stations, and a lumberyard. Also noted were services more typical of courthouse squares, such as a bank and post office. In many isolated communities the post office is the only daily meeting place for otherwise distant neighbors.

Several modified schemes include squares that serve more limited civic functions and are removed from most commercial development. An

Figure 13 Claude in Armstrong County. Although the area around this modified Shelbyville square is incompletely developed, the courthouse square maintains the central focus of this small ranching community.

THE COURTHOUSE SQUARE IN TEXAS

interesting example is Panhandle in Carson County, with churches on three corners opposite the courthouse. Across the street from the courthouse are a local history museum and library. Other modified squares are characterized by substantial residential development on adjoining blocks.

Other less-developed squares are indeed forlorn and vacant. Paint Rock in Concho County, with a town population below 350 and county population of 2,800, maintains a tidy courthouse and fenced lawn, but there is little else except vacant storefronts and unpaved streets. A county or town in decline is a problem beyond the reach of a quaint, homelike courthouse or neatly kept square.

Another example of an underdeveloped square is Mertzon in Irion County. Sparsely populated, this "big country" county seat has a courthouse sited on a hilltop square in an imposing landscape of wide open spaces. Purposely removed from the highway by its WPA planners when Mertzon became the county seat in 1936, the courthouse presides over a ghostlike grid of vacant lots. A fire station and United States Department of Agriculture (USDA) office are the courthouse's only companions on the square. Across the street stands a small frame church and a single house. Sited on a distant hilltop is the town's other significant building, a stone schoolhouse. Mertzon's planners obviously intended to provide an imposing courthouse, but the square's remoteness was not what was desired. Instead of focusing on the hilltop courthouse, the town's businesses and growth followed the activity along the highway below. Many rural towns are witness to similar episodes of competition between town squares and development along the highway.

Other deviations from the prototype are those county seats that have outgrown the space provided by the courthouse and placed annexes or additions on the square. This incremental development is very common: 50 percent of the Shelbyville squares have been altered in this way. Some squares are crowded with buildings, such as the small east Texas town of Centerville (Figure 14) in Leon County, where a small brick antebellum courthouse shares the square with both the old and new jail buildings and a separate sheriff's office. More in keeping with tradition, a gazebo is also positioned on the square.

Other examples, such as the Hutchinson County Courthouse in Stinnett, have a single but no less disruptive addition. In Stinnett a low, windowless jail building unceremoniously abuts an otherwise impressive

Figure 14 Centerville in Leon County. This small antebellum courthouse shares the square with a gazebo as well as other county buildings. Old county jails are common sights on modified squares.

courthouse sited on the center of its hilltop block. In other instances, an annex may dwarf or engulf the courthouse. Additions in Conroe in Montgomery County and an annex in Kerrville in Kerr County are two examples. Kerrville is more fortunate, with a large open lawn in front of its courthouse, but Conroe's modern addition leaves little of the former square intact.

Obscured architecturally and with reduced open space, courthouse squares such as these begin to merge with the surrounding blocks and urban fabric and thereby play a reduced architectural role. This occurs as a result of shortened set-backs from the street, loss of open space, and loss of a distinct building type that is readily identifiable as the courthouse. Problems such as these are not exclusive to modified squares, but they are typical of numerous county seats in Texas.

Shelbyville-Related Patterns

Sixteen county seats have block patterns closely related to the Shelbyville (Figure 15). These include five squares that mimic the prototypical pattern, but surround the courthouse square with a symmetrical combination of full and partial blocks. The other eleven squares vary and involve irregularities in the location of courthouses, street intersections, or block sizes. Despite such variation, all sixteen squares approximate the appearance and pattern of the Shelbyville and thus are counted in this category. However, only one of these squares was verified by on-site survey; the others were classified according to historical data only (Table 10).

The five squares that elaborate on the block pattern around the square are Archer City, Brownwood, Cleburne, Denton (Figure 16), and Jacksboro. With the exception of Archer City, where the courthouse is placed on one of four equal squares centered in the town's grid, the plans for the other four are remarkably similar. These towns feature a

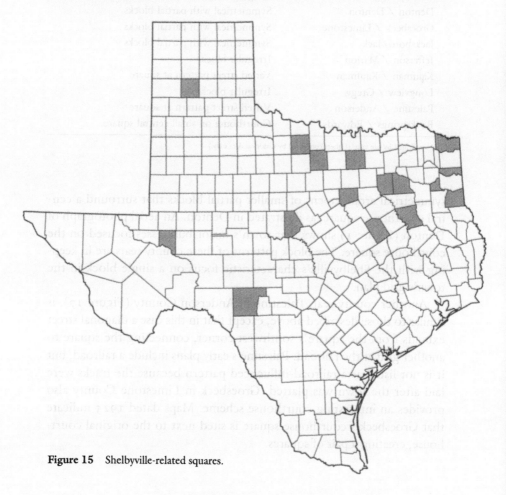

Figure 15 Shelbyville-related squares.

Anglo-American Courthouse Squares

Table 10. Shelbyville-Related Patterns

COUNTY SEAT / COUNTY	DESCRIPTION OF PATTERN AT SQUARE
Archer City / Archer	Symmetrical single square
Boston / Bowie	Irregular blocks
Brownwood / Brown	Symmetrical with partial blocks
Canton / Van Zandt	Varied street pattern at square
Canyon* / Randall	New courthouse adjacent to square
Carthage / Panola	Courthouse on small central square
Cleburne / Johnson	Symmetrical with partial blocks
Crane / Crane	Irregular blocks
Denton / Denton	Symmetrical with partial blocks
Groesbeck / Limestone	Symmetrical with partial blocks
Jacksboro/Jack	Symmetrical with partial blocks
Jefferson / Marion	Irregular blocks
Kaufman / Kaufman	Varied street pattern at square
Longview / Gregg	Irregular blocks
Palestine / Anderson	Varied street pattern at square
Rocksprings / Edwards	Courthouse on small central square

*Confirmed by site visit. (Others confirmed by historical data only.)

symmetrical arrangement of smaller partial blocks that surround a central courthouse square, as illustrated in Denton. An aerial photograph of Denton (Figure 1) shows that town's major businesses focused on the courthouse square. The block patterns of these county seats are in keeping with the Shelbyville's characteristic focus on a single block in the town's grid plan.

Another county seat, Palestine in Anderson County (Figure 17), is similar to those described above, except that in this case a diagonal street extends from the square's southwest corner, connecting the square to another grid at the railroad. Palestine's early plans include a railroad, but it is not listed as a railroad-influenced pattern because the tracks were laid after the town was platted. Groesbeck in Limestone County also provides an interesting courthouse scheme. Maps dated 1925 indicate that Groesbeck's courthouse square is sited next to the original courthouse, creating a pair of squares.

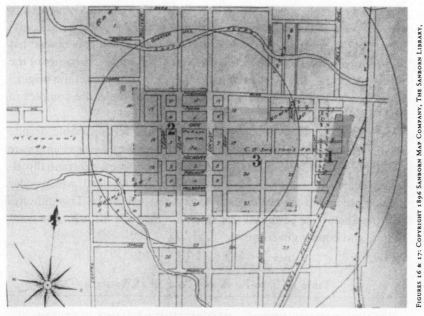

Figure 16　Plan of Denton in 1896 showing an elaborated Shelbyville pattern. The courthouse is sited on a single central square in the grid, like all Shelbyvilles. However, the surrounding blocks deviate from the prototypical pattern.

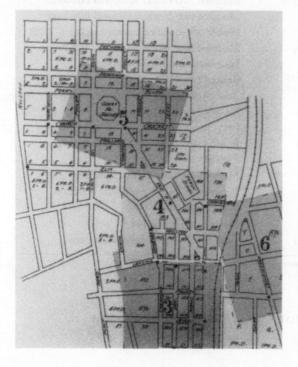

Figure 17　Partial plan of Palestine in Anderson County in 1896 with octagonal square surrounded by partial blocks of the city's grid. According to later maps, the polygon was lost by 1935, but the diagonal street at the southwest corner tying the square to the railroad remained.

A final example worth noting is in Canyon in Randall County. Here annexes were added to both the north and south ends of the old courthouse; but these too have been outgrown, and a new courthouse has just been completed on the block diagonal to the southeast corner of the square. Although largely supplanted by the new courthouse, the original courthouse is still in use and remains the focus of the entire complex of buildings.

The fact that many Shelbyvilles and variants remain viable despite change indicates the inherent strength of the pattern. Some changes are inevitable, and several former Shelbyvilles have been substantially altered. Three of these are in Houston, Dallas, and Midland, which today include plazas and are no longer classified as Shelbyvilles. This indicates that the Shelbyville pattern is not alone in offering a focus for the community and county government.

Table 11. Two-Block and Four-Block Patterns

COUNTY SEAT / COUNTY	DESCRIPTION OF BLOCK PATTERNS
Angleton* / Brazoria	Modified two-block: additional buildings
Ballinger* / Runnels	Modified two-block: additional buildings
Beaumont* / Jefferson	Modified two-block: additional buildings
Brady* / McCulloch	Modified two-block: additional buildings
Edinburg* / Hidalgo	Four-block modified to two-block
Eldorado* / Schleicher	Modified four-block: additional buildings
Farwell* / Parmer	Four-block modified to two-block
Gilmer / Upshur	Related two-block: NA
Graham* / Young	Related two-block: additional buildings
Groveton* / Trinity	Modified two-block: additional buildings
Jayton / Kent	Four-block: NA
Karnes City* / Karnes	Related two-block: additional buildings
Lubbock / Lubbock	Two-block: NA
Mason* / Mason	Modified two-block: additional buildings
Plains* / Yoakum	Related two-block: additional buildings
Quitman / Wood	Related two-block: NA
Tyler / Smith	Related two-block: NA
Weatherford* / Parker	Four-block: central courthouse only

*Confirmed by site visit. (Others confirmed by historical data only.)
NA: No current data available.

TWO-BLOCK AND FOUR-BLOCK SQUARES

The two-block and four-block patterns share features with the Shelbyville square, but more than a single block is reserved for the courthouse. In Texas there are fifteen two-block squares and three with four blocks (Table 11), although two of those currently classified as two-blocks, Edinburg and Farwell, were laid out originally as four-block squares.

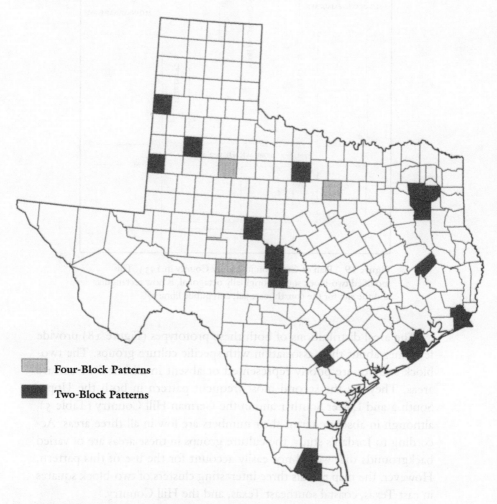

Four-Block Patterns

Two-Block Patterns

Figure 18   Two-block and four-block courthouse squares.

Anglo-American Courthouse Squares

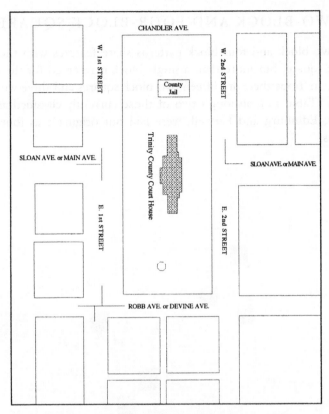

Figure 19 Plan of Groveton in Trinity County in 1933. This
modified two-block square, originally octagonal, is now rectangular
and the site for the courthouse, jail, and public library.

The areal distributions of both these prototypes (Figure 18) provide
few clues about their association with specific culture groups. The two-
block squares are poorly represented or absent in all but four culture
areas. They are the second most frequent pattern in both the Upper
South 2 and Lower South 1 and in the German Hill Country (Table 5),
although in absolute terms their numbers are low in all three areas. According to Jordan's study, the culture groups in these areas are of varied
backgrounds that would not easily account for the use of this pattern.
However, the map reveals three interesting clusters of two-block squares
in east Texas, coastal southeast Texas, and the Hill Country.

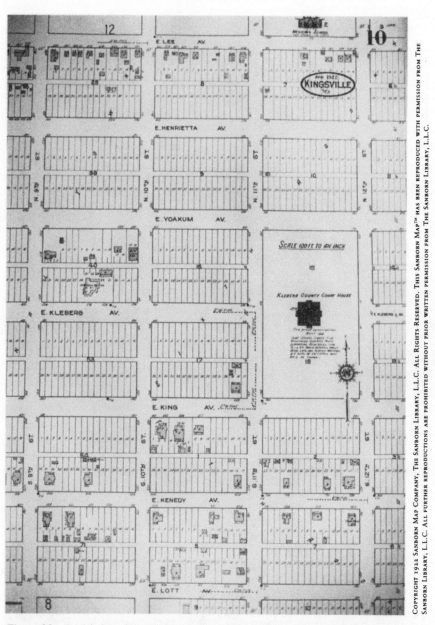

Figure 20 Partial plan of Kingsville in Kleberg County in 1922. The block pattern here is typical of two-block squares, but the town's major business district is located several blocks to the west near the railroad.

Anglo-American Courthouse Squares

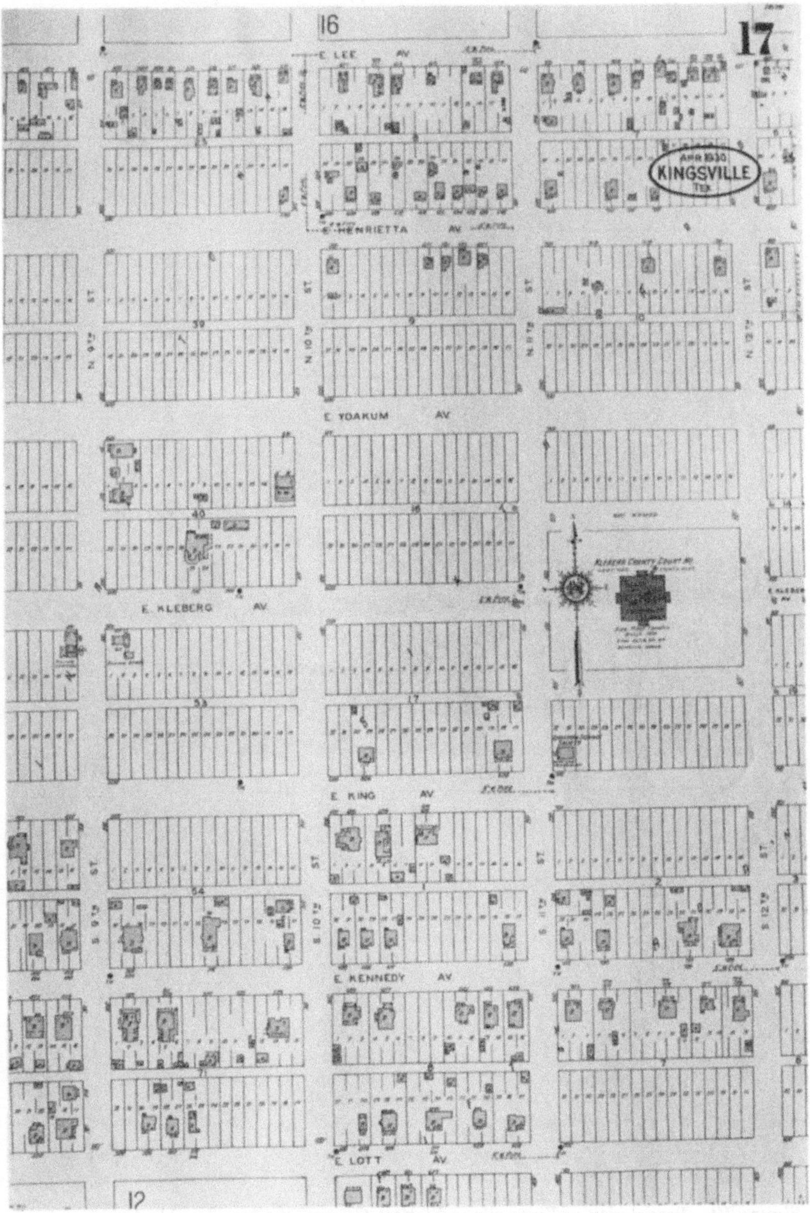

Figure 21 Partial plan of Kingsville in Kleberg County in 1930. The original two-block scheme was altered by division of the square, which is now classified as a Harrisonburg square.

THE COURTHOUSE SQUARE IN TEXAS

The four-block types occur most often in west Texas counties in the Upper South 3, especially if Farwell's square, originally a four-block, is included. Again, the relative scarcity of this pattern frustrates any attempt to relate four-block squares to any single culture area.

Many two-block plans assume the characteristics of single squares with the courthouse situated in the center, such as Groveton in Trinity County (Figure 19), which is classified as a modified two-block. In some cases, separate blocks were joined to form a two-block square. This occurred in Angleton in Brazoria County and Beaumont in Jefferson County.

Because of the ample grounds typically afforded to these squares, many two-block schemes are now the sites of additional buildings. All of the two-block squares surveyed in the field have additional buildings (Table 11). Graham in Young County is an extreme example where the original two-block square was split by a street, placing the courthouse on the north side and the post office, two jails, sheriff's office, annex, and chamber of commerce on the south. Two other original two-block schemes that changed significantly are Kingsville in Kleberg County, which became a variant of the Harrisonburg square (Figures 20 and 21), and Fort Worth in Tarrant County. Fort Worth eventually developed a plaza next to the courthouse. Both county seats are listed in other categories.

Despite the number of two-block schemes listed above, none present the hallmark features of the prototypical pattern because few two-block patterns have retained the ideal of a single building—the courthouse—on the square. Changes in street patterns that alter the original form of some of these squares are another factor. Many two-block courthouse squares, however, remain the central focus of their communities.

Those county seats originally planned as four-block squares are Edinburg in Hidalgo County, Eldorado in Schleicher County, Farwell in Parmer County, Jayton in Kent County, and Weatherford in Parker County. All have witnessed substantial changes. Edinburg's courthouse was originally sited in the center of a four-square space (Figure 22) and now is located on two blocks that face a parking lot on the remaining two blocks. In the case of Farwell (Figure 23), churches now occupy two of the original four blocks and a public park takes up most of the third. The courthouse, however, maintains a central location. The Weatherford courthouse retains its position in the center of a four-block space, but most of the space is now devoted to parking lots and traffic

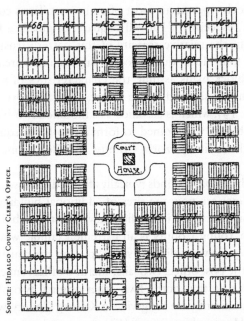

Figure 22 Portion of an early plan for Edinburg
in Hidalgo County. This scheme shown is an
elaboration of the typical four-block pattern.

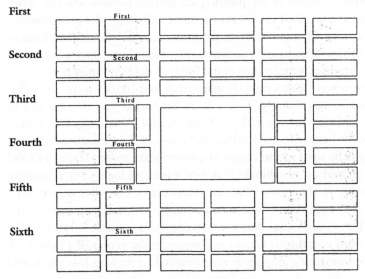

Figure 23 Portion of plat of Farwell in Parmer County in 1910.
Today the original four-block square accommodates the courthouse,
two churches, and a public park.

Figure 24 Courthouse in Weatherford in Parker County. Although the historic courthouse still occupies a central location on this four-block square, it is now surrounded by parking lots and traffic islands—a fate common to many squares.

control islands for the major highways that converge on the square (Figure 24). Eldorado is the least changed square, with all four blocks dotted with county buildings.

The arrangement of commercial land use around these large squares is varied. Both Eldorado and Farwell have a compact, traditional main street aligned with the centrally located courthouse. The other blocks facing the squares include churches and residential development. Edinburg and Weatherford, which are larger, more prosperous towns, are surrounded by commercial land use on all four blocks. As a rule, the four-block and two-block plans are capable of retaining a prominent position in their townscapes; but most two-block squares have fared better than the four-blocks, probably because the ample space afforded by four-block schemes often invites greater intrusion.

HARRISONBURG SQUARES

The Harrisonburg pattern occurs in fourteen Texas county seats. Two basic models have been found in Texas (Figure 25). One is the prototypical Harrisonburg square described by Price that requires nine city blocks of the town's grid. The other is a modified pattern, which uses a combination of half-blocks and full blocks and requires only six blocks. Five county seats follow the prototype, while five employ the modified scheme (Table 12). Four others adopt various related patterns. Common to all is a main street aligned with the midpoint of the square and

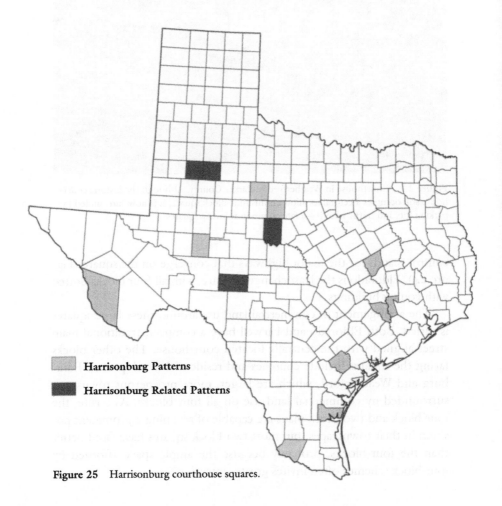

Figure 25 Harrisonburg courthouse squares.

THE COURTHOUSE SQUARE IN TEXAS

Table 12. Harrisonburg Patterns

COUNTY SEAT / COUNTY	DESCRIPTION OF PATTERN AND SQUARE
Anson / Jones	Modified: NA
Baird / Callahan	Modified: NA
Bellville* / Austin	Prototype: Fully developed square
Big Lake* / Reagan	Prototype: Incomplete development
Coleman / Coleman	Related: NA
Franklin / Robertson	Related: NA
Goliad* / Goliad	Prototype: Fully developed square
Hempstead* / Waller	Modified: Incomplete development
Kingsville* / Kleberg	Modified: Incomplete development
Marfa* / Presidio	Prototype: Incomplete development
Post / Garza	Prototype: NA
Rio Grande City* / Starr	Modified: Incomplete development
Sonora* / Sutton	Related: Incomplete development
Tahoka / Lynn	Related: NA

*Confirmed by site visit. (Others confirmed by historical data only.)
NA: No current data available.

focused on the courthouse. As in all central courthouse squares, the Harrisonburg's block patterns and lot lines reinforce the prominence of the courthouse square in the townscape.

The areal distribution of the Harrisonburg squares suggests few correlations with specific culture areas. Seven occur in the Upper South areas of west Texas, three in the Spanish-Mexican borderlands, and two each in the Lower South and central Texas Mixed culture areas (Table 5). Those located in the area of Spanish-Mexican influence typically are a consequence of later Anglo-American settlement and dominance. For example, Goliad, which was established in 1829 near a Spanish mission, adopted the prototypical Harrisonburg pattern. Those squares classified as related patterns are found in west Texas counties.

After Goliad, the two earliest examples of Harrisonburg squares in Texas are Rio Grande City in Starr County, planned in 1847, and Bellville in Austin County, laid out in 1848. Bellville adopted the prototypical pattern (Figure 26) with full blocks fronting the square. One of the first counties in Texas, Austin County was also the site of the first Anglo settlement, San Felipe de Austin. Following that town's destruction dur-

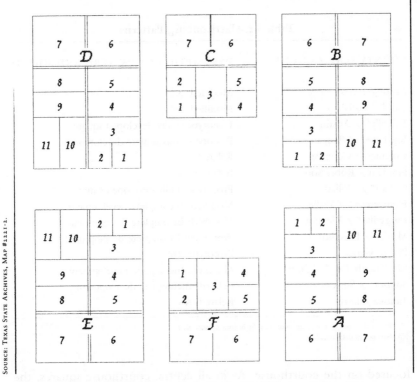

Figure 26 Plan of Bellville's square in Austin County. This plan, darkened by age, depicts the prototypical Harrisonburg pattern that requires the space of nine city blocks.

Figure 27 The courthouse in Bellville. Typical of all Harrisonburg squares, the main street is aligned with the central axis of the square and focuses attention on the courthouse.

ing Texas' war for independence, Bellville was selected as the new county seat on land donated by the Bell brothers.

Bellville's square is sited on a hilltop and surrounded by traditional storefronts. Three courthouses have stood on the square. The most recent was erected in 1960 following a fire that destroyed the 1854 structure. Today's modern and mostly windowless courthouse (Figure 27) occupies its original central position on the square, but much of the surrounding space is now occupied by parking lots and highway intersections.

The modified Harrisonburg plan causes less disruption of the grid because it requires fewer blocks. Kingsville (Figures 20 and 21), which originally developed from a two-block model, today employs two half-blocks on either side of a full-block square. Another town with this pattern is Rio Grande City. In this case, a boulevard and modest mall tie the courthouse to a small plaza and pavilion several blocks away on the town's main street. In both instances, the courthouses are removed from the CBD.

Six of the eight Harrisonburg squares surveyed are incompletely developed or removed from the CBD. This may be the result of more complicated plans, at least in comparison to Shelbyville or plaza patterns. It may also reflect the fact that many Harrisonburg and related patterns (for example, in Kingsville, Marfa, and Sonora) place the CBD along the main street leading to the courthouse square and not on the blocks surrounding the square. This is contrary to the defined pattern described by Price. Only two county seats, Bellville and Goliad, follow the prototypical Harrisonburg pattern defined by Price.

An interesting modification of the prototype's pattern occurs with respect to the lot lines in Post in Garza County (Figure 28). In what appears to be a unique configuration, all corner lots are square and oriented to both the square and the main street. The remaining lots are extremely narrow, becoming progressively shorter at the corners, and do not allow for any connections to an alley. The problems of access to these lots are obvious and suggest why this scheme was rarely employed.

In general, the Harrisonburg squares and their related patterns are successful in focusing the main street's axis on the courthouse. However, as a group, Harrisonburg squares are less likely to be surrounded by the town's major businesses, although most of these squares serve as an anchor or terminus for a linear CBD.

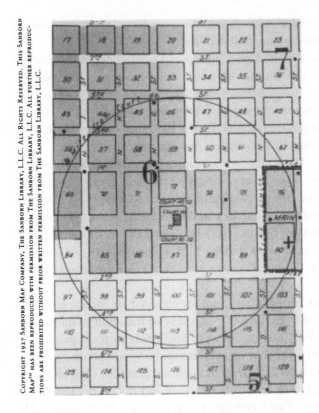

Figure 28 Plan of Post in Garza County in 1927. A unique feature of this plan is the arrangement of lots at the corners facing the square.

LANCASTER SQUARES

The Lancaster square is the most complex of central courthouse plans. The prototypical plan calls for the merging of four streets at the square's midpoint and provides a clear focus on the courthouse. However, in practical terms this plan is difficult to implement because it creates blocks with inside corners. This causes many problems for conventional land use and may account for the fact that only four county seats in Texas (Anderson in Grimes County, Henderson in Rusk County, Jourdanton in Atascosa County, and Marshall in Harrison County) have chosen Lancaster-like patterns, and all deviate from the prototypes cited by Price. Three of the four occur in east Texas and may suggest an early introduction by Lower South groups (Figure 29).

In Anderson commercial activity was originally aligned along a main

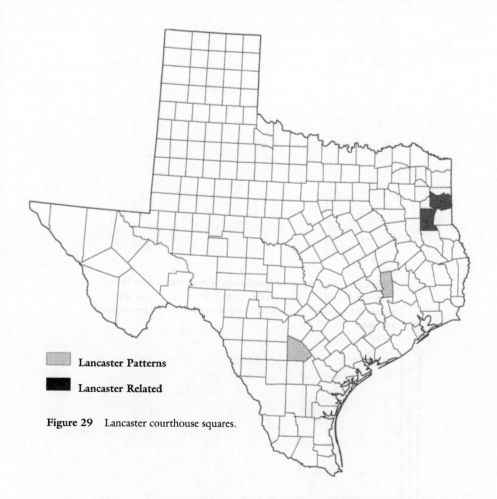

Lancaster Patterns

Lancaster Related

Figure 29   Lancaster courthouse squares.

street leading to the courthouse, but moved west one block to front the highway. Today only county annexes and law offices surround the square. The case in Jourdanton (Figure 30) is similar, with vacant lots and little commercial activity, although a public park is nearby. Anderson's courthouse maintains its prominent hilltop position, but Jourdanton's is clearly peripheral to the life of the community.

Two other squares are classified as Lancaster-related patterns because each has four streets merging on the courthouse square, similar to the prototypical plan. These are Henderson (Figure 31) and Marshall (Figure 32). Both schemes are more elaborate and include partial blocks at the square. The similarities in these two plans suggest a shared origin. Marshall's square was identified by T. G. Jordan as a distinct type, but is

Anglo-American Courthouse Squares

59

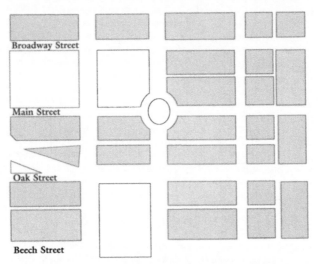

Figure 30 Partial plan of Jourdanton in Atascosa County in 1974. The courthouse is located on the circle. The intersecting of four streets at the courthouse square is a characteristic of the prototypical Lancaster.

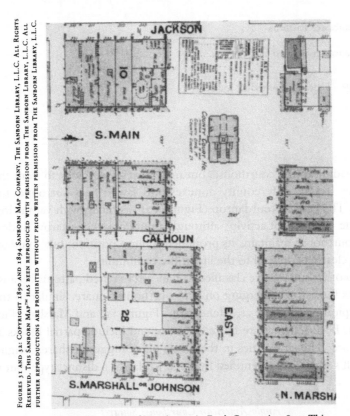

Figure 31 Plan of Henderson in Rusk County in 1890. This early scheme depicts a pattern that is related to the Lancaster square, but with the addition of smaller blocks around the square.

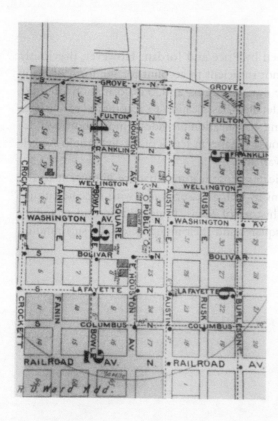

Figure 32 Plan of Marshall in Harrison County in 1894. Marshall's courthouse square is very similar to that of its neighbor, Henderson.

classified here as a Lancaster-related pattern because of its street pattern at the square.

Both Henderson and Marshall are classified as Lancaster-related patterns on the premise that elaborations of a prototype are best described in terms of that pattern. This was done with the other categories as well. It is reasonable to assume that these and other related patterns could be listed as separate types; however, for the purposes of this classification, further subdivision was not necessary.

THE SIGNIFICANCE OF ANGLO-AMERICAN PATTERNS AND THEIR VARIANTS

The data discussed above testify to the dominance of Anglo-American courthouse square patterns in Texas. Most of these derive from the prototypes originally described by Price and Jordan. However, previously defined prototypes were not sufficient to account for the form of many courthouse squares. The varied origins and transformation of these squares required a more detailed classification to accommodate changes in the square. The resulting classification provides a more thorough description of Texas courthouse squares in terms of the five Anglo-American prototypes and their variants.

This classification indicates those features that are important to the retention of these patterns as well as associations with specific culture areas and the settlement history of Texas. It also aids in understanding the forces acting on the squares and their influence on the surrounding urban landscape.

Chapter Four

Origins of the Anglo-American
Courthouse Squares

The courthouse square in Texas is an urban form derived from diverse sources. The plans of most courthouse squares were the result of Anglo-American settlement. However, a significant number of Texas county seats observe planning traditions that did not originally include a courthouse square. In reviewing and weighing these influences, three points should be stressed. The first is that Texas remained a frontier for several centuries and much of its early settlement was based upon planning traditions developed for new towns in both the Old and New Worlds. Second, Hispanic, European, and Anglo-American town planning traditions in Texas typically relied on the grid-pattern plan and public square. Third, when Texas came to be rapidly settled, it was largely by Anglo-Americans from states with established systems of county government and central courthouse squares. These Anglo-American central courthouse squares became the model for most county seats in Texas.

To place the Anglo-American courthouse square in its proper context requires review of the planning precedents available to the European settler in the New World, particularly those involving the grid-pattern plan and town square. Reps noted the potential range of European models available when he stated:

> One unifying theme running through the diverse strains of western cities
> is the prevailing use of the gridiron . . . While we may think of this as typ-
> ically American, it has been the plan-form used in all great periods of
> mass town founding in the past: Mediterranean colonization by the
> Greeks and Romans; medieval urban settlement in southwestern France,

Poland, and eastern Germany; Spanish subjugation of Latin America; and English occupation of Northern Ireland. (Reps 1979, x)

In light of these many influences, the grid-pattern town in the Americas should be viewed as the product of both importation from various sources of Old World origin and invention in response to New World rationalism and expansionism. The widespread use of the grid in the Americas resulted from application and adaptation of this well-known form to an ever-expanding frontier.

How the grid came to be the preferred form for new towns in both the Old and New Worlds is the subject of continuing debate (Kubler 1978). Many have suggested the importance of Roman town planning and its characteristic order. Some researchers have noted the role of the church in bridging the centuries between Roman town plans and medieval ones (Dupree 1968; Braunfels 1988).

Others have argued against the role of the Roman model, favoring the advent of the grid in new town plans and infatuation with ideal city plans during the Renaissance. An urban historian, Wolfgang Braunfels, addressed the difficulty of tracing the influence of the Roman grid in urban history as well as the role of the church in rebuilding ancient towns. He remarked that

> there is no dividing line between antiquity and the Middle Ages. The process took a different course in different provinces and in each of their towns between the 4th and 11th centuries . . . In a few [provinces and towns], . . . the Roman era lasted until the 8th century: in others, . . . all that the first missionaries found . . . were neglected ruins and grass-grown streets. (Braunfels 1988, 12)

Another researcher, Hunter Dupree, documented one way in which the church may have preserved use of the grid. Through observations on the construction of the Abbey of Saint Gall in Switzerland around 820, Dupree noted use of the Roman pace as a measurement and the orthogonal organization of spaces. The regular unit of measure and grid-like arrangement of the abbey's plan (Figure 33) represent a link between Roman custom and medieval church construction (Dupree 1968, 19). The use of the grid in laying out and constructing large monastic complexes might also have served as a model for later planning efforts, as well as preserving aspects of Latin-based order. Thus, the church through its perseverance may have provided the basis for reemergence of the grid in Europe.

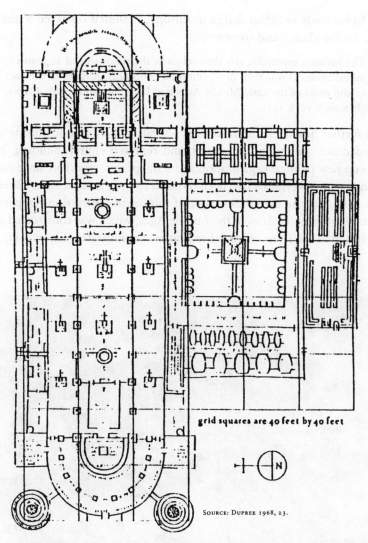

grid squares are 40 feet by 40 feet

N

SOURCE: DUPREE 1968, 23.

Figure 33 Plan of the Abbey of Saint Gall, Switzerland, in 820. Dupree suggested that the construction of the monastery was based upon Roman-derived principles of measurement and orthogonal planning. The grid lines on the plan indicate the use of a 40-foot module or eight Roman paces.

Origins of the Anglo-American Courthouse Squares

In his study of urban design in Europe, Braunfels observed a similar role for the church and commented:

> The bishops, especially, saw themselves as the successors of Roman administration. It was they that promoted continuity. Almost all the successful cities of the early Middle Ages had been Roman cathedral cities. (Braunfels 1988, 13)

He further noted that architectural revival of the cities of Europe depended not only upon the church and renewed church building, but also on new political organization and royal power, especially since most Roman cities previously had been reduced to their ancient cores (Braunfels 1988, 13). An extreme example of this urban contraction is apparent in an illustration of Arles in the Middle Ages, which was constructed entirely within the ruins of an earlier Roman amphitheater (Figure 34).

SOURCE: BENEVOLO 1981, 257.

Figure 34 Drawing of medieval Arles, France. Built within the ruins of an ancient Roman amphitheater, Arles characterizes the loss of the Roman urban planning legacy during the feudal period.

THE COURTHOUSE SQUARE IN TEXAS

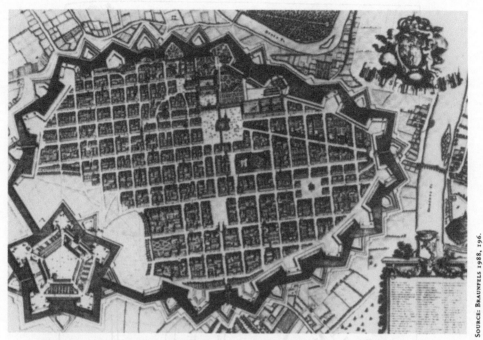

SOURCE: BRAUNFELS 1988, 196.

Figure 35   Plan of Turin, Italy, in 1682. Turin illustrates revival of a Roman grid plan. Although large areas were in ruins or vacant, the city was revived in 1599 and the grid enlarged in 1673, following royal preferences for formal planning by local princes.

Planning scholars like Paul Zucker also observed that the Roman grid underlying many European towns was largely forgotten or obscured and that it was new town plans and not the Roman grid that served as models for planners of grid-patterned towns (Zucker 1959). A notable exception was Turin (Figure 35), which reinstated its long dormant but largely intact Roman grid beginning in 1599 (Braunfels 1988, 197). Ancient towns like Turin were able to return to their Roman street plans not because they had been purposefully preserved, but because of decline or neglect, which left their grids largely undisturbed and available for later use by a royal family (Braunfels 1988, 196).

More deliberate uses of the grid-pattern came about as the result of planning for new towns. Some models for new towns were based on utopian or fortified planning schemes. Plans for "ideal towns" by Leon Battista Alberti, Filarete (Antonio di Pietro Averlino), Pietro Cataneo,

Origins of the Anglo-American Courthouse Squares

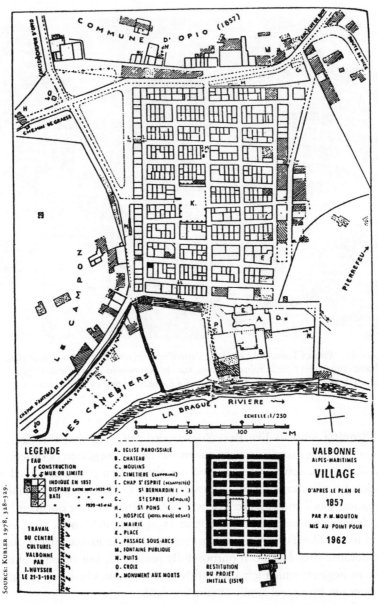

Figure 36 Plan of Valbonne, France, in 1857 with an inset detailing the plan of 1519. Note the regular grid-pattern plan and central "place." Kubler believed such towns, which were rebuilt after the plagues, may have reintroduced the grid-pattern plan to urban planning and predated published plans of ideal towns typically cited by planning scholars.

THE COURTHOUSE SQUARE IN TEXAS

and Vincenzo Scamozzi combined the rationalism and symbolism of fifteenth- and sixteenth-century Italy that valued formal planning techniques for military and sociopolitical reasons. One such scheme was Filarete's plan for Sforzinda in Italy, which Zucker called the "idée fixe" of utopian projects: "This general scheme is of decisive importance for many future plans, from Palma Nuova and Granmichele in Italy to Washington D.C." (Zucker 1959, 102).

However, use of ideal towns as models must have been the exception. Both Jorge Hardoy and George Kubler noted earlier, more commonplace and numerous uses of the grid in Europe (Hardoy 1978; Kubler 1978). Citing French, English, and Spanish grid-patterned towns, they pointed to hundreds of lesser-known new or reestablished towns in Europe that adopted the grid to accommodate growing economies and populations. Kubler specifically made the case for "new, unwalled gridiron towns" (Kubler 1978, 328–329) rebuilt by Benedictines after a century's abandonment during the plagues. One such town was Valbonne in France in 1519 (Figure 36), which used a regular grid-pattern plan with a central open square (Kubler 1978, 328–329). Again, the church's preservation of ancient knowledge may have informed the Benedictines' tasks of town building for expanding populations.

Hardoy noted such pragmatic issues: "The need to enlarge and remodel existing cities at this time resulted in the development of partial urban aggregates and in the adoption of complete town-planning schemes" (Hardoy 1978, 220). He also commented on why these schemes may have been overlooked and on the need for such planning:

Undoubtedly it is a less resplendent theme than others generally favored by historians of cities . . . [Yet] The sixteenth century saw the spread in Europe of designs of straight streets crossing at right or almost right angles, with orderly squares and complete plans for sufficient space to absorb population growth. (Hardoy 1978, 222)

Other influential European new towns were based on the grid and central square. The new town of Charleville (Figure 37) was designed and built between 1608 and 1620. Zucker described it as a combination of Italian theoretical notions and noted that "Charleville is based upon the gridiron . . . its straight streets connect its central square with six subordinate squares" (Zucker 1959, 167). This grid plan with multiple squares would be reiterated in the town plans of Charleston in 1624 and

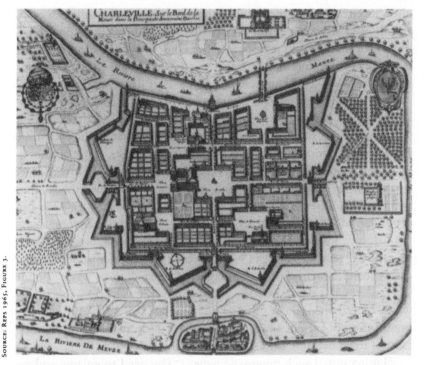

Figure 37 Plan of Charleville, France, in 1656, showing the new town surrounded by fortified ramparts. The plan features a central square and general orthogonal arrangement.

in James Oglethorpe's plan for Savannah in 1733, which made a virtue of multiple squares (Speck 1985, 12–13).

What is apparent from these examples is that town planners, lay and professional alike, turned to the grid and square. Similar planning traditions were carried by the colonial powers to the New World and formed the basis for both the Anglo-American square and courthouse plans derived from other precedents.

ANGLO-AMERICAN PRECEDENTS

To understand the evolution of many of the courthouse squares in Texas requires a brief review of the historical precedents for the square in Anglo-American culture. The institutions of the county and county courthouse are distinctly Anglo-American and are well represented in the siting and planning of many Texas towns. Anglo-American practices of town building were based on centuries of experience by a population of English stock who settled North America and, interestingly, by English colonial experiments in places such as Ireland. Anglo-American culture in colonial America is often studied in terms of major culture areas: the New England states, the Mid-Atlantic states (which included New York, Pennsylvania, and later the Upper South), and two other traditions: the Tidewater and Plantation cultures in the Lower South. All shared an urban landscape that at times utilized the grid and square.

Several of these groups influenced the urban landscape of Texas, including the planning of courthouse squares. The planning traditions of these culture groups evolved as settlers moved from the colonies across the United States and, later, into Texas. Many of these practices can be linked with the five Anglo-American block patterns described previously (Shelbyvilles, Harrisonburgs, Lancasters, and two- and four-block squares). The Mid-Atlantic culture areas, including the Upper South, had the most influence on material culture in Texas, including the preference for central courthouse squares.

Mid-Atlantic Planning Traditions

The Mid-Atlantic area contained two of the most significant and influential cities in American town planning: New York and Philadelphia (Reps 1969, 184). Both popularized the use of the grid now synonymous with American cities. Each town also included a prominent public park or square, although Philadelphia's plan was more significant in terms of influence on the courthouse square.

New York's first extensive use of the grid occurred in 1785 and again in 1796 under supervision of the city surveyor, Casimir Goerck, although a rectangular scheme by Francis Maerschalck was used for earlier developments in the 1760s. Later, in 1811, a New York state commission formalized and expanded Goerck's grid to include a total of 12 hundred-foot-wide north-south avenues and 155 sixty-foot-wide east-west streets, completing Manhattan's familiar grid pattern (Reps 1969, 194–196).

In contrast, Philadelphia (Figure 38) was planned from the outset following William Penn's guidelines, dated September 30, 1681, which were laid out in 1682 by Captain Thomas Holme (Reps 1969, 207). The dominant features of the plan are the grid, the ten-acre central public square, and the four additional squares of eight acres each. The central square is approached from two main streets that converge at the midpoints of the public square in a manner similar to the Lancaster block pattern.

Donald Meinig quoted early reports that "the formal and spacious symmetry of Philadelphia showed it 'to be a product of Baroque London [and] the first important example in America of the order so desired by the merchant and the trader'" (Meinig 1986, 140). Reps commented on several possible precedents for Penn's plan. One was the plan for Londonderry (Figure 39) in Northern Ireland that was laid out in the 1620s with a central square sited at the convergence of the town's major streets. Another potential precedent for Philadelphia's plan was Richard Newcourt's design scheme for rebuilding a portion of London after the Great Fire of 1666. This plan featured the use of five public squares (Figure 40). Reps suggested that Penn would probably have been aware of both designs from his previous experience in England, which included

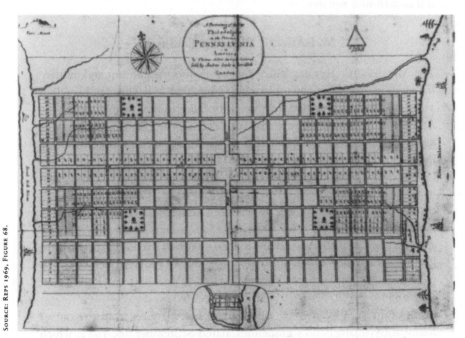

Figure 38 Plan of Philadelphia in 1683. The central square was placed midway along the main street. Philadelphia became one of the most influential plans in America in terms of its extensive use of the grid and prominent siting of public squares.

THE COURTHOUSE SQUARE IN TEXAS

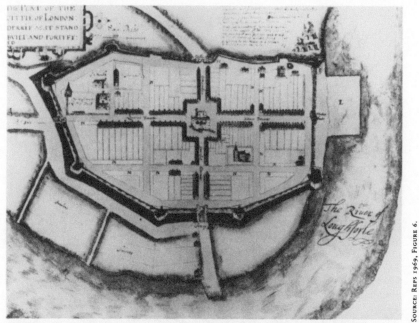

Figure 39 Plan of Londonderry in Northern Ireland in 1622, a colonial city. Note the plan's focus upon the central square and the main streets converging at the midpoints of the square. Note, too, that the square is occupied by an imposing structure. This pattern was also to emerge in the American colonies.

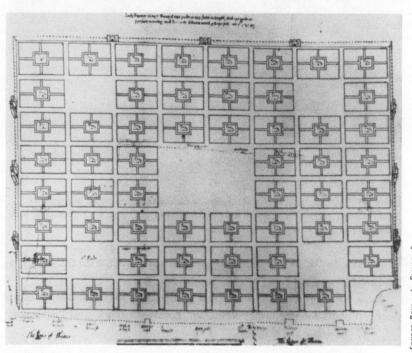

Figure 40 Plan for London by Richard Newcourt. After the Great Fire of 1666, numerous plans were considered for the rebuilding of London. Newcourt called for a series of rectangular blocks and courts arranged around five open squares. This scheme may have influenced William Penn's plans for Philadelphia and indirectly, perhaps, the plan of Texas' capital city, Austin.

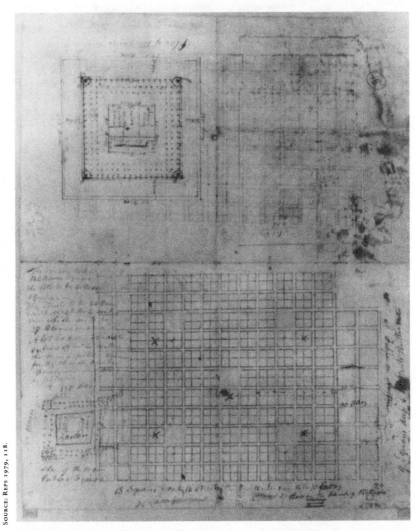

SOURCE: REPS 1979, 118.

Figure 41 Unexecuted plan for San Felipe de Austin as first proposed by Stephen F. Austin in 1824. Scholars have noted its resemblance to Penn's plan for Philadelphia, with a central square and four smaller satellite squares.

tenure as director of two "undistinguished" settlements on the Jersey Islands (Reps 1969, 212).

Reps also noted that Philadelphia's pattern of streets and squares influenced plans for Reading, Allentown, Lancaster, York, and Pittsburgh, as well as the capitals of Raleigh (1792) and Tallahassee (1824). He stated, "The single open square in the center of the town became the typical expression of the Philadelphia plan as it was transplanted west" (Reps 1969, 223). However, these squares did not always remain open, as in the case of Lancaster, which was identified by Price as one of five prototypes of central courthouse squares.

Aspects of Newcourt's London scheme and Penn's plan for Philadelphia's can be found in Stephen F. Austin's original design for San Felipe de Austin (Figure 41) and later in Mirabeau B. Lamar's and Edwin Waller's plan for the capital of Texas, named in honor of Austin. San Felipe was the first Anglo town in Texas and the capital of Austin's colony in what was then Mexican territory. Austin's plan for San Felipe called for a central public square and four additional squares. The similarities to Newcourt's and Penn's plans are obvious. The plan shown also indicates that the locations of the squares were shifted slightly by Austin, but to little avail: the Mexican authorities did not approve his plan. The final form of the short-lived town followed Hispanic planning precedents (discussed below).

By the time the city of Austin was surveyed in 1839, Texas was independent and Anglo preferences prevailed. Yet, despite the influence of the Philadelphia pattern in the plan for the capital, few courthouse squares in Texas used such schemes. The most popular Anglo-American pattern is the Shelbyville square, which according to Price is named for its prototype in Tennessee. Although this pattern is found throughout the Mid-Atlantic culture area, especially in the Upper South, earlier precedents can be found in the county seats of other culture areas, such as those of the Lower South.

The Lower South and Plantation Planning Traditions

Planning traditions in the Lower South also contributed to the form of rural Texas county seats. The county seat became the distinctive community type of the South, as Meinig observed: "the physical and social patterns of the southern county [seat] were the rural American counterpart of the European baroque capital, the city of the palace and the parade" (Meinig 1986, 156). He further noted that many county seats were not very different from the early state capitals of Annapolis and Williamsburg, with "wide avenues and squares, imposing capitols, governor's houses, and colleges" (Meinig 1986, 156), even though rural free-standing courthouses were often the rule in the counties of the southern coastal plains.

Two towns in the Lower South have distinctive plans: Charleston and Savannah. Both were planned towns that benefited from a policy of centralized planning. Charleston was begun in 1672 and by 1680 included a courthouse centered on a two-acre square with four streets focused on the center of the square (Reps 1969, 225).

Savannah was subdivided into wards of four tythings each. Each tything consisted of ten house lots of 60 x 90 feet each (Reps 1969, 242). More importantly, each ward contained an open, parklike space of 270 x 315 feet for the owners of the forty house lots situated in each ward. The consistent pattern of alternating open spaces was unique to Savannah. The application of this elaborate scheme of streets and squares was perhaps too formal and rigid for many frontier planners.

In some ways Savannah's plan recalls elements of Newcourt's scheme. However, Reps noted a written account that suggested Oglethorpe himself had attributed his design to colonial town plans in Northern Ireland (Reps 1969, 251). Whatever the source, Savannah's extensive system of squares did not become a model for later American cities, although some towns applied similar street patterns to a single square.

Reps reported on another early example of a central courthouse square in New Bern, North Carolina, which was laid out in 1710 (Reps 1969, 230). County seats planned around a central courthouse square such as those of New Bern or Charleston influenced plans for county seats from the Eastern Seaboard to Texas. Charleston's plan echoes the Lancaster pattern, while New Bern's is more similar to the prolific Shelbyville.

Tidewater Planning Traditions

The Tidewater culture associated with Virginia and Maryland only indirectly influenced planning in Texas. Town building in the Tidewater region began with the founding of colonial trading centers and public acts concerning establishment of new towns. These acts, which were later repealed, specified site selection, planning, land acquisition, valuation, taxation, and layout of public buildings and town lots (Reps 1969, 116). Typical of these laws, Maryland's new town act specifically stipulated that each site be

> marcked staked out and devided into Convenient streets, Laines, & allies, with Open Space places to be left on which may be Erected Church or Chappell, & Marckett house, or other publick buildings, & the remaining part of the said One hundred acres of Land as neare as may be into One hundred equall Lotts. (Reps 1969, 118)

However, before such planning directives were changed, a few towns were established, such as Alexandria in Virginia in 1748 and Charlestown in Maryland in 1742. Charlestown (Figure 42), a county seat, was surveyed with three distinct squares: a market square and two public squares. All three squares were approached by streets focused on their midpoints, as had been the case in Philadelphia and Londonderry. However, Charlestown's courthouse was not located on any of the squares, but rather on a half-block reserved for the government of the colony.

Observations on the Origins of Anglo-American Patterns

The plans for many courthouse squares are derived from Anglo-American urban forms that evolved from plans for colonial capitals and county seats in the states as well as in Northern Ireland. Even though the English had few centralized or defined settlement policies comparable to those of the Spanish, and no distinct regional organization like that of the French, they did have the county and county seat. This form of self-government with its unique blend of local and central policies was adapted to life in the colonies.

County government and county seats were of less consequence in New England, where the township with its meeting hall and commons was the "primary local unit" (Meinig 1986, 237). However, in the Upper and Lower South the county seat was often a planned, centrally located feature, sometimes alone in a rural landscape, such as Appomattox Court House in Virginia. The Mid-Atlantic states offered numerous models, from imposing and influential plans, such as Philadelphia's, to more straightforward schemes like the Shelbyville.

Many elaborate prototypes touted by scholars as influential proved to be the exception rather than the rule in Texas, which favored more pragmatic versions. Yet, however simple or elaborate, these patterns share a focus on the courthouse. In Texas the Anglo-American form of central courthouse squares became the dominant feature of many townscapes.

Origins of the Anglo-American Courthouse Squares

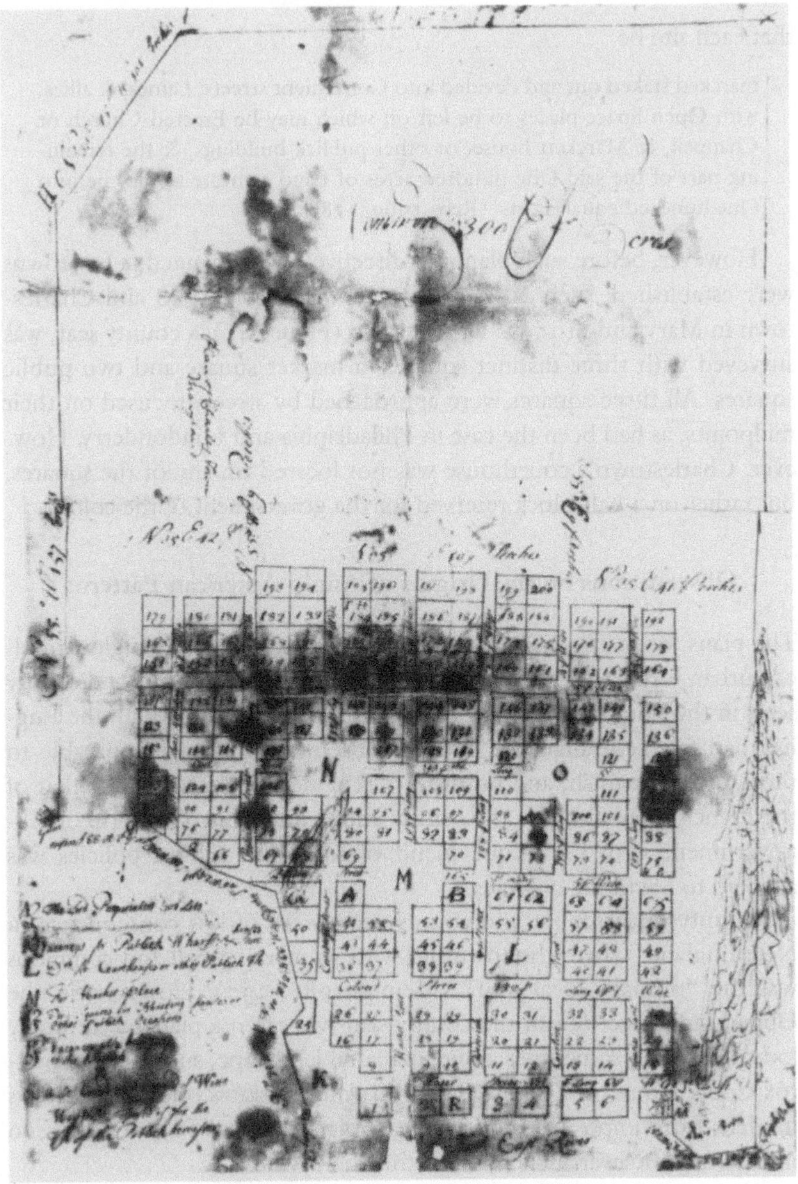

Figure 42 Plan for the county seat of Charlestown, Maryland, in 1742. An early example of town planning principles in the Tidewater calling for open public squares and use of the grid. Two public squares are marked with "N" and "O." An "M" indicates the market square. The courthouse block is marked "L," and the blocks noted as "A" and "B" on the Market Square were reserved for the lord proprietors of the colony.

THE COURTHOUSE SQUARE IN TEXAS

Even though many of the Anglo-American models for courthouse squares had elements in common with English precedents, they were often expressed more freely and expansively in the colonies. Perhaps the greatest legacy of the English, with respect to Anglo-American town planning, was a lack of any sustained policy or system of planning, which allowed for a diversity and flexibility that would prove crucial in adapting the grid-pattern to a frontier landscape. Meinig commented upon this fact: "Thus the English colonies in America displayed something of the diversities of their antecedents, the marked variety of their initiators, and the continued vitality of the English genius for adaptation" (Meinig 1986, 239).

Chapter Five

Squares Derived from Spanish Precedents
and Other Planning Traditions

Many squares developed from planning traditions other than those adopted by Anglo-American settlers. The Anglo-American patterns were unique insofar as they were intended specifically for siting a central courthouse in a town's plan; but many towns were platted for different reasons, and plans had to be adapted to include a courthouse. In these cases, the courthouse was sited according to other planning traditions and precedents. This is the first study to consider these other five types of squares in detail. Plaza squares, railroad-influenced plans, quarter-block and half-block schemes, and irregular-block plans account for nearly one-quarter of the state's county seats.

Previous studies passed over these squares because they are derived from sources unassociated with Anglo-American central courthouse squares. The Anglo-American squares have gained perhaps more than their share of attention because they are diagnostic of the material culture of certain groups that moved across the United States. Plans derived from other precedents are no less interesting, however. The adaptation of other planning traditions provides insight into the influence of other cultural groups on the landscape of Texas. These patterns are far more varied than their Anglo-American counterparts precisely because they reflect the influence of a wider range of cultural groups, including Spanish, Mexican, and German populations, with different settlement histories. The modification of these plans lends additional insights into the malleability of urban design and the ways in which designers sought to develop new civic spaces from the existing urban fabric. These designers were striving toward many of the same goals manifest in the Anglo-American patterns—such as the reinforcement of the square's prominence and centripetal influence—but had to base their solutions on other precedents. The hybrid patterns that resulted offer an interesting study in the history of Texan and American town planning.

PLAZA COURTHOUSES

Apart from the Shelbyville, the plaza courthouse is the most widely accepted pattern in Texas and accounts for some of the oldest and newest civic spaces in the state (Figure 43). Most Texas plazas evolved from Hispanic, European, or Anglo-American prototypes. The first plazas were associated with Hispanic town plans. Other European settlers in

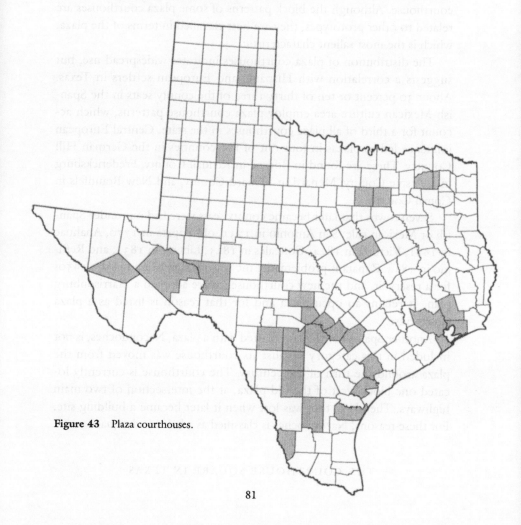

Figure 43   Plaza courthouses.

Texas, such as the Germans, employed central plazas too. The most influential Anglo-American plaza plan was Penn's scheme for Philadelphia (Price 1968; Reps 1979; Meinig 1989). In the twentieth century urban plazas were created in response to other influences, such as those designed by the WPA in the 1930s and by urban planners in more recent years.

Thirty-three county seats are classified as plaza courthouses (Table 13). No single prototype exists for these spaces, which are defined by this study as a courthouse sited adjacent to an open public space. Fifteen county seats fit this description. Ten have plazas next to their courthouses, but these have been modified by the addition of public or private buildings. Eight are related patterns because of their proximity to open plazas. Several have small urban plazas that were added to the courthouse. Although the block patterns of some plaza courthouses are related to other prototypes, they are best classified in terms of the plaza, which is the most salient characteristic.

The distribution of plaza courthouses indicates widespread use, but suggests a correlation with Hispanic and European settlers in Texas. About 30 percent or ten of thirty-three of the county seats in the Spanish-Mexican culture area employ plaza courthouse patterns, which account for a third of all plaza courthouses in the state. Central European influence led to plazas in four out of five counties in the German Hill Country. These are found in Boerne in Kendall County, Fredericksburg in Gillespie County, Menard in Menard County, and New Braunfels in Comal County.

Seven towns that later became county seats were laid out under Spanish or Mexican rule: San Antonio in 1731, old Zapata in 1770, Anahuac in 1821, Victoria in 1824, Gonzales in 1825, Liberty in 1831, and Refugio in 1834. Zapata is problematic: the town was relocated in the 1950s for a reservoir, and the new courthouse square adopted a Harrisonburg plan. It retains an open plaza and for that reason is listed as a plaza courthouse.

Another Spanish settlement platted with a plaza, Nacogdoches, is not included in this category because its courthouse was moved from the plaza around the turn of the century. The courthouse is currently located one block west of the old plaza, at the intersection of two main highways. The plaza, too, was lost when it later became a building site. For these reasons, Nacogdoches is classified as a half-block square.

Table 13. Plaza Patterns

COUNTY SEAT / COUNTY	DESCRIPTION OF PATTERN AND PLAZA
Anahuac* / Chambers	Modified: Former plaza with public building
Aspermont / Stonewall	Prototype: (1934 Sanborn Map)
Austin* / Travis	Prototype: Open with lawn, gazebo
Boerne* / Kendall	Related: One block from open plaza
Corpus Christi* / Nueces	Related: Urban plaza with fountain, monument
Cotulla* / La Salle	Prototype: Open with lawn, gazebo
Crosbyton* / Crosby	Modified: Former plaza with public building
Dallas* / Dallas	Prototype: Open with fountain, monument
Fort Davis* / Jeff Davis	Related: Near open irregular plaza
Fort Stockton* / Pecos	Prototype: Open with monuments
Fort Worth / Tarrant	Prototype: (1945 Sanborn Map)
Fredericksburg* / Gillespie	Modified: Partly open with public building
Galveston* / Galveston	Modified: Open with lawn, fountain, monument
Gonzales* / Gonzales	Modified: Partly open with monument
Hondo* / Medina	Modified: Former plaza with public building
Houston* / Harris	Related: Small urban plaza
Liberty* / Liberty	Modified: Former plaza with public building
Menard* / Menard	Modified: Partly open—recreational
Midland* / Midland	Related: Small urban plaza, fountain
Mount Vernon / Franklin	Prototype: (1923 Sanborn Map)
New Braunfels* / Comal	Prototype: Open plaza with lawn, gazebo
Ozona* / Crockett	Prototype: Open plaza with lawn, monument
Pampa / Gray	Modified: (1949 Sanborn Map)
Pearsall* / Frio	Related: Partly open—recreational
Refugio* / Refugio	Modified: Public building, lawn, gazebo
San Antonio* / Bexar	Prototype: Open plaza with fountain, monument
San Diego* / Duval	Related: Partly open—recreational
Seguin* / Guadalupe	Prototype: lawn, fountain, monument
Sulphur Springs / Hopkins	Prototype: (1915 Sanborn Map)
Uvalde* / Uvalde	Prototype: Open with lawn, gazebo, monument
Victoria* / Victoria	Prototype: Open with lawn, gazebo, monument
Waco* / McLennan	Related: Urban plaza with parking lots
Zapata* / Zapata	Prototype: Open with lawn, gazebo, monument

*Confirmed by site visit. (Others confirmed by historical data only.)

Squares Derived from Spanish Precedents and Other Traditions

Other courthouses that do not occupy full blocks opposite the plaza are Crosbyton, Fredericksburg, Menard, New Braunfels, Ozona, and Refugio. Crosbyton's and Refugio's courthouses are both located on half-blocks. The remainder of their blocks are shared with private land use. Menard's courthouse sits on a long block that combines a site for the school and public park. Ozona's court building is sited in the middle of a block across from the public park that is surrounded by a mix of land uses. New Braunfels' courthouse is placed on a corner lot. Fredericksburg's current structure shares a vast block—originally designed as a market and church square before the town became a county seat—with other public buildings, including the former courthouse (now a history museum and library). Refugio also erected a library on a portion of its plaza. The remainder of the space is reserved for lawn, monuments, and a gazebo, which are typical of many courthouse squares. Today many of the plazas include some type of public structure or monument.

Of twenty-eight plaza courthouses visited (Table 13), sixteen have plazas that remain open or partly open. Another six county seats with formerly open plazas have been obscured by a combination of public or private buildings. Four county seats visited had modern urban plazas, which are usually smaller, paved spaces that are closely associated with public buildings: Corpus Christi, Houston, Midland, and Waco. Two other sites, Boerne and Fort Davis, had courthouses located within a block of an open public space.

Prototypical Plaza Courthouses

The prototypical plaza courthouse is characterized by an open, public space or park bounded by streets on all sides and fronted by the courthouse. Fifteen county seats are counted in this category, although there is no typical block pattern (Table 13). In most cases, the courthouse sits on a separate block opposite a plaza, as in Seguin (Figure 44). Like many plaza types, Seguin is a hybrid form. The courthouse square and open plaza occupy equal blocks in a uniform grid and appear to address the Hispanic preference for an open plaza and the Anglo-American tradition calling for a central courthouse square.

One of the earliest examples of a prototypical plaza courthouse can be found in San Antonio (Figure 45). Originally laid out by Spanish officials in 1731 according to many of the planning principles contained in

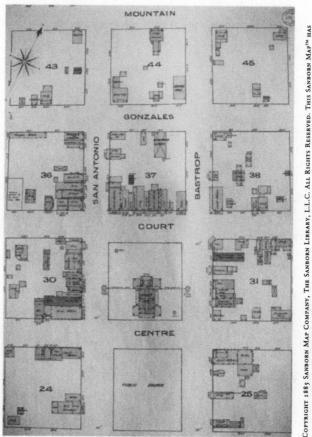

Figure 44   Plan of Seguin in Guadalupe County in 1885. This map depicts a central courthouse square fronting an open plaza. This plan is typical of many courthouse plaza patterns.

the Laws of the Indies, San Antonio's Main Plaza remains open (Figure 46). Today shade trees and a fountain stand opposite the present courthouse, which was erected in 1892 on the plaza's southern end. Numerous additions to the courthouse and changes in the street plan at the Main Plaza have not altered the basic form or relationship between the courthouse and plaza in San Antonio. The importance of this civic space is reinforced by the cathedral, also sited on the plaza, and the city hall one block west. However, given the significance of the Alamo in Anglo-Texas history, its larger plaza attracts more attention and activity.

Other prototypical plazas located in the Spanish-Mexican culture

Squares Derived from Spanish Precedents and Other Traditions

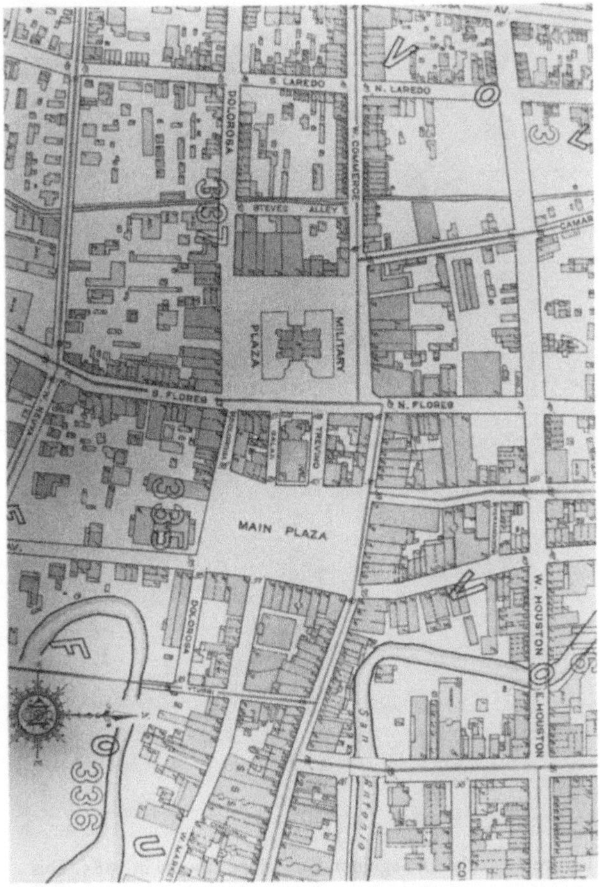

Figure 45 Plan of San Antonio in Bexar County in 1911. The Main Plaza in San Antonio remains open. The courthouse complex is located on the south side of the plaza. Military Plaza became the site of the city hall in 1910.

area include Cotulla, Fort Stockton, Uvalde, Victoria, and Zapata, although not all were planned strictly according to Hispanic tradition. All have open parklike plazas, but varied block patterns and land use. Cotulla was laid out in the 1880s with a hilltop courthouse and plaza that form a formal axis terminating at the central business district situated downhill along the railroad tracks. Fort Stockton's courthouse and plaza are located in the historic part of town away from most commercial ac-

THE COURTHOUSE SQUARE IN TEXAS

tivity. The old plaza is dominated by monuments and markers and is surrounded by county offices and a historic church.

Uvalde employs a more extensive arrangement of four central blocks: one for the public square, another for the courthouse, and one each for the city hall and post office (Figure 47). All four blocks are surrounded by storefronts, with the most prominent businesses fronting the plaza and courthouse block. Victoria's plaza, which dates to 1824, is also open and formal, but the courthouse block is cluttered with county buildings. Several high-rise buildings surround the plaza. Zapata was first planned in 1770 with an open plaza. In the 1950s the town was relocated and rebuilt to make way for the International Falcon Reservoir. In an attempt to retain an open plaza, a half-block of the modified Harrisonburg scheme was dedicated as a park. Today the courthouse and plaza remain less well developed than in Uvalde or Victoria in terms of commercial activity.

Figure 46 Main Plaza in San Antonio. The view is to the south, with the plaza's fountain in the foreground and the courthouse beyond.

Squares Derived from Spanish Precedents and Other Traditions

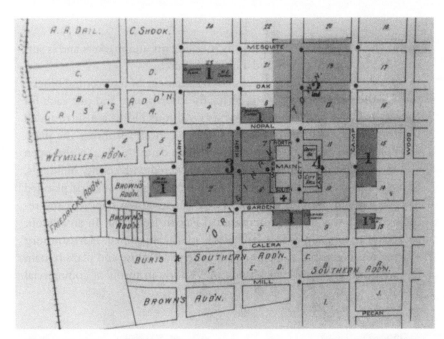

Figure 47 Partial plan of Uvalde in Uvalde County. The courthouse square and open plaza occupy two of four centrally located blocks.

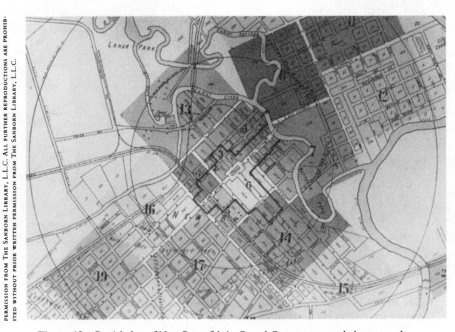

Figure 48 Partial plan of New Braunfels in Comal County as recorded on an early Sanborn map. The open main plaza is located at the intersection of the town's two main streets: San Antonio and Seguin.

During early statehood, a number of towns were planned with plazas. Two of these were founded by Germans: New Braunfels in 1845 and Fredericksburg in 1846. Both eventually became county seats. New Braunfels (Figure 48) is classified as a prototype plaza, while Fredericksburg's plaza has been substantially modified and is discussed later. New

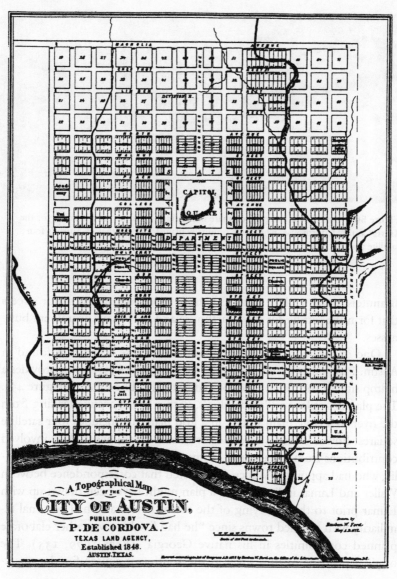

SOURCE: REPS 1965, 37.

Figure 49   Plan of Austin in 1839.

Figure 50 Courthouse and public square in Austin. This is the third location for the Travis County Courthouse, which was originally planned for another of Austin's four satellite squares. The present courthouse, shown here, was a WPA project.

Braunfels' narrow plaza occurs at the intersection of two major streets that form the setting for the courthouse and the town's prominent businesses.

One of the most interesting plaza courthouse schemes is found in Austin. Planned as a national capital for Texas in 1839, Austin provides a hilltop site for the capitol and four additional public squares (Figure 49). The plan is similar to Philadelphia's, with a broad avenue leading from the river to a large main square in a grid plan that includes four satellite squares. Edwin Waller is credited for Austin's plan, but it likely involved contributions from Mirabeau B. Lamar, second president of the Republic, who had appointed Waller. Reps noted that correspondence between Waller and Lamar indicated that a plan might have been drawn up with Lamar prior to the surveying of the town. Lamar also had personal familiarity with planned towns since "he had lived in two rather elaborate planned communities in his native Georgia" (Reps 1979, 135). The original plan for Austin reserved the southwest square for the courthouse. Later it sat opposite the capitol at the head of Congress Avenue. In the 1930s the courthouse was relocated to its present site alongside Wooldridge Park (Figure 50).

Two other plaza courthouses that benefited from WPA projects are in Dallas and Fort Worth. In Dallas several phases of urban renewal added plazas to the courthouse complex. Dealey Plaza, located to the west of both the old and new courthouses, was developed by the WPA (Figure 51). The assassination of President John F. Kennedy at Dealey Plaza resulted in further changes (Figure 52). A plaza was created to the east of the old courthouse as the site of a memorial to Kennedy.

Fort Worth was originally laid out as a two-block square and like Dallas was sited on a bluff overlooking the Trinity River. As in Dallas, the area between the courthouse and bluff became a plaza. Because of the significance and prominence of their plazas, these cities are classified as plaza courthouses even though both were planned according to other patterns.

Figure 51 Dealey Plaza in Dallas. Note the turreted old courthouse on the bluff. The new courthouse is a high-rise office tower situated on two blocks immediately south of the old courthouse.

Squares Derived from Spanish Precedents and Other Traditions

Three additional prototypical courthouse plazas have been identified by historical data only, in Aspermont in Stonewall County, Mount Vernon in Franklin County, and Sulphur Springs in Hopkins County. According to Sanborn Company maps, each appears to have an open plaza fronted by a courthouse. All three are located in Upper Southern culture areas, not typically associated with plazas.

Many of the fifteen prototypical plaza courthouses described above vary in form and precedent. In some cases, they have undergone significant changes. However, they all combine a separate block for public space with a nearby site for the courthouse. The result is added prestige and presence for both.

Modified Plaza Courthouses

There are ten county seats with modified plazas, characterized by the obscuring of formerly open spaces next to the courthouse: Anahuac, Crosbyton, Fredericksburg, Galveston, Gonzales, Hondo, Liberty, Menard,

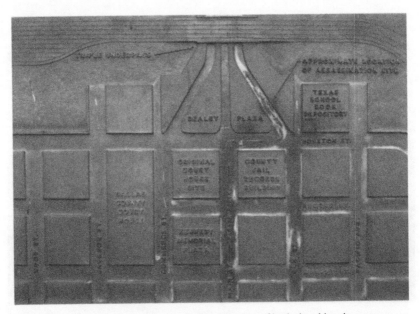

Figure 52 Plaque in Dealey Plaza in Dallas. The sites of both the old and new courthouses are indicated, along with several open plazas. Note the additional plazas to the east of the courthouse.

Pampa, and Refugio (Table 13). Typically, the plazas in these towns became the location for other public uses such as libraries, jails, churches, museums, parks, or parking lots. Open plazas encourage such use by providing an area of publicly owned land adjacent to existing government facilities. Despite these changes, most former plazas maintain a civic role and for that reason are included in this classification and described as modified plaza patterns.

Anahuac, Gonzales, Liberty, and Refugio owe their original plazas to Hispanic influence. Anahuac's courthouse square is located across from a public park that contains a number of historic structures and a recent county jail. Both blocks are situated on a bluff above the waterway that ties the town's port to Galveston Bay.

Liberty's original plan called for five contiguous squares to be placed all in a row. None remain totally open. Today the courthouse occupies the middle square. Another just east of the courthouse is completely obscured by private development. The city hall and other public buildings take up the remaining three squares. Squares for the city hall and courthouse are partly open and convey a civic presence.

Although Anahuac and Liberty retain little of their former plazas, both are listed here because of the continued public use of the plazas near the courthouse. In comparison, Refugio's plaza fares better despite the inclusion of a public library. The plazas in all four of these towns predate the courthouses that came to be associated with them.

Gonzales' plan (Figure 53) is a hybrid form that observes both Hispanic and Anglo-American traditions. First planned by Missourian James Kerr in 1825 for *empresario* Green DeWitt, Gonzales was actually surveyed in 1832 by Kerr's successor, Byrd Lockhart. Situated on the Guadalupe River, the inner town contained forty-nine blocks arranged seven blocks on a side. At the center of the inner town, five public squares lay in a cruciform pattern composed of an open central square and four others. Originally these were designated as Jail Square, Church Square, Military Square, and the Plaza. Two other squares, two blocks east and west, were reserved for a cemetery and market, respectively. Two broad public avenues or commons extended north and east of the inner town. Mexican law called for multiple squares, an open plaza, and a commons, but Kerr's arrangement of the requisite features appears to be unique.

Gonzales' first courthouse, a temporary frame structure, was sited to

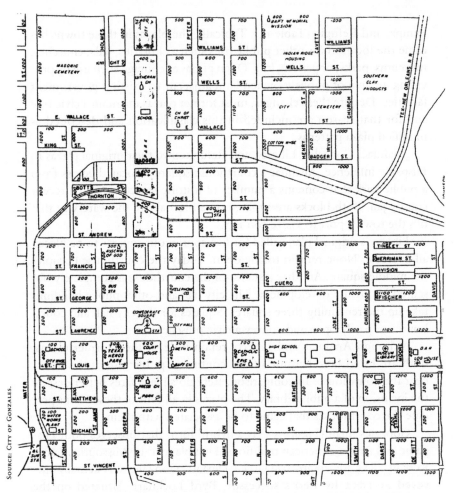

Figure 53 Plan of Gonzales in Gonzales County in 1956, indicating that the original plazas, first planned by James Kerr in 1825, remain in public hands. However, their uses have changed. What was originally Jail Square on the north is now known as Confederate Square, the plaza on the west is now Texas Heroes Park, and Military Square is the site of a church. The courthouse stands on the former central open square. Only Church Square retains its original use.

the west of the central plaza. A second, more permanent courthouse was placed in the middle of the central plaza in 1849. This was followed in 1896 by the current structure (Figure 54), which was designed by James Riely Gordon, the noted Texas architect.

Today Church Square continues its original role, but both Military

Figure 54 Courthouse square in Gonzales looking east to the courthouse from one of the remaining open plazas, now known as Texas Heroes Park. The courthouse, designed by James Riely Gordon and built in 1896, still dominates the townscape.

Square and the cemetery are the site of additional churches. What were once Plaza and Jail Squares are now public plazas with parking lots and monuments. The commons, too, have remained public, but not as open as before. All manner of public spaces from a city hall to schools, stadiums, museums, and parks occupy the commons today.

This legacy of civic space is unusual, but may be explained by the fact that the town was intended as a capital for an entire colony. Kerr's original plan for Gonzales appears to have anticipated placement of the courthouse on the central square. His ambitious plan has proven to be an enduring one that combines Hispanic tradition calling for multiple squares with Anglo-American preferences for a central courthouse square.

Another modified plaza courthouse worthy of note is that of Fredericksburg (Figure 55), which was founded by John O. Meusebach, who selected and planned the site (King 1967, 750). The town was laid out in 1846 by T. Charles Doebner and consisted of a linear grid of blocks and a vast plaza. One observer in 1847 noted, "When following the main street, one comes to the market square which appears to be large enough to accommodate a city of ten to twelve thousand inhabitants" (Roemer 1935, 229). Very early on, the plaza became the site for the community's first meeting house, an octagonal structure that served as town hall, church, and schoolhouse.

After Fredericksburg became Gillespie County's seat, a series of courthouses occupied the square. Two of these still stand amid other

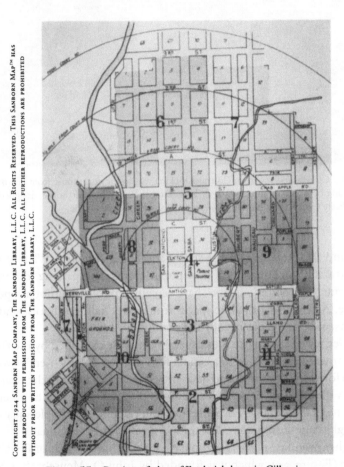

Figure 55   Portion of plan of Fredericksburg in Gillespie County showing the linear town grid and public square. The courthouse is located opposite the block designated for the square. The original scheme for the plaza would have included both blocks, with the town's meeting house centered on the main street.

THE COURTHOUSE SQUARE IN TEXAS

public and private buildings that now take up much of the square. A replica of the first meeting house, the Vereins-Kirche, is sited across the street on the northern half of the square, which is often the location for local cultural and historical events.

Three other county seats—Crosbyton in Crosby County, Hondo in Medina County, and Pampa in Gray County—lost their open squares opposite the courthouse in exchange for city halls or municipal buildings. Crosbyton's scheme is unusual because the courthouse is located diagonally across from the park on a half-block. Today the former open plaza is the site for numerous community activities and buildings, including a history museum and library.

Other modified plaza courthouses are found in Galveston and Menard. In each case, the public square was combined with the courthouse block by vacating a street separating the two. In Menard the park developed into a recreational center complete with swimming pool. Only a shaded lawn separates the courthouse from the park. Galveston's plaza retained its formality and symmetry through the use of fountains and monuments. The motive for the modification of Galveston's plaza was construction and expansion of a new courthouse complex. This scheme effectively subordinates the plaza to the courthouse and represents a transition from the original open square to a smaller urban plaza more typical of related plaza patterns.

Related Plaza Courthouses

There are eight county seats with block patterns that indicate some relationship between the courthouse and a nearby plaza. These related plaza patterns are found in Boerne, Corpus Christi, Fort Davis, Houston, Midland, Pearsall, San Diego, and Waco (Table 13). Four of these county seats are located in the Spanish-Mexican culture area, but none features a courthouse opposite a well-defined plaza.

San Diego in Duval County does have such a plaza, but it is the site for the city hall. The parklike courthouse square is located several blocks to the east of this older, Hispanic-inspired plaza. The courthouse fronts a block immediately to the north that is reserved for public use, which includes a parking lot and tennis courts. San Diego has another, more active public park, leaving the space opposite the courthouse underused and ill-kept.

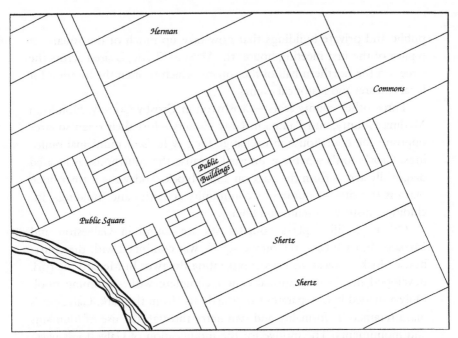

Figure 56   Partial plan of Boerne in Kendall County in 1856. The block designated for public buildings is the site of the courthouse. The public square is located one block away on the riverfront.

Two other county seats in the Spanish-Mexican area, Fort Davis and Pearsall, also have courthouses associated with unconventional plazas. In Fort Davis the courthouse square is placed near an irregular paved plaza that serves as the town's focal point. A small landscaped island with a historical marker is centered in this space, which is fronted by the post office and other prominent businesses. Pearsall's courthouse is located away from the town's commercial activity on a small residential block that is adjacent to a large park and recreation area. Other state and county offices are situated nearby.

Another county seat with a historic plaza is Boerne in Kendall County (Figure 56), founded in 1851 in the German Hill Country area. Boerne's original plan featured a commons with two avenues leading to the linear public square. The courthouse was placed on a block reserved for public buildings, located between the avenues and one block from the plaza. The courthouse still occupies this block. The square, which was oriented to the river, is the focus for both historic and present-day buildings.

Three of the county seats in this group—Corpus Christi, Houston, and Midland—were originally Shelbyville squares, but because of the addition of small urban plazas they are classified with the plaza courthouses. Waco, too, includes a small paved plaza or mall opposite the courthouse, although it is surrounded by large parking lots. The perception of this space is ambiguous, but the fact that major banks and businesses also front this space argues for its inclusion in this category.

The Nueces County Courthouse in Corpus Christi was relocated from its original square. Built in 1976, the present courthouse is a high-rise megastructure covering several blocks and surrounded by parking

Figure 57 The high-rise courthouse and plaza in Corpus Christi. This small urban plaza serves as a pedestrian link to the street, a modest park, and a place for monuments and memorials.

Squares Derived from Spanish Precedents and Other Traditions

lots. An intensively landscaped plaza connects the main entrance of the courthouse complex to the street (Figure 57). This plaza includes a large fountain and numerous monuments, but its connection to the building's entry is ambiguous, and few visitors see this space because the parking entrances are more accessible and obvious.

Houston and Midland are more conventional. Both retain their Shelbyville block patterns, but include paved urban plazas that were added to an adjacent block. Houston's square (Figure 58) has become a center for county government and is surrounded by high-rise buildings housing county offices and agencies. The nearby plaza resulted from the construction of one of these office blocks and was an attempt to make an ar-

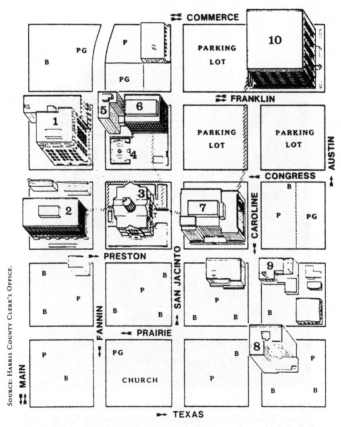

Figure 58 Plan of Houston's courthouse complex, which includes a small urban plaza adjacent to the old courthouse.

THE COURTHOUSE SQUARE IN TEXAS

chitectural gesture to the courthouse. Midland's plaza came about with construction of a civic center next to the extensively remodeled courthouse (Figure 59). The small paved plaza and fountain serve as a link between the two public buildings.

Significance of Plaza Courthouses

The plaza courthouses described here are a diverse group. Most have in common an open space associated with the courthouse that continues to serve a civic role. These patterns are significant because they are the most popular Texas courthouse schemes after the Shelbyville. They also represent a wide range of planning traditions and culture groups. In addition, they account for the oldest and newest patterns found at the square, including eighteenth-century Hispanic plazas, nineteenth-century German plazas, and twentieth-century U.S. versions. Finally, plaza courthouses concentrate public activities and land uses at the square—a key factor in the square's centripetal influence.

Figure 59 Midland County Courthouse and plaza in Midland. The paved plaza next to the courthouse links that building to the civic center across the street.

Squares Derived from Spanish Precedents and Other Traditions

RAILROAD-INFLUENCED
COURTHOUSE SQUARES

More than forty county seats were planned by railroads or their agents. Many more have rail links, but only those county seats that have courthouses placed next to the tracks or those with squares directly influenced by the placement of the rails are included in this category (Figure 60). Eighteen county seats fit these criteria (Table 14). Ten of these were visited and surveyed for features found at the square that relate to the railroad. The remaining eight (Colorado City, Daingerfield, Falfurrias, Lip-

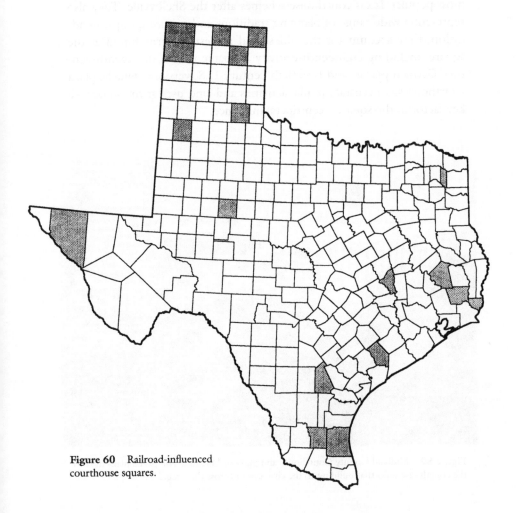

Figure 60   Railroad-influenced
courthouse squares.

Table 14. Railroad-Influenced Courthouse Squares

COUNTY SEAT / COUNTY	DESCRIPTION OF PATTERN & SQUARE	DISTANCE BETWEEN COURTHOUSE & RAILROAD
Bryan* / Brazos	Prototype (Symmetric)	1 block
Channing* / Hartley	Prototype (Symmetric)	Adjacent (RR abandoned)
Colorado City / Mitchell	Modified T-Town pattern	3 blocks (1896 data)
Dalhart* / Dallam	Related to T-Town (unique pattern)	4 blocks
Daingerfield / Morris	Related to symmetric pattern	Adjacent (1926 data)
Edna* / Jackson	Related to symmetric pattern	Adjacent
Falfurrias / Brooks	Modified orthogonal pattern	1/2 block (1930 data)
George West* / Live Oak	Modified T-Town pattern	3 blocks
Kountze* / Hardin	Related to symmetric pattern	Adjacent (RR abandoned)
Lipscomb / Lipscomb	Prototype (Symmetric)	Adjacent (RR abandoned?)
Littlefield / Lamb	Related to T-Town pattern	4 blocks (1932 data)
Livingston* / Polk	Related to orthogonal pattern	Adjacent
Memphis / Hall	Modified orthogonal pattern	1/2 block (1931 data)
Miami / Roberts	Modified orthogonal pattern	1/2 block (1929 data)
Orange* / Orange	Related to symmetric pattern	1 block
Sarita* / Kenedy	Modified symmetric pattern	Adjacent
Sierra Blanca / Hudspeth	Related to orthogonal pattern	NA
Spearman* / Hansford	Related to T-Town (unique pattern)	3 blocks

*Confirmed by site visit. (Others confirmed by historical data only.)
NA: No current data are available.

scomb, Littlefield, Memphis, Miami, and Sierra Blanca) were classified solely on the basis of historical data, primarily early Sanborn maps or plats in county clerks' offices.

The railroad-influenced squares are widely distributed, but are not associated with any single culture group (Figure 2). The Midwest culture area does show a high percentage (50 percent or three of six) of county seats with railroad patterns. This reflects the importance of the railroad town in the settlement of the Midwest in general. Of the eighteen county

Squares Derived from Spanish Precedents and Other Traditions

seats in this diverse classification, most are located at the periphery of the state: in the Panhandle, the Valley, or the far west and southeast. This pattern may represent varied phases of rail development in the state. Following the general trend of Texas settlement, railroad towns in the east such as Daingerfield, which was founded in the 1840s, preceded those in the west like Spearman, which was not planned until 1917.

Another factor shared by these communities is a reciprocal relationship between the prosperity of the railroad and the town. Recognizing the economic value of county government to a community's development, railroad planners often sought to secure a county seat. J. C. Hudson (1985) studied railroad towns in the American West and documented a number of these cases. Although Hudson was not concerned specifically with the location of the courthouse, he did discuss the importance of county seats and town squares in the success of many railroad towns (Hudson 1985, 190). More importantly, he described a typology of three basic plans (Figure 61) adopted by planners of railroad towns (Hudson 1982, 1985).

Many of the towns classified in this analysis of Texas squares exhibit patterns similar to those first noted by Hudson, which were based on the relationship of the tracks, the location of main street, and the resulting arrangement of blocks. Hudson determined that the earliest railroad plans followed "symmetric" schemes, characterized by alignment of the town's businesses and blocks with the tracks. Another pattern, the "orthogonal," was defined by a main street running perpendicular to and across the railroad's right-of-way. A third type, the "T-town," proved the most stable and successful. In these communities the main street was also placed perpendicular to the railroad, but continued in only one direction from the depot, thus forming a "T" pattern (Hudson 1985, 88).

These three prototypes were adopted for this analysis because they delineate features of importance to the town and describe a variety of block patterns which included a square for the courthouse. Variations of all three prototypes are found in Texas, as well as several schemes that appear to be unique. Some of these squares present modified or related patterns that are discussed in terms of Hudson's prototypical railroad plans.

Many other county seats share some relationship with the rails, but their courthouse squares display less connection to the railroad. These are better described in other categories. The eclipse of the railroad and

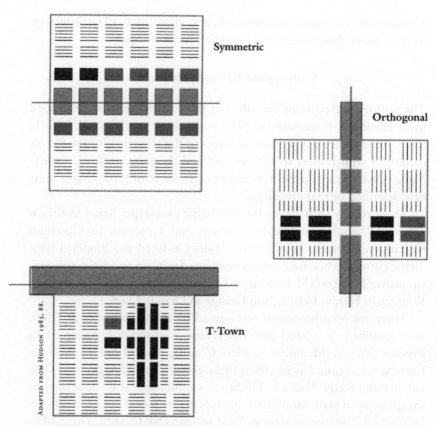

Figure 61 Types of railroad towns. Hudson described three planning schemes for railroad towns based on the location of a town's main street relative to the tracks.

its diminished role in most county seats argue for such a classification. For example, Sinton's courthouse, relocated from its original block alongside a railroad, is listed as a Shelbyville. Alice and Kingsville also represent railroad plans, but their courthouse squares are less impacted by the tracks and are listed with other block patterns. Alice follows a symmetric pattern, with the tracks parallel to the town's main street and business district. The courthouse is sited several blocks from the railroad. Kingsville's plan is an elaboration of an orthogonal scheme, with a main street running perpendicular to the rails. The axis formed by Main Street's crossing of the tracks is terminated at one end by the courthouse and at the other by a prominent school building. Despite this interesting

Squares Derived from Spanish Precedents and Other Traditions

arrangement, the courthouse square is best classified as a Harrisonburg, which is more descriptive of the square's block pattern.

Prototypical Railroad Patterns

The prototypical patterns described in this classification are developed from Hudson's three railroad plans: symmetric, orthogonal, and T-town. All three are defined here in terms of the alignment of the town's main grid with respect to the railroad and the location of the courthouse. Each of these patterns is discussed in terms of those county seats best described by that prototype.

Three county seats follow the symmetric prototype: Bryan in Brazos County, Channing in Hartley County, and Lipscomb in Lipscomb County. Another, Sarita in Kenedy County, is listed as a modified symmetric pattern, while four county seats are described as related symmetric plans: Daingerfield in Morris County, Edna in Jackson County, Kountze in Hardin County, and Orange in Orange County.

There are no prototypical orthogonal or T-town schemes in Texas, only modified or related patterns. Three county seats, Falfurrias in Brooks County, Memphis in Hall County, and Miami in Roberts County, are counted as modified orthogonal plans. Livingston in Polk County and Sierra Blanca in Hudspeth County appear to be related to the orthogonal plan. Modified T-town plans are found in Colorado City in Mitchell County and George West in Live Oak County. Three additional county seats, Dalhart in Dallam County, Littlefield in Lamb County, and Spearman in Hansford County, are listed as related T-town plans, although they present unique variations on that theme.

The only county seats in Texas that observe a prototypical pattern are those that follow a symmetric design. Three towns fit this description; although the rails and depots are abandoned or little used, their basic symmetric patterns remain.

A clear example of a symmetric prototype is found in Channing (Figure 62). The plat for this Panhandle community indicates that all of the town's blocks were aligned with the tracks. The courthouse is located adjacent to the tracks, indicating the planner's intentions to provide a connection between the railroad and the town's most prominent building. Visual inspection of the site today indicates that little of the original grid was developed. The courthouse and jail still occupy the block along

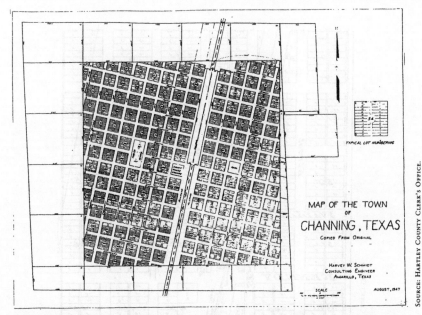

Figure 62 Plat of Channing in Hartley County. This map, dated August 1947, details the plan's emphasis on the railroad, which required reorientation of the grid from the original rectangular survey to alignment with the tracks. As is typical of many "symmetric" patterns, the courthouse fronts the railroad tracks.

the railroad right-of-way, which like the town is mostly vacant. The other main public spaces, such as the school and park, remain set back from the now abandoned tracks.

In Lipscomb, another Panhandle town, the grid was split in two equal halves with the rails running down the middle. Like Channing, the town did not fulfill original expectations. The courthouse remains situated on a half-block fronting the town's main street and former railroad right-of-way. Another symmetric scheme is found in Bryan. Here the courthouse is sited one block off the main street, which is shared by the tracks. An early Sanborn map shows Bryan's city hall located on Main Street immediately next to the railroad. The town's original symmetric scheme remains evident today.

Modified Railroad Patterns

Six county seats with railroad-influenced courthouse squares are classified as modified patterns because of changes or deviations from the prototypical plans. These include one modified symmetric pattern, three

Squares Derived from Spanish Precedents and Other Traditions

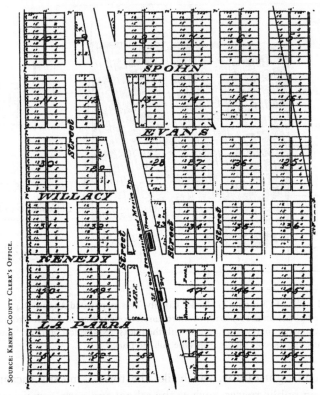

Figure 63 Plan of Sarita in Kenedy County in 1907. This plan is typical of the modified railroad-influenced county seats with the courthouse sited along the tracks, which here cut diagonally through the town.

modified orthogonal schemes, and two modified T-town plans. Modified T-towns are found in Colorado City in Mitchell County and George West in Live Oak County. The three modified orthogonal plans include Falfurrias in Brooks County, Memphis in Hall County, and Miami in Roberts County. The single modified symmetric pattern is Sarita in Kenedy County.

Sarita's plan (Figure 63) clearly indicates a modification of the symmetric prototype because the railroad cuts a diagonal path through the settlement's grid, forming a series of irregular blocks, the only exception being the block for the courthouse square. Sarita's courthouse was situated immediately opposite the train depot on what the 1907 plan calls Kenedy Park. Today an open recreational area bears that name and sits

THE COURTHOUSE SQUARE IN TEXAS

across the tracks from the courthouse. The only other buildings in town include several brick structures housing the Kenedy Ranch headquarters, a modest museum dedicated to that local ranch family, a post office, and a few dwellings. Like several other very small county seats, Sarita exists solely as a ranch headquarters and former train depot. It remains one of the county's few communities.

Three county seats are described as modified orthogonal plans. Two are in Memphis and Miami, which are located in northwest Texas. The third, Falfurrias, is situated in the Rio Grande Valley. All three are classified according to Sanborn maps only. Maps drawn in 1930 for Falfurrias indicate several gridlike sections aligned on both sides of the tracks. The courthouse is sited on a large block near the railroad, but on the opposite side, away from the tracks.

The railroad in Memphis runs diagonally through the town's otherwise regular grid. A Sanborn map dated 1931 indicates that the courthouse is located one block from the tracks near the train station. Based on data compiled by Sanborn's agents in 1929, Miami's courthouse is also located one block from the tracks, but several blocks from the passenger station. Miami also differs from Memphis by having a more varied block arrangement, including the courthouse square, which is irregularly shaped. Elements in common in the two county seats are proximity of their courthouse squares to the railroad and the fact that each town's main street runs across the tracks.

Two other county seats, George West and Colorado City, exhibit modified T-town plans. Colorado City combines features of both the symmetric and T-town patterns. A plat from 1896 indicates a definite "T" relationship between the railroad and the town's grid, but the main street is parallel to the tracks, a feature consistent with symmetric plans but contrary to prototypical T-towns. The plat also locates the courthouse on a quarter-block square three blocks from the railroad.

A better example of a T-town plan is George West (Figure 64) in Live Oak County, although the prototypical pattern has been modified today by an extension of the town's grid northeast across the railroad. The courthouse still occupies the square first reserved for its use in 1914. As in Colorado City, the courthouse square in George West is located three blocks from the depot. In other respects, the square is similar to a Shelbyville model. Classification as a railroad-influenced square reflects the plan's fidelity to Hudson's "T-town" prototype, the courthouse's proximity to the tracks, and its location along the town's main street leading to the train station. Little evidence remains of the logic of the town's layout, as two intersecting highways bypass the community's original grid and courthouse square.

MAP OF THE TOWN OF GEORGE WEST – LIVE OAK COUNTY, TEXAS.

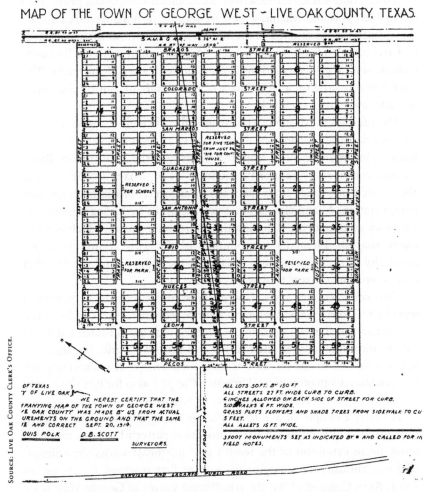

Figure 64 Plat of George West in Live Oak County in 1914. The plan for the town anticipated the formation of Live Oak County from Bexar County and reserved a public square for the courthouse. The scheme represents a prototypical "T-town" pattern noted by Hudson, although modified today.

THE COURTHOUSE SQUARE IN TEXAS

Related Railroad Patterns

The county seats classified as related patterns constitute a more diverse subgroup than those already discussed. In addition, these squares deviate more substantially from the three prototypical plans. Despite such differences, all nine county seats classified here as related patterns share an association between the location of the railroad and the courthouse that reflects elements of the three prototypical patterns. Today, however, the rails play a diminished role in these communities.

Four county seats are considered related to a symmetric pattern: Daingerfield in Morris County, Edna in Jackson County, Kountze in Hardin County, and Orange in Orange County. Three are found in east Texas. The fourth, Edna, is located along the middle Gulf Coast. In each case, the railroad and courthouse square share a close relationship.

Only two towns' patterns appear to be related to an orthogonal scheme: Livingston in Polk County and Sierra Blanca in Hudspeth County. The two exhibit few similarities, except that in each town's early plats the railroad passes near the courthouse and divides the town's grid in a fashion similar to the orthogonal prototype.

Perhaps the most interesting railroad-influenced courthouse squares are those classified as related T-town patterns: Dalhart in Dallam County, Littlefield in Lamb County, and Spearman in Hansford County. Each of these displays a pattern unlike any other in the state, but they share features related to the T-town plan.

The four county seats with patterns related to symmetric plans indicate a close relationship between the railroad right-of-way and alignment of their courthouse squares, which originally were adjacent to the tracks. Although their locations were altered in many instances, these courthouse squares retain a strong connection to the railroad. Consistent with the basic theme of a symmetric plan, most of the major buildings in these towns were also oriented toward the tracks and the courthouse.

In Daingerfield the railroad's path cuts haphazardly through the town's central business district and along the courthouse square. As a consequence, the blocks in this northeast Texas county seat are very irregular, including the courthouse square. A 1926 Sanborn map indicated that most of the town's major buildings fronted the railroad.

Edna's town grid is more regular, but the blocks near the intersection of the courthouse square and the old depot are irregularly shaped be-

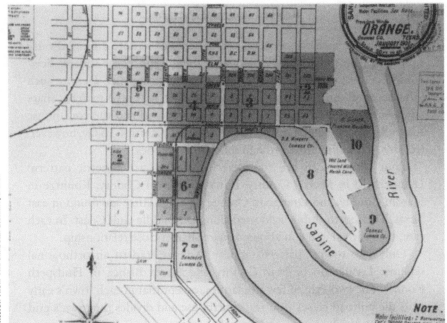

Figure 65 Plan of Orange in Orange County. This 1901 map shows the importance of the Sabine River to this port town. In earlier times the railroad, too, played a significant role. The courthouse square was located near the intersection of two rail lines that terminated at the port and the depot, which fronted the river. The line nearest the courthouse is gone now, but the tracks along Front Street remain. The alignment of blocks and businesses with the tracks is a pattern related to Hudson's "symmetric" railroad town.

cause of the railroad's right-of-way. Today a 1950s-era courthouse sits on a tree-shaded lawn surrounded by the town's major businesses on three sides, while on the fourth a derelict train depot remains. Based on the railroad signals next to the courthouse, the tracks still carry traffic, although freeway connections to Houston have replaced most of the railroad's former functions.

Kountze, in southeast Texas, also possesses a modern courthouse sited a half-block from the railroad right-of-way. New highway routes and intersections also changed the focus of the town, which used to front the tracks. Although the present courthouse square fronts one of these major roadways, it is well apart from the commercial activity of the town. Ironically, the railroad today serves to reinforce the isolation of the courthouse from the town's business district.

Early plans for Orange, located in far southeast Texas, present an intriguing picture of the relationship between natural topography, the town's grid, and the railroad (Figure 65). Here both the rails and town's grid follow the course of the Sabine River. Today the tracks on the east side of the courthouse have been removed, but those along Front Street remain. The courthouse square is still located on Division Street, which marks the dividing line between this port town's two major grids. Tracks along Front Street separate the present WPA-era courthouse from a civic complex located two blocks north on Main Street. This complex is linked visually to the courthouse and includes a city hall, two museums, and several historic churches and homes. Despite this connection, the civic complex and not the courthouse dominates the townscape.

Two county seats loosely related to the orthogonal pattern are Livingston in Polk County and Sierra Blanca in Hudspeth County. The plans of the two towns, located at opposite ends of the state, share little other than the proximity of their courthouse to the tracks. Livingston was surveyed in the field, but data for Sierra Blanca are less conclusive.

In Livingston the courthouse square is the central feature of the city's regular grid pattern, much like a Shelbyville. However, the railroad cuts diagonally through the town and severs a block adjacent to the courthouse, thus altering what might otherwise be a traditional pattern. As is typical of most orthogonal plans, Livingston's major business thoroughfare runs perpendicular to the main rail line. This street, Church Street, passes by the courthouse and the city hall, which is located just across the tracks from the courthouse square.

The information available on Sierra Blanca in far west Texas indicates an irregular block pattern that in times past included active rail connections. The courthouse square was sited on an oversize block near the tracks. It is included in this discussion because Texas Department of Transportation maps suggest an orthogonal arrangement between the railroad and the town's grid. Correspondence with the county clerk's office confirmed that the community did not conform to any traditional pattern.

The final three railroad-influenced county seats to be discussed are Dalhart, Littlefield, and Spearman. As disparate as these three are, they bear some resemblance to Hudson's T-town plan. The main characteristic of that prototype was a main street originating at a "T" intersection with the railroad. All of the county seats in this subgroup include a courthouse square located on a main street that intersects the tracks, although in Dalhart's case there is no "T" connection.

Dalhart's plan (Figure 66) might best be described as an "X" pattern. Two major rail lines that intersect north of the town's center form that pattern and effectively divide the town into four grids. The courthouse is located on a half-block square several blocks south of the crossing of the rail lines forming the "X." Despite its reduced block size and blank exposure on its north facade, the courthouse square serves as the community's cultural center. Immediately adjacent is the museum of the famous XIT Ranch and a county library.

A clear elaboration of the T-town pattern can be found in Littlefield in Lamb County. Here the "T" is formed by a large boulevard-like block arrangement running perpendicularly from the railroad to a public

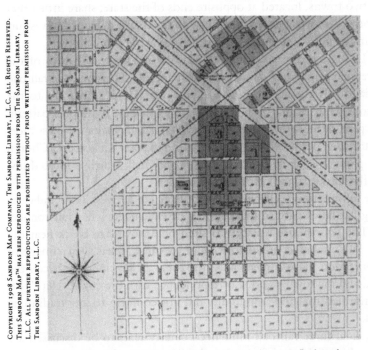

Figure 66 Plan of Dalhart in Dallam County in 1908. Perhaps best described as an "X-town" plan, Dalhart features intersecting rail lines that create a unique geometry for the town's grid, but one which is related to Hudson's "T-town" prototype. The courthouse is located on a half-block square three blocks south of the "X."

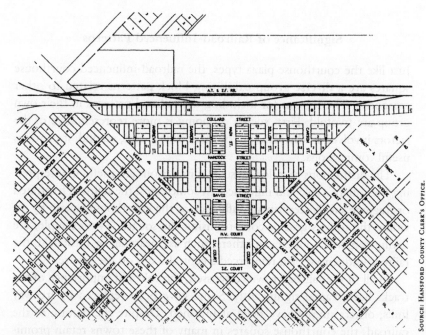

Figure 67 Plan of Spearman in Hansford County. Platted by the railroad in 1917, Spearman's plan is unique. Combining aspects of the railroad's "T-town" with the traditional central courthouse square found all over the state, this plan reflects the importance of two institutions: the railroad and the courthouse.

square. According to Sanborn maps dated 1932 and 1950, this block was originally two separate half-blocks, which were joined later to form a single public square that accommodates both a courthouse and city hall.

The most striking T-town related plan is that of Spearman in Hansford County (Figure 67). Planned by the railroad in 1917, Spearman's courthouse square was linked to the depot by Main Street and to the town's grid by diagonal streets projecting from each corner of the square. This unique arrangement placed the town's two primary institutions, the train depot and county courthouse, at opposite ends of Main Street. The commercial district was oriented along this street, while the town's remaining blocks formed another grid aligned with the cardinal directions. The community's compact business district has remained viable, and the courthouse square is still the town's central focus. Few railroad planners recognized the public role of the courthouse as explicitly as Spearman's, a fact that remains evident today.

Squares Derived from Spanish Precedents and Other Traditions

Significance of Railroad-Influenced Patterns

Just like the courthouse plaza types, the railroad-influenced courthouse squares are a diverse group exhibiting block patterns related to other categories. The reasons for including the railroad patterns in their own group are twofold. First, such a grouping is more representative of the factors involved in the planning of these towns; and, second, it provides useful comparisons.

The distinctions revealed by such comparisons are useful in interpreting the square's role and influence. In some cases, the railroad frustrated or fragmented the centripetal influence of the courthouse square by dividing the town's grid or compromising the square. Two examples are Livingston and Kountze. In others, such as Spearman or Littlefield, the railroad-influenced plan reinforced a central focus on the square.

In all of the railroad towns discussed, the role and importance of the tracks have waned significantly. Some have been replaced by freeway links; others simply have been abandoned. Despite the demise of the railroad, the courthouse squares in many of these towns retain prominent positions in their communities.

IRREGULAR BLOCKS, HALF-BLOCKS, AND QUARTER-BLOCKS

The final three categories of nontraditional squares lack any prototype and are classified as irregular-block, half-block, or quarter-block (Figure 68). These terms are self-descriptive and provide a means to assess those few courthouse squares that cannot be accommodated in previous classifications. Just as with previous categories, the most obvious criteria derive from the form of the squares. This survey identified five irregular-block patterns, three half-blocks, and two quarter-blocks (Table 15). Several courthouse squares in this group approximate the appearance of a traditional square, with prominent structures, set-backs, and parklike settings. Others make little effort in that regard and can claim few characteristics of conventional courthouse squares.

As might be expected from such a heterogeneous group, their geographic distribution also suggests few relationships, except for the irregular blocks. Three contiguous county seats exhibit irregular-block pat-

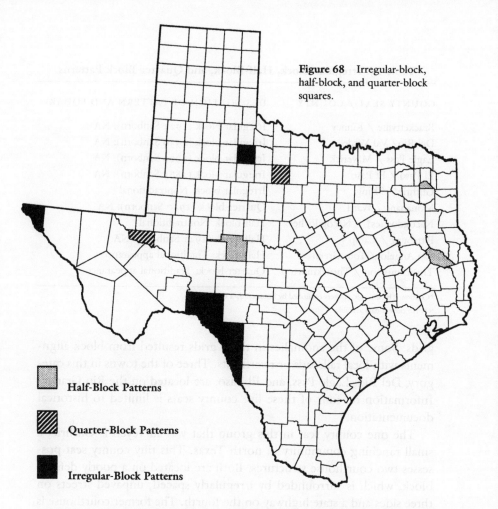

Figure 68 Irregular-block, half-block, and quarter-block squares.

■ **Half-Block Patterns**

▨ **Quarter-Block Patterns**

■ **Irregular-Block Patterns**

terns: Brackettville in Kinney County, Del Rio in Val Verde County, and Eagle Pass in Maverick County. Two more irregular-block patterns are found in El Paso in far west Texas and Guthrie in north Texas. Four of the five are found in the Spanish-Mexican culture area, which may indicate an ambivalence toward Anglo-American patterns in these towns. The half- and quarter-block squares display no conclusive geographic relationships.

Irregular-Block Patterns

The most difficult group of squares to assess are those with a courthouse located on or next to an irregular block. Most of the irregular blocks appear to be created by the intersection of diagonal streets or competing

Squares Derived from Spanish Precedents and Other Traditions

Table 15. Irregular-Block, Half-Block, and Quarter-Block Patterns

COUNTY SEAT / COUNTY	DESCRIPTION OF PATTERN AND SQUARE
Brackettville / Kinney	Irregular-block (1924 Sanborn): NA
Del Rio/ Val Verde	Irregular-block (1930 Sanborn): NA
Eagle Pass / Maverick	Irregular-block (1900 Sanborn): NA
El Paso / El Paso	Irregular-block (1885 Sanborn): NA
Guthrie* / King	Irregular-block: Nontraditional
Monahans / Ward	Quarter-block (1940 Sanborn): NA
Nacogdoches* / Nacogdoches	Half-block: Nontraditional
Pittsburg / Camp	Half-block (1921 Sanborn): NA
San Angelo / Tom Green	Half-block: Traditional appearance
Throckmorton / Throckmorton	Quarter-block: Traditional appearance

*Confirmed by site visit. (Others confirmed by historical data only.)
NA: No current data available.

grids. Some of the anomalies in these grids resulted from block alignments with local railroads or riverfronts. Three of the towns in this category, Del Rio, Eagle Pass, and El Paso, are located on the Rio Grande. Information on four of these five county seats is limited to historical documentation.

The one county seat in this group that was surveyed is Guthrie, a small ranching community in north Texas. This tiny county seat possesses two courthouse structures. Both are located on a poorly defined block, which is surrounded by irregularly spaced, unpaved streets on three sides and a state highway on the fourth. The former courthouse is enclosed by a short iron fence that attempts to establish a presence for the modest two-story structure. The new courthouse is a featureless, single-story building located next to its predecessor. The town's most prominent buildings are an imposing ranch house sited on a nearby hill and an active ranch store located within sight of the courthouse.

According to Sanborn maps dated 1894 and 1924, Brackettville's courthouse block (Figure 69) is trapezoidal and placed opposite a triangular block where two diagonal streets come together. These maps also indicate that the courthouse was originally located to one side of its block. However, by 1924, a later courthouse held a more prominent position fronting the smaller, triangular block. In addition to being a larger structure, the relocated courthouse suggests more formal recognition of its role in the community. Nearby structures that reinforce the square's public presence include a county jail, post office, and church.

The courthouses in Del Rio and El Paso are sited on more regular blocks. However, in both instances the courthouse square is next to an irregular block. Plans of Del Rio in 1900, 1909, and 1930 exhibit a number of different grids that appear to follow local watercourses and later the railroad. The courthouse square is located at the juncture of two of these grids that create a series of irregular blocks.

El Paso's courthouse is also situated at the intersection of two competing grids that form irregular blocks adjacent to the square. Historical documentation for Del Rio, Eagle Pass, and El Paso also indicates the presence of railroads and open plazas. However, none of the courthouse locations or block patterns in these towns suggest any relationship to the rails or the plazas. A Sanborn map dated 1900 for Eagle Pass places the courthouse square in an area of irregular blocks distant from both the rail line and the old plaza.

As a group, the irregular block patterns appear to provide the least definition for the courthouse square and promote the most ambivalence

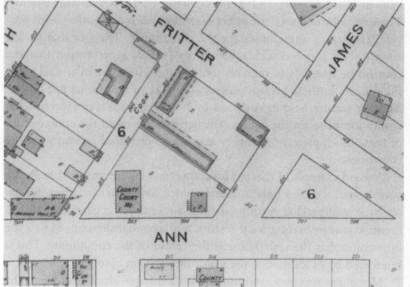

Figure 69   Plan of Brackettville in Kinney County in 1924. This map clearly indicates an irregular-block pattern for the courthouse square.

Squares Derived from Spanish Precedents and Other Traditions

in terms of other prominent features in their respective townscapes. In addition, the irregular courthouse blocks show the least relationship to known traditional models or to other nontraditional patterns described in this analysis.

The irregularities displayed by these squares often can lead to ambiguity in the courthouse's role in the community. While it is sometimes true that discontinuities in a monotonous grid might emphasize a feature in a townscape, few of the courthouses in this group appear to benefit from such siting. However, in spite of their irregular-block patterns, several of the courthouses in this category provide a conventional appearance. This is accomplished by customary practices requiring building setbacks, as well as reserving the square for county buildings—primarily the courthouse.

Half-Block and Quarter-Block Patterns

Three county seats are classified as half-blocks: Nacogdoches in Nacogdoches County, Pittsburg in Camp County, and San Angelo in Tom Green County. Two county seats are counted as quarter-blocks: Monahans in Ward County and Throckmorton in Throckmorton County. There are obvious similarities between these two categories: both provide less than a single block for the courthouse. The fact that so few county seats adopted such schemes may reflect a perception that the courthouse deserves or requires more space. However, in several cases, the squares in these groups project an image of traditional full-blocks. Another feature held in common by both groups is a predilection for corner locations for the square. Corner sites are often the consequence of these block patterns, but they also afford increased exposure for the courthouse.

A good example of this is Throckmorton (Figure 70). Although the courthouse occupies only a quarter-block, its corner location, formal set-back, and parklike setting establish a traditional appearance. Monuments commemorating local history and accomplishments add to the impression that the courthouse is the center of the community. This is reinforced by its location at the major intersection in town.

Monahans was also established with a quarter-block plan when the county seat was moved there, although this has since been changed.

Several half-block squares also favor corner locations. One of the

Figure 70 The courthouse in Throckmorton County. Sited on only a quarter-block at Throckmorton's major intersection, the courthouse still has the appearance of a traditional square with an imposing structure, parklike setting, and civic monuments.

least fortunate is the courthouse square in Nacogdoches. Originally located opposite the town's historic plaza, the courthouse was moved to a half-block location around the turn of the century. Although situated on a major intersection, the present courthouse does not really address the corner. Built in 1958 in a style recalling that of simpler historic structures, the courthouse appears more like a motel or nursing home. Its low scale and nondescript facade do not provide sufficient presence.

San Angelo's half-block, however, projects the appearance of a traditional courthouse square owing to the large scale of the block, its generous set-back, and the formal neoclassical style of the courthouse. San Angelo's square does suffer from a lack of focus on the square—that is, lot lines and land uses at the square are oriented toward the street and not the courthouse.

A similar pattern is found in Pittsburg in Camp County. According to Sanborn maps dated 1921 and 1934, Pittsburg's courthouse and county

Squares Derived from Spanish Precedents and Other Traditions

jail occupy a half-block on Church Street. As with other courthouses in this group, land use on the remaining half of the block is not oriented to the courthouse. The same was true for the quarter-block patterns. This exposes an inherent problem with partial block arrangements—the inability to provide a clear four-sided focus on the courthouse.

SIGNIFICANCE OF PATTERNS DERIVED
FROM OTHER PRECEDENTS

The squares surveyed in this chapter are significant for a number of reasons. First, these five types—plaza patterns, railroad-influenced squares, irregular blocks, half-blocks, and quarter-blocks—account for almost 25 percent of the county seats in Texas. Second, all are indicative of an evolving process of urban design based upon both convention and innovation. Finally, these patterns demonstrate that several different planning traditions could be adapted to accommodate courthouses. Many present unique solutions.

The patterns discussed illustrate the desire of most town planners and townspeople to imbue the courthouse square with special significance. The extent and variety of those attempts have been described above in terms of block patterns. The plans of most Texas courthouse squares depict several common themes: a central location for the square, focus on the courthouse, and an expression of shared ideas about community life. Each of these themes can be manifest in concrete terms in the urban morphology of the square.

Chapter Six

Origins of Squares Derived from Spanish Precedents and Other Planning Traditions

Almost a quarter of Texas courthouse squares evolved from sources other than the Anglo-American planning tradition. The Anglo-American tradition was unique insofar as it was clearly intended to hold a court-house on a square. Other planning traditions required that designers find space for the courthouse in other ways. Typically, existing open squares or plazas planned for other reasons were taken over by court-houses. Some towns were originally platted under Spanish and Mexican regimes and designed with open plazas. To a lesser extent both French and German town plans featured open squares, although there are exceptions to these patterns. Also included in this category are towns laid out by railroad companies, although several of these followed Anglo-American preferences for central courthouse squares. All of these non-traditional courthouse squares are as capable of providing a central focus for their communities as their Anglo-American counterparts.

SPAIN'S INFLUENCE

Spanish town planning reflected an evolving urban emphasis and settlement policy that became typical of the Spanish in the New World. The Spanish codified planning policies and predated other colonial powers with settlements in America by more than a century. Hispaniola was founded in 1493, and the first Spanish settlement in North America was established in 1565 at St. Augustine, Florida. The Spanish also founded other present-day North American cities such as San Antonio, Laredo,

Santa Fe, Albuquerque, Tucson, San Diego, San Francisco, Santa Barbara, and Monterey (Reps 1979, 35). Typical of these towns was a central plaza surrounded by a gridlike arrangement of blocks and streets.

The Spanish system of settlement involved three primary institutions, each with different jurisdictions and purposes. All three found expression in Texas. The *presidio* or fort secured territory. The *mission* brought clerics to convert native people and provide sacraments to settlers. The *pueblo* or town settlement stabilized the frontier (Cruz 1988). The most enduring and often overlooked of these, the town or municipality, instituted laws and elements of self-rule (Cruz 1988). Plans of the missions and forts were often bound more by site and circumstance and less by law. However, civil settlements and towns typically were planned according to specific sets of laws evolved over several centuries in Spain.

During the years of Spanish rule in Texas from 1521 to 1821, a small number of settlements were constructed as the indirect result of presidios and missions as well as those specifically founded as pueblos or

SOURCE: "TEXAS AND ADJACENT REGIONS IN THE EIGHTEENTH CENTURY," IN *Let there be towns: Spanish municipal origins in the American Southwest, 1610–1810,* BY GILBERT R. CRUZ. COURTESY OF TEXAS A&M UNIVERSITY PRESS.

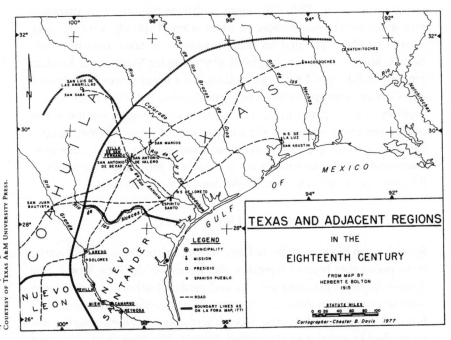

Figure 71 Northern New Spain, showing the provinces of Texas, Coahuila, Nuevo León, and Nuevo Santander and locations of civil settlements, presidios, and missions.

THE COURTHOUSE SQUARE IN TEXAS

towns (Figure 71). It should be noted that the present borders of the state of Texas are far more extensive than those of the province of Texas under Spanish or Mexican rule. The earliest Spanish presence within present-day boundaries occurred in the far west around El Paso in 1659 and later in the east along the Neches River by 1690. Two missions were established in 1682 near El Paso: Isleta and Socorro. Missions in the east included San Francisco de los Tejas and El Santísimo de Nombre María, both of which dated from 1690. Also in the east, in present-day Louisiana, the mission of San Miguel de Linares de los Adaes was founded in 1716. It became the site of a settlement and the first provincial capital of Texas in 1722, although it was abandoned by 1773.

The most significant settlements in terms of population and influence were San Antonio, La Bahía near Goliad, and Nacogdoches in east Texas (Jones 1979, 38–46). As late as 1803, the population of San Antonio was 2,500. La Bahía had 618 inhabitants and Nacogdoches 770 (Hatcher 1927, 67). San Antonio's first mission was San Antonio de Valero (1718), which later became known as the Alamo, and four more were established during the next thirteen years.

La Bahía contained a presidio and mission that was relocated near Goliad in 1749, west of its original siting in 1722 on the ruins of La Salle's Fort Saint Louis. Other nearby missions were Rosario (1754) and Refugio (1793).

Nacogdoches began as a presidio and mission in 1716, but did not include a pueblo until 1779. Additional missions in the vicinity were Concepción (1716), San José de Nazones (1716), Nuestra Señora de los Dolores de los Ais (1716), and San Francisco de los Neches (1721).

Also worthy of mention, but located outside Spanish Texas along the Río Grande, were settlements that acted as gateways from other parts of New Spain: San Juan Bautista in Coahuila (mission founded in 1699 and presidio in 1701), El Paso del Norte in New Mexico (mission of Nuestra Señora de Guadalupe del Paso established in 1659 and presidio in 1683), and Laredo (pueblo settled in 1755), then in the province of Nuevo Santander (Jones 1979, 38–46).

The two earliest permanent town settlements that attained the status of municipality in Texas were San Antonio in 1731 and Laredo in 1767. Both towns' plans indicated a preference for the grid and the square (Cruz 1988). San Antonio also later attained the status of *ciudad* in 1811, the only city in the present United States to receive the highest

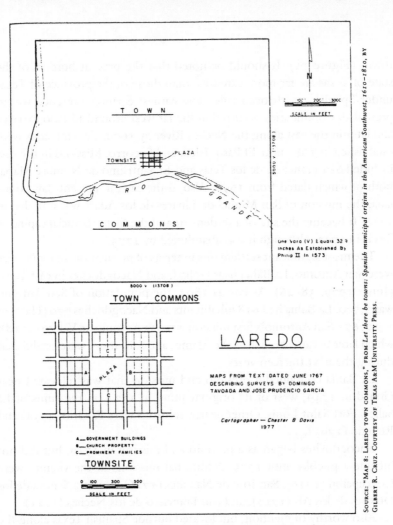

SOURCE: "MAP 8: LAREDO TOWN COMMONS," FROM *Let there be towns: Spanish municipal origins in the American Southwest, 1610–1810,* BY GILBERT R. CRUZ. COURTESY OF TEXAS A&M UNIVERSITY PRESS.

Figure 72 Plan of Laredo in 1767 showing the regular pattern of streets around the central plaza. Jones noted that later ordinances for frontier settlements, which dated from 1789, called for "symmetrical arrangement of streets" (Jones 1979, 10).

rank in the Spanish urban hierarchy (Jones 1979, 259). Laredo (Figure 72), which was not surveyed officially until 1767, observed prescriptions similar to San Antonio's with similar results, even though Laredo was funded solely by private interests and had no prior presidio or mission (Cruz 1988).

To appreciate the influence of Spanish town planning in Texas requires an understanding of the evolution of those traditions. In Spain

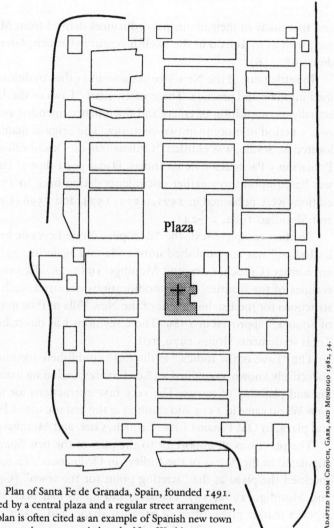

Plaza

Figure 73 Plan of Santa Fe de Granada, Spain, founded 1491. Characterized by a central plaza and a regular street arrangement, the town's plan is often cited as an example of Spanish new town planning schemes that were carried to the New World.

new towns and town planning traditions date back to the eighth century and parallel the centuries-long reconquest of Iberia from the Moors (Cruz 1988). One of these new towns in Spain, Santa Fe de Granada (Figure 73), was founded in 1491 and used a gridlike street pattern and square that typified Spanish traditions born out of Roman, Moorish, and Iberian experience. Some scholars of Spanish urban planning have stated that the "Iberians became a municipal people during the reconquest"

Origins of Squares Derived from Spanish and Other Traditions

and that many of their municipal ordinances derived from Moorish contact, such as in Toledo in the twelfth century (Crouch, Garr, and Mundigo 1982, 36).

In settlement of the New World these and other traditions were codified into law and practice. These often-cited "Laws of the Indies" were actually a compilation of edicts and documents amended and published over a period of more than two centuries. The original manuscript, now located in Seville, was entitled "Ordenanzas de Descubrimiento, Nueva Población y Pacificación de las Indias, Dadas por Felipe II en 1573" and was based upon three earlier documents dating back to 1521. Various editions were published in 1571, 1573, 1574, and 1596 (Crouch, Garr, and Mundigo 1982, 23–24).

The first complete text, the "Recopilación de Leyes de los Reynos de las Indias," was not published until 1681 and again in 1791 in a different format (Crouch, Garr, and Mundigo 1982, 26). Responding to the realities of the frontier, other modifications occurred, such as the "Instructions for the Establishment of the New Villa of Pitic in the Province of Sonora," approved in 1789. These revisions had direct bearing upon Texas settlements (Jones 1979, 10).

The "Laws of the Indies," as the earlier published documents became collectively known, contained 148 ordinances, including many on the siting and planning of towns. The very first instructions for towns in the New World came in 1513 and resulted in the first use of the Hispanic grid and plaza, in Old Panama City (Crouch, Garr, and Mundigo 1982, 38).

The plaza was all-important to the plan of the new Spanish town as stipulated in the "Laws of the Indies" in Ordinances 112 to 117, which specified the plaza as the "starting point for the town" (Crouch, Garr, and Mundigo 1982, 39). Plazas in old Spain had been of two basic types: a market plaza, often of irregular shape, and a later monumental plaza of formal design. The New World plaza combined aspects of both types and became the "center for secular, religious, political, social, and other ceremonial activities . . . [and] also the point at which civic identity was expressed" (Crouch, Garr, and Mundigo 1982, 42). Thus, as the focus of frontier life, the central plaza and grid brought order to the landscape of the New World.

The grid-pattern plan, which became characteristic of the Spanish, derived from Ordinance 110, which stipulated that "a plan for the site [of a new town] is to be made, dividing it into squares, streets, and building lots, using cord and ruler" (Crouch, Garr, and Mundigo 1982, 13). In 1789, in the "Instructions for the Establishment of the New Villa of Pitic in the Province of Sonora," the grid was also specified in Article 8, which required that "streets shall run in a straight line . . . their symmetry and regularity contributing to the beauty and cleanliness of the new settlement" (Hatcher 1927, 316–317).

Recommendations for plazas were recorded in Ordinances 112 and 113, which preferred rectangular proportions with a length

> one and half times its width [and] not less than two hundred feet wide and three hundred feet long, nor larger than eight hundred feet long and five hundred and thirty-two feet wide. A good proportion is six hundred feet long and four hundred wide. (Crouch, Garr, and Mundigo 1982, 13)

The plazas were required to remain open: locations of major churches and buildings were also prescribed by law; they were "not [to] be placed on the square," while the *cabildo* or town council was to be placed "near" the church and "next to the main plaza" (Ordinance 124; Crouch, Garr, and Mundigo 1982, 15). Although the ordinances did not specify this, the church was often placed on the east of the main plaza and the *casa real* on the west.

In San Antonio this convention was reversed, with the church on the west of what became Main Plaza, although the church was on the east side of the earlier Military Plaza. Laredo's plan of 1767 indicated a church on the east and government buildings on the west side of the plaza as prescribed. Contrary to Ordinance 126, which stated that "no lots [on the plaza] shall be assigned to private individuals: instead, they shall be used for the buildings of the church and royal houses and for city use" (Crouch, Garr, and Mundigo 1982, 15), both Laredo and San Antonio early on allowed prominent residences on the main plaza. Yet the overall pattern of a regular grid and public plaza was consistent.

Thus, the "Laws of the Indies" and later ordinances provided for a systematic process of settlement with rules for siting towns, laying out public plazas and streets, distributing lots, dictating land uses, and establishing governance. While local conditions and preferences may have deviated from the letter of the law, a tradition of town planning evolved that depended upon the grid pattern and the plaza for both the practical and symbolic needs of Spanish settlers in the New World.

However, despite a code for founding and administering towns,

Spanish policy toward immigration in Texas varied greatly, alternating between encouraging and forbidding foreign settlement. Near the end of Spain's rule there were few viable communities in Texas. In 1819 Texas was home to as few as 2,000 settlers, excluding soldiers and missionaries (Hatcher 1927, 271).

In that same year the Crown began to distribute royal lands to settlers, although the Cortes, a constitutionally established legal body, had earlier instituted colonization contracts in Texas. The first such colonization contract had been approved in November 1813 and awarded to Colonel R. R. Keene, a U.S. citizen and the "first real empresario for Texas" (Hatcher 1927, 241–242). However, the most successful grant to eventually result in a lasting presence in Texas was conveyed in 1821 to Moses Austin, who previously had received a Spanish land grant in Louisiana in 1797. Yet full implementation of the *empresario* system, as well as the founding of more communities, would await Mexico's rule of Texas.

MEXICO'S INFLUENCE

Spanish control of town planning in Texas officially ended when Mexico declared its independence from Spain on February 24, 1821, but many Hispanic traditions continued under Mexican law and practice. Mexico assumed Spain's little-used *empresario* program of settlement that provided land grants to those who established permanent settlements in Texas. Mexico's Colonization Laws of 1824, 1825, and 1827 also contained provisions for the planning of towns. Towns were to have a "Principal or Constitutional" plaza 120 varas (1 vara = 33.33 inches) square and straight streets 20 varas wide running north to south and east to west (Reps 1979, 117). In addition, blocks were to be provided east of the main square for the church and west of the square for the town hall, as well as separate blocks for a jail, school, and cemetery (Reps 1979, 117).

Early Texas towns included Anahuac (1821), Velasco (1821), San Felipe de Austin (1824), Victoria (1824), Gonzales (1825), Mina or Bastrop (1827), Matagorda (1827), Goliad (1829), Liberty (1831), San Patricio de Hibernia (1831), and Refugio (1834). Most of these towns were surveyed and laid out under the jurisdiction of Mexican authorities in Texas. In keeping with the colonization laws, many of these towns

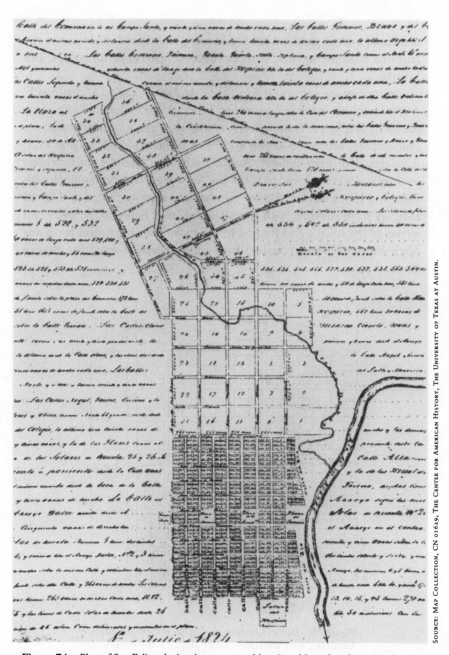

Figure 74 Plan of San Felipe de Austin as surveyed in 1824. Note that the main plaza replacing Austin's central square fronts the river, following Hispanic custom. Note also additional squares for other institutional uses.

Origins of Squares Derived from Spanish and Other Traditions

contained a main plaza within a grid plan, and several made use of the required multiple squares, such as those of San Felipe, Gonzales, and Liberty.

An interesting example is San Felipe de Austin, capital of Stephen F. Austin's colony, assumed from his father, Moses Austin. Early plans drawn by Stephen F. Austin closely resembled Penn's influential plan for Philadelphia, which was similar to British colonial models such as Londonderry, Northern Ireland. Austin's scheme called for four satellite squares and a central square as the site for a group of community buildings. The Hispanic plan (Figure 74) that was approved in 1824 differed radically from Austin's, with three plazas placed between the two main streets of the town's grid leading to the river. The larger main plaza was open and (like many Hispanic river- or seaports) fronted the Brazos River.

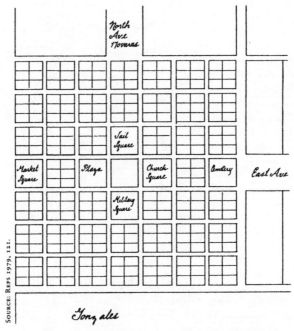

Figure 75 Plan of Gonzales, the capital of DeWitt's Anglo-American colony established under Mexico's *empresario* system of settlement. In Gonzales the multiple squares, typical of many Hispanic towns, are organized in an elaborate cruciform pattern planned by James Kerr in 1825.

THE COURTHOUSE SQUARE IN TEXAS

Gonzales, discussed in the previous chapter, is another example of the unusual *empresario* plans (Figure 75). Plans for Gonzales, like those for San Felipe de Austin, had to be approved by Mexican authorities, who, as noted earlier, were not averse to changing or challenging the plans submitted by the colonists to meet Mexican law. In the case of Gonzales, *empresario* Green DeWitt's choice of James Kerr as official surveyor was judged illegal (Rather 1904, 115). Later, when Kerr's plan was to be surveyed by Byrd Lockhart, the authorities again objected because the plan did not conform to the letter of the law. However, since it had been approved when originally submitted on December 12, 1825, Lockhart was permitted to lay out the town in May 1832 (Rather 1904, 120).

Although exceptional in its elaborate use of plazas and malls, Gonzales is indicative of Mexico's legacy in Texas, which continued the use of Hispanic grid-pattern plans and open plazas. Perhaps more importantly, Mexico opened Texas to further settlement, accomplishing more in fifteen years than Spain had in three centuries. After independence from Mexico, Anglo-American settlement and town building increased. However, the Americans were not alone, as both French and German immigrants became a factor in the settlement of Texas during the nineteenth century.

GERMAN INFLUENCE

German settlement brought yet another European-based set of planning traditions to Texas. German influence on Texas town planning, like the French influence, was both direct and indirect. The primary, indirect influence resulted from early German immigration to America in the seventeenth and eighteenth centuries. Their customs contributed significantly to evolving Anglo-American traditions in the Mid-Atlantic area, some of which eventually found expression in Texas. More immediate influence was provided in the mid-nineteenth century by immigrants who entered Texas directly from Germany. These later groups of settlers contributed substantially to the early population and culture of the state, and members of these groups planned and settled a number of communities.

Despite the fact that many of the German colonists came from settlements of irregular, clustered farm villages (Jordan 1966) or small linear towns, there were both historical and contemporary models of German town planning traditions using regular blocks and squares that Germanic

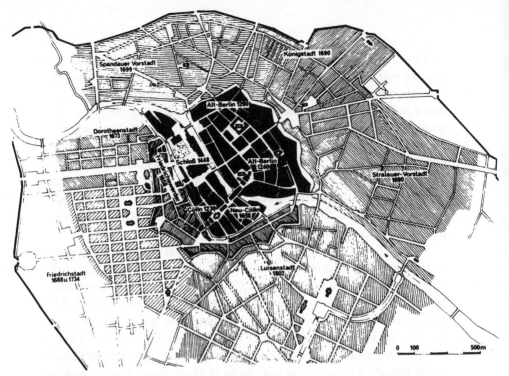

SOURCE: W. BRAUNFELS, *Urban design in western Europe: Regime and architecture, 900–1900,* TRANSLATED BY K. J. NORTHCOTT, PUBLISHED BY THE UNIVERSITY OF CHICAGO PRESS. ©1988 BY THE UNIVERSITY OF CHICAGO.

Figure 76   Plan of Berlin and surrounding new towns around 1800. Increasingly regular, especially to the west, these new towns may have provided inspiration for the planning of several German communities in Texas.

settlers could have drawn upon. Older towns such as Bern, founded in 1190 (Braunfels 1988, 156), as well as other planned towns from the thirteenth century displayed grids and central squares. Many of these squares were fronted by a town hall or church. Some occupied the square or parts of it (Zucker 1959).

In addition, there were substantial enlargements of existing cities that followed orthogonal urban design schemes, and later Baroque plans were applied to existing urban fabrics. Both Berlin and Potsdam exhibited elements of Baroque design. Berlin (Figure 76), in particular, is notable for its new towns, especially Friedrichswerder (1658), Dorotheenstadt (1673), and Friedrichstadt (1688–1734). These were west of the old city, and each was more regular and orderly than its predecessor. Potsdam and Berlin, however, were centrally controlled towns (Braunfels 1988, 216–217) and like many other European capitals were reflective of royal patronage and large-scale planning. Unlike the German settlers' traditional ways of laying out settlements, these formally planned examples may have influenced town planners in Texas in terms of street patterns and public spaces.

One organization that was responsible for the settlement of thousands of Germans in Texas was the Society for the Protection of German Immigrants in Texas. This group was first organized in 1842, but did not receive the aid it sought from the Prussian government and was reorganized on March 25, 1844 (King 1967, 33–34). This society, which became known as the Adelsverein because it consisted of many aristocratic members such as Prince Carl of Solms-Braunfels, eventually came into possession of Texas land through purchases of land grants issued by the Republic.

The largest was the troublesome Fisher-Miller grant, located deep in hostile, unsettled territory. The provisions of that grant required the so-

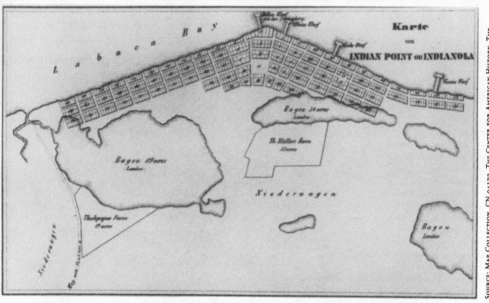

Figure 77 Plan of the port of Indianola. The town was also known as Carlshafen by the Society for the Protection of German Immigrants in Texas, who planned it as their port of entry. Note the linear grid of streets and central square set back from the waterfront. This contrasts with the plans of Spanish and French ports, which usually employed plazas fronting the water.

Origins of Squares Derived from Spanish and Other Traditions

ciety to settle 6,000 families by August of 1847 in order to receive over 4 million acres of land, half of which could be retained by member-investors of the society (King 1967, 43). The society's primary motive was obvious, but was often confused with desires that ranged from establishing a new German state to an individual's seeking a new start in a new world.

Despite official mismanagement, unrealistic expectations, and constant indebtedness, the society sought other land grants and did secure title for many of its colonists. More importantly, the society founded several towns, including the port of Indianola on the coast, New Braunfels (1845) in Comal County, and Fredericksburg (1846), the first settlement within the society's original land grant.

Indianola (Figure 77), also called Carlshafen, served as port of entry for the society and was planned with a linear grid aligned along the shore

SOURCE: MAP COLLECTION, CN 09641, THE CENTER FOR AMERICAN HISTORY, THE UNIVERSITY OF TEXAS AT AUSTIN.

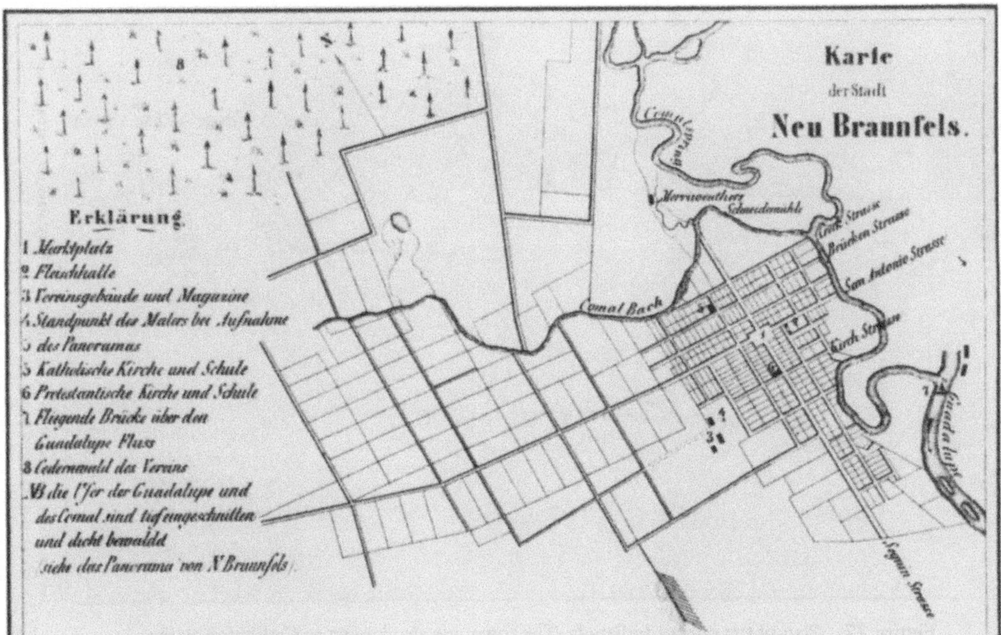

Figure 78 Early plan of New Braunfels, which was one of the first German settlements in Texas. Note the use of a central open plaza.

THE COURTHOUSE SQUARE IN TEXAS

of Lavaca Bay. In this regard it was similar to linear plans employed by Spanish and French ports, yet it differed from these since its main square was set back from the waterfront. The German port town was short-lived: after a series of devastating storms, Indianola was abandoned.

New Braunfels, after the lean years of the society's patronage, prospered because of its more central location between San Antonio and Austin. By 1850 New Braunfels was the fourth largest town in Texas, with 1,298 inhabitants, led by Galveston with 4,177, San Antonio with 3,488, and Houston with 2,396 (Reps 1979, 145). The town was established in 1845 for the Adelsverein by Prince Carl of Solms-Braunfels. The town's plan featured a rectangular central plaza (Figure 78) at the intersection of two main streets, San Antonio and Seguin. The grid-pattern plan and open plaza indicate the influence of formal planning traditions and in many respects are similar to the Lancaster square. In the

Figure 79   Main plaza in New Braunfels today. The square's significance is marked by prominent buildings, including the courthouse, which remains opposite the square.

Origins of Squares Derived from Spanish and Other Traditions

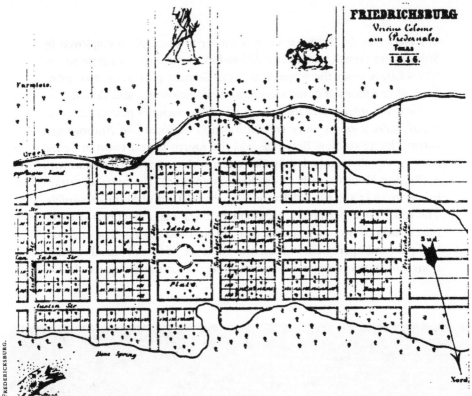

Figure 80 Plan of Fredericksburg showing the linear town grid and central square, noted here as Adolphs Platz and later known as Markt Platz. The octagonal meeting house, the Vereins-Kirche, was placed in the middle of the main street, which passed through the plaza.

case of New Braunfels, however, the plaza is very small and linear and was never intended for a courthouse. The small plaza (Figure 79) remained open except for a gazebo and was eventually surrounded by the town's prominent buildings. Over time, two courthouses, placed at different corners, have faced the plaza.

The next most prominent town of the society, Fredericksburg, was founded by John O. Meusebach. Originally known as Baron Ottfried Hans von Meusebach, he came to Texas as the society's second general commissioner, replacing Prince Carl of Solms-Braunfels. Fredericksburg's site was selected and planned by Meusebach (King 1967, 75). The town was laid out in 1846 by T. Charles Doebner, the surveyor for the German Emigration Company, which had assumed the business of the bankrupt Adelsverein. The plan for the town (Figure 80) consisted of a linear grid of blocks with a very large square located along the main street. Originally, the plaza was open; as one observer in 1847 noted, "When following the main street, one comes to the market square which appears to be large enough to accommodate a city of ten to twelve thousand inhabitants" (Roemer 1935, 229).

Shortly thereafter, the Vereins-Kirche was erected in the middle of the plaza. A frame octagonal structure with a cupola, the building was used as church, town hall, and schoolhouse for some fifty years before being demolished in 1897. A replica was later built opposite the courthouse (Figure 81). There is some question as to the design of the structure. Most accounts maintain that Dr. Friedrich A. Schubert, the first director of the colony, designed the building (Wisseman 1971, 59). However, Meusebach's biographer refers to a conversation in which the founder mentions his directions for laying out the town, its central park, and the Vereins-Kirche (King 1967, 169–171).

Figure 81 Fredericksburg's main square and replica of the Vereins-Kirche. The original structure was demolished in 1897, and a replica was placed near the original site in 1934.

Origins of Squares Derived from Spanish and Other Traditions

Additional circumstantial evidence contained in Meusebach's biography suggests his involvement. Meusebach was familiar with urban spaces in Germany. He knew Berlin well and was likely aware of its *Achteck* (Figure 82) or octagonal plaza along the main route he used to visit his parents in Potsdam. Together known as Leipziger Platz, the Potsdammer Tor and the octagonal *Achteck* were a major ceremonial entrance to Berlin. Also nearby were two prominent octagonal churches, each located in the middle of the street. In addition, Meusebach's first official position was in Aachen, site of one of the most famous octagonal churches in Europe—Charlemagne's Palatine Chapel, built around 800. Meusebach may have relied upon all of these precedents in planning

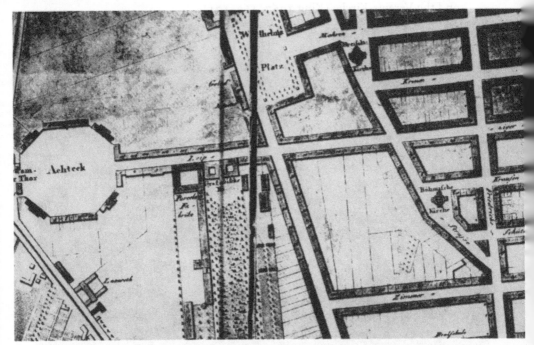

Figure 82   Plan of Leipziger Platz in Berlin, Germany. Note the *Achteck* or octagonal plaza and Potsdammer Tor, one of the major entrances to the city of Berlin. Note also the two octagonal churches, each placed in the middle of the street two blocks east of the *Achteck*. The octagonal church is a German building type that dates back to Charlemagne.

Fredericksburg, directing others to survey the town, and designing prominent public spaces.

The Society for the Protection of German Immigrants in Texas brought in more than five thousand settlers and founded numerous settlements and towns. Yet these were only a part of the stream of Germans and Central Europeans that entered Texas from Europe during the nineteenth and early twentieth century. Revolution and depression on the continent led many to seek new lands and lives—and Texas was a popular destination.

THE RAILROAD'S INFLUENCE

Two factors in development of the state worthy of special mention are the railroad and railroad town. Railroads received the largest amount of land for internal improvements, with over 32,000,000 acres donated by the state legislature. This was a practice shared by many states, as the federal government also transferred title of public lands to railroads. The railroads were also important because along with their tracks they laid out and developed numerous Texas towns (Table 16). Besides the obvious but belated benefits to the state's economy, rail companies also fostered urban development in two ways. First, they boosted the economies of existing towns. Second, they planned and promoted new towns along their routes. Their influence on new towns is of most interest to this discussion.

Many railroad towns became county seats, as the commerce and growth associated with the railroad assured a dominant role in the county. The function of the railroad in Texas was similar to that in the West as outlined by Hudson (1985). Although the rails often came later in Texas, railroad companies and speculators planned and platted many new towns. As in other western states, established towns and county seats sought rail links and the commerce they promised. The rail line and town plan formed a "commercial geometry" that maximized both rail traffic and land value (Hudson 1985, 15–16).

Hudson traced the railroad's impact on town building in the West and noted that "town platting thus became the function of the railroad corporations, . . . [their] agents, and individual speculators" (Hudson 1985, 10). Whereas the railroad's measure of success was traffic, the town's success was measured by land values and lot sales (Hudson 1985,

Origins of Squares Derived from Spanish and Other Traditions

Table 16. County Seats Established by Railroads

COUNTY SEAT / COUNTY   DATE

Abilene / Taylor	1881	Lufkin / Angelina	1882
Alice / Jim Wells	1888	Marfa / Presidio	1881
Alpine / Brewster	1882	Mertzon / Irion	1910
Ballinger / Runnels	1886	Miami /Roberts	1887
Big Lake / Reagan	1911	Monahans / Ward	1880?
Channing / Hartley	1891	Odessa / Ector	1886
Daingerfield / Morris	1840?	Pampa / Gray	1888
Dalhart / Dallam	1901	Panhandle / Carson	1887
Edna / Jackson	1882	Pearsall / Frio	1880
Floresville/ Wilson	1885	Pecos / Reeves	1881
Franklin / Robertson	1871	Quanah / Hardeman	1886
Goldthwaite / Mills	1885	Raymondville / Willacy	1904
Groesbeck / Limestone	1870	Sanderson / Terrell	1882
Hebbronville / Jim Hogg	1881	Sarita / Kenedy	1904
Hempstead / Waller	1857	Sierra Blanca / Hudspeth	1881
Jayton / Kent	?	Sinton / San Patricio	1885
Jourdanton / Atascosa	1908	Spearman / Hansford	1917
Kingsville / Kleberg	1904	Stanton / Martin	1881
Kountze / Hardin	1881	Sweetwater / Nolan	1882
Littlefield / Lamb	1912	Van Horn / Culberson	1912
Longview / Gregg	1870	Vega / Oldham	1900

Source: Compiled by author from Webb et al., 1952.

103). The form of these towns evolved from the 1850s to the 1920s as planners and speculators learned more about the features for a successful venture. Hudson's study of North Dakota railroad towns determined a "common look" based on the grid-pattern plan (Hudson 1985, 87).

Hudson described three types of urban morphology for railroad towns (see Chapter 5). The earliest form, the "symmetric," featured the railroad track as the central focus of the town, which was split in two equal halves by the tracks. In practice, however, one side of the tracks was often favored, and land values and even social status were adversely affected. This plan also placed all the best commercial lots along the tracks, a scheme that did not survive long past the 1890s in the West (Hudson 1985, 89).

The town plan that followed attempted to correct the problems of having two parallel main streets on either side of the tracks. The "orthogonal" plan placed its main street perpendicular to the tracks, allowing for a commercial street with businesses along both sides. However, the railroad's division of the town and main street persisted.

Improvement came after 1890, when the "T-town" became the dominant model:

> This [plan] proved to be a stable solution, more acceptable both to railroads and to townspeople. The elimination of crossings in the business district was a relief . . . and the isolation of the tracks to one side of town made them less conspicuous to residents. (Hudson 1985, 90)

The T-town allowed for two further developments in the urban design of railroad towns. One was "reintroduction" of the central square, a long-favored feature of urban design; and the second was placement of a major cross-street intersecting the main street and forming a four-way commercial intersection (Hudson 1985, 190). These developments provided a new focus for the town as the railroad became a less dominant feature in the townscape.

These changes also allowed greater freedom for the railroad to control property next to its tracks and increased land values at the square or major business intersection. Banks were typical purchasers of these lots (Hudson 1985, 90). County seats, too, were frequent beneficiaries of such town planning schemes, as speculators realized the value of county government to the economic vitality of their ventures by donating a square for the county courthouse. The number of county seats planned or associated with the building of the railroads provides an indication of the reciprocal nature of their relationship.

Towns and county seats hoping to prosper and maintain their dominance often sought rail connections; and railroad speculators recognizing the economic and political pull of the county seat returned the favor by reserving blocks for county government in hopes of securing a county capital. Many of these towns featured a prominent location for the courthouse square, either adjacent to the tracks and depot or at the end of a main street running perpendicular to the tracks. Examples of both types remain in the urban landscape of Texas and reflect the centripetal influence of the courthouse and of the county seat.

Chapter Seven

The Centripetal Role
of the Courthouse Square

Long after they have been platted, courthouse squares exert influence on town life and on the surrounding townscape. This can be characterized as a centripetal influence that attracts to the square everyday activities associated with commerce (and the creation of a central business district) as well as public and ceremonial events important to the community as a whole. The square's civic role is one of a gathering point for community life. Many courthouse squares act centripetally, but there is considerable variation in the degree to which they focus activity. One way to assess this role is to record and analyze land use around the square, taking into account the square's relationship to the town's CBD, concentration of land uses, city size, planning traditions, block patterns, structures on the square, courthouse location, the square's setting, and the placement of monuments and memorials. In specific contexts these features can either reinforce or weaken a square's influence on the surrounding urban landscape. In order to assess the role of selected Texas courthouse squares, data on these features were collected during site visits to 139 county seats (Figure 83 and Tables 6, 7, and 17).

Site visits involved recording land uses and other features of the urban landscape at the square, including retail businesses, offices, high-rise buildings, banks and financial institutions, government buildings, residences, and churches. Additional building types and uses included funeral homes, gas stations, vacant lots, and abandoned structures (Table 18). Sketch maps for each site surveyed noted the type and locations of land use relative to the courthouse square. The survey also

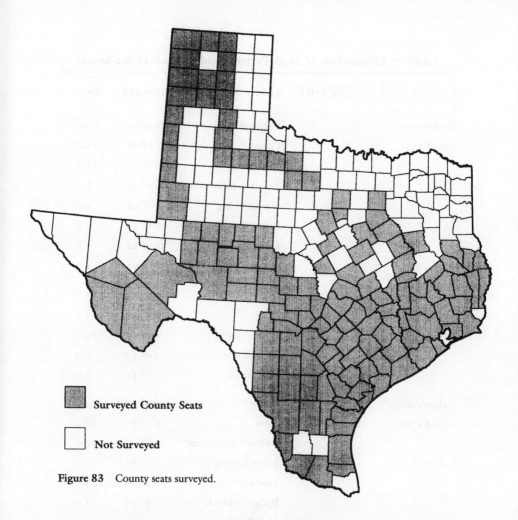

Figure 83 County seats surveyed.

Surveyed County Seats

Not Surveyed

recorded other features on the square, such as major monuments and gazebos, as well as parklike or hilltop settings (Appendix 2). Many of these features play a part in reinforcing the special character of the square, suggesting certain relationships between the courthouse square and community.

On the basis of these surveys of land use and features found at the square, each site was classified into one of three categories describing the square's role (Table 18). Of 139 county seats surveyed, 92 courthouse squares were defined as *predominant* (Figure 84). Squares in this category retain a central focus in their community and often dominate their townscapes. Some squares in this group lack certain features associated

The Centripetal Role of the Courthouse Square

Table 17. Comparison of Block Patterns and the Role of the Square

COURTHOUSE SQUARE ROLE	BLOCK PATTERNS	NUMBER	%*
Predominant	Shelbyville	57 of 92	62.0
(92 of 139)	Plaza	11 of 92	12.0
	Two-Block	10 of 92	11.0
	Railroad-Influenced	6 of 92	7.0
	Harrisonburg	4 of 92	4.0
	Four-Block	2 of 92	2.0
	Lancaster	1 of 92	1.0
	Quarter-Block	1 of 92	1.0
Codominant	Shelbyville	2 of 17	12.0
(17 of 139)	Plaza	11 of 17	65.0
	Harrisonburg	2 of 17	12.0
	Two-Block	1 of 17	6.0
	Half-Block	1 of 17	6.0
Subordinate	Shelbyville	16 of 30	53.0
(30 of 139)	Plaza	6 of 30	20.0
	Railroad-Influenced	3 of 30	10.0
	Harrisonburg	2 of 30	7.0
	Lancaster	1 of 30	3.0
	Irregular-Block	1 of 30	3.0
	Half-Block	1 of 30	3.0

*Percentage of county seats surveyed only (excludes fractions).

with traditional block patterns or play limited central roles, but their significance is generally unquestioned.

Seventeen courthouse squares were classified as *codominant*. These squares share aspects of their community role with one or more sites within the town's landscape. These may include other significant civic spaces or features that constitute multiple foci in the community, such as major public buildings, plazas, or parks. This situation is often found in cities where the city hall is an important civic space and the scene of public events.

Table 18. Land Use Survey at the Courthouse Squares

ROLE	LAND USE	NUMBER	%
Predominant	Banks or S&Ls	69 of 92	75.0
(92 of 139)	Churches	27 of 92	29.0
	Government	72 of 92	78.0
	Retail & Office	83 of 92	90.0
	Office-Only	4 of 92	4.0
	High-Rise	3 of 92	3.0
	Residential	41 of 92	45.0
	Vacant Property	29 of 92	32.0
Codominant	Banks or S&Ls	6 of 17	35.0
(17 of 139)	Churches	6 of 17	35.0
	Government	17 of 17	100
	Retail & Office	7 of 17	41.0
	Office-Only	10 of 17	59.0
	High-Rise	9 of 17	53.0
	Residential	6 of 17	35.0
	Vacant Property	4 of 17	24.0
Subordinate	Banks and S&Ls	7 of 30	23.0
(30 of 139)	Churches	17 of 30	57.0
	Government	20 of 30	67.0
	Retail & Office	12 of 30	40.0
	Office-Only	18 of 30	60.0
	High-Rise	3 of 30	10.0
	Residential	20 of 30	67.0
	Vacant Property	13 of 30	43.0

Thirty courthouse squares were categorized as *subordinate*. These county seats are more ambiguous in character and lack focus. Their roles in the activities of the community are very limited. These squares are typically more removed both literally and figuratively from the life of the community. The distinctions among these three groups of squares and the roles they play within their respective communities become apparent through comparison of specific types of land uses and urban features.

The Centripetal Role of the Courthouse Square

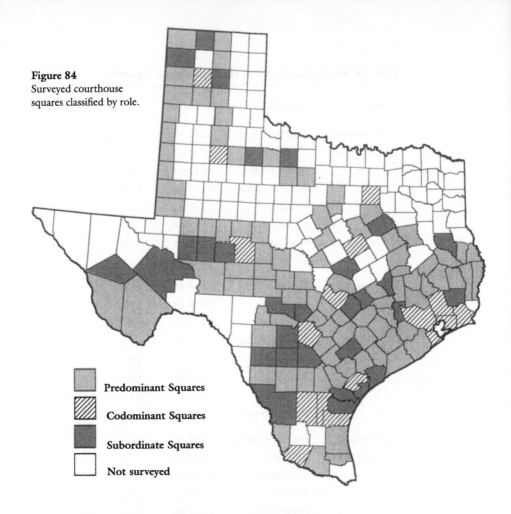

Figure 84
Surveyed courthouse
squares classified by role.

Predominant Squares

Codominant Squares

Subordinate Squares

Not surveyed

Field surveys noted nine related features that can be divided into three groups based on (1) the function or use of the square, (2) the square's urban form, and (3) specific characteristics or attributes of the square and courthouse (Table 19). The first grouping includes the square's association with the central business district, concentration of significant land use, and the size of the community. The second set relates to the square's tradition, block patterns, and the number of buildings located on the square itself. The third set of features is composed of specific site conditions such as the courthouse's placement on the square, the square's setting, and the monuments or memorials found on the square. All of these features can be related to the square's connection to the community and its role as civic space.

Table 19. Comparison of Selected Features of Surveyed Courthouse Squares

FEATURE	PREDOMINANT n=92	CODOMINANT n=17	SUBORDINATE n=30
Relationship of square to CBD			
Center of CBD (May be incomplete)	66.0%	18.0%	00.0%
Adjacent to CBD	24.0%	23.0%	27.0%
Removed from CBD (or no CBD)	10.0%	59.0%	73.0%
Concentration of significant land use			
Enclosure by storefronts	39.0%	00.0%	00.0%
Near enclosure, free-standing bldg.	37.0%	65.0%	13.0%
Less enclosure, free-standing bldg.	24.0%	35.0%	87.0%
Population of the county seat			
100,000+	00.0%	41.0%	10.0%
25,001 to 100,000	09.0%	18.0%	03.0%
5,001 to 25,000	35.0%	18.0%	33.0%
1,001 to 5,000	41.0%	23.0%	44.0%
1,000 or less	15.0%	00.0%	10.0%
Courthouse square tradition			
Traditional block patterns	80.0%	29.5%	63.0%
Nontraditional block patterns	20.0%	70.5%	37.0%
Urban morphology or block patterns			
Shelbyvilles and related patterns	62.0%	00.0%	53.0%
Plazas and related patterns	12.0%	65.0%	20.0%
All other block patterns	26.0%	35.0%	27.0%
Structures on the square			
Courthouse only major structure	46.0%	69.0%	47.0%
Additional bldg. on square	54.0%	31.0%	53.0%
Courthouse location at square			
Centered and/or set-back	53.0%	47.0%	40.0%
Modest set-back	39.0%	23.5%	27.0%
Little or no set-back	08.0%	29.5%	33.0%
Setting of courthouse square			
Parklike setting, lawn or trees	44.5%	41.0%	16.0%
Modest parklike setting	44.5%	41.0%	37.0%
Parking lots and street only	11.0%	18.0%	47.0%
Monuments and memorials on square			
Monuments/memorials	74.0%	82.0%	60.0%
No major monuments/memorials	26.0%	18.0%	40.0%

Many of these features provided the basis for the morphological clas-sification of courthouse squares already discussed, and most of them, in varying degree, characterize central courthouse squares. However, nu-merous centrifugal factors, such as decentralization, decline of urban centers, suburbanization, and other socioeconomic changes, have al-tered or transformed the role of some squares. Yet squares derived from all planning precedents discussed in preceding chapters—as well as their variants—are capable of dominating or anchoring their local townscape. Discussion of these features and land uses demonstrates how this domi-nance is accomplished.

PREDOMINANT COURTHOUSE SQUARES: INFLUENCE AND ROLE

Squares with predominant roles that were determined by field study in-volve a large group of county seats with diverse patterns and features. These squares can be found throughout Texas (Figure 84) and include examples of block patterns derived from Anglo-American and other planning traditions (Table 20). What they have in common is their cen-tripetal role in focusing important urban functions and features at the courthouse square as well as providing a focal point for the urban land-scape. Predominant squares can be determined by observing street pat-terns that converge at the square, land uses that concentrate significant buildings and activities around the square, prominent siting of the courthouse, and presence of significant monuments. A prime example of a predominant square is Georgetown in Williamson County (Figure 85).

Despite varied origins and plans, predominant squares share a num-ber of specific features (Table 21) that account for their influence and special role. The most obvious is the common practice of reserving an honored space for civil authority in the community. These spaces typi-cally involve a centrally located square or plaza and often require special emphasis by street or block patterns to accomplish a central focus. Tradi-tion often placed the courthouse in the most prestigious position and el-evated government's role above that of other features in the urban land-scape.

Predominant squares constitute 66 percent (92 of 139) of the sites surveyed. This figure indicates the continued viability of these squares

Figure 85 Williamson County Courthouse and square in Georgetown. Typical of many predominant squares, this courthouse dominates a parklike square surrounded by traditional storefronts.

despite the forces that erode their traditional function. Predominant squares are associated with Anglo-American block patterns in 80 percent of the sites and with other block patterns in 20 percent of the surveyed counties.

The predominant group is dominated by Shelbyville patterns (Table 20), which account for 62 percent of the surveyed squares. This is the same percentage of Shelbyvilles counted in the state as a whole. There is

Table 20. Predominant Courthouse Squares by Block Pattern

COUNTY SEAT / COUNTY

Shelbyvilles or Related Patterns: 57 of 92 (62.0%)

Alpine*** / Brewster	Johnson City* / Blanco
Andrews*** / Andrews	Junction* / Kimble
Bandera*** / Bandera	La Grange / Fayette
Bay City / Matagorda	Lampasas / Lampasas
Beeville* / Bee	Leakey*** / Real
Benjamin* / Knox	Llano** / Llano
Brenham / Washington	Lockhart / Caldwell
Caldwell / Burleson	Lufkin** / Angelina
Canyon*** / Randall	Madisonville / Madison
Carrizo Springs / Dimmit	Morton* / Cochran
Centerville*** / Leon	Muleshoe*** / Bailey
Claude* / Armstrong	Newton*** / Newton
Coldspring* / San Jacinto	Paint Rock* / Concho
Columbus* / Colorado	Raymondville*** / Willacy
Conroe** / Montgomery	Richmond*** / Fort Bend
Dickens*** / Dickens	Robert Lee*** / Coke
Fairfield* / Freestone	San Augustine** / San Augustine
Floresville*** / Wilson	San Marcos / Hays
Floydada** / Floyd	Seminole** / Gaines
Garden City*** / Glasscock	Silverton*** / Briscoe
Georgetown / Williamson	Stephenville / Erath
Granbury / Hood	Sterling City*** / Sterling
Hallettsville / Lavaca	Stinnett*** / Hutchinson
Hamilton / Hamilton	Tilden*** / McMullen
Hemphill** / Sabine	Vega*** / Oldham
Hereford*** / Deaf Smith	Waxahachie / Ellis
Hillsboro / Hill	Wharton / Wharton
Huntsville / Walker	Woodville*** / Tyler
Jasper** / Jasper	

Plazas or Related Patterns: 11 of 92 (12.0%)

Cotulla* / La Salle	Ozona** / Crockett
Fredericksburg*** / Gillespie	Seguin / Guadalupe
Gonzales*** / Gonzales	Uvalde / Uvalde
Menard*** / Menard	Victoria*** / Victoria
Midland* / Midland	Zapata* / Zapata
New Braunfels** / Comal	

Two-Blocks or Related Patterns: 10 of 92 (11.0%)

Angelton*** / Brazoria   Graham** / Young
Ballinger*** / Runnels   Groveton*** / Trinity
Brady / McCulloch   Karnes City*** / Karnes
Edinburg / Hidalgo   Mason** / Mason
Farwell*** / Parmer   Plains*** / Yoakum

Railroad-Influenced Patterns: 6 of 92 (7.0%)

Dalhart* / Dallam   Livingston*** / Polk
Edna* / Jackson   Sarita* / Kenedy
George West*** / Live Oak   Spearman*** / Hansford

Harrisonburgs or Related Patterns: 4 of 92 (4.0%)

Bellville / Austin   Marfa* / Presidio
Goliad* / Goliad   Sonora*** / Sutton

Four-Blocks or Related Patterns: 2 of 92 (2.0%)

Eldorado*** / Schleicher   Weatherford / Parker

Lancasters or Related Patterns: 1 of 92 (1.0%)

Anderson* / Grimes

Quarter-Blocks and Related Patterns: 1 of 92 (1.0%)

Throckmorton* / Throckmorton

---

*Incomplete or inconsistent development around the square.
**Additional buildings on the courthouse square.
***Both incomplete development and additional buildings.

a similar correspondence between the other most popular block patterns in this group as well. Plaza patterns are found in 12 percent of the predominant squares and 13 percent of all county seats; and railroad-influenced squares total 7 percent of the predominant role group and 7 percent of the state total.

Of fifty-seven Shelbyvilles interpreted as predominant squares, seventeen exhibit a prototypical pattern with courthouses centered on their squares. These are found in Bay City, Brenham, Caldwell, Carrizo Springs, Georgetown, Granbury, Hallettsville, Hamilton, Hillsboro, La Grange, Lampasas, Lockhart, Madisonville, San Marcos, Stephenville, Waxahachie, and Wharton. Eleven of these towns retain prominent nineteenth-century courthouses.

There are eleven plaza courthouses in this group of predominant

The Centripetal Role of the Courthouse Square

Table 21. Selected Features of Predominant Squares

SELECTED FEATURE	NUMBER	%*
Relationship of square to CBD		
Center of CBD (May be incomplete)	61 of 92	66.0
Adjacent to CBD	22 of 92	24.0
Removed from CBD (or no CBD)	9 of 92	10.0
Concentration of significant land use		
Enclosure by common-wall building	36 of 92	39.0
Near enclosure & free-standing building	34 of 92	37.0
Less enclosure & free-standing building	22 of 92	24.0
Population of the county seat		
100,000+	0 of 92	0.0
25,001 to 100,000	8 of 92	9.0
5,001 to 25,000	32 of 92	35.0
1,001 to 5,000	38 of 92	41.0
1,000 or less	14 of 92	15.0
Courthouse square tradition		
Traditional block patterns	74 of 92	80.0
Nontraditional block patterns	18 of 92	20.0
Urban morphology or block patterns		
Shelbyvilles and related patterns	57 of 92	62.0
Plazas and related patterns	11 of 92	12.0
All other block patterns	24 of 92	26.0
Structures on the square		
Courthouse only major structure	42 of 92	46.0
Additional building on square	50 of 92	54.0
Courthouse location at square		
Centered and/or set-back	49 of 92	53.0
Modest set-back	36 of 92	39.0
Little or no set-back	7 of 92	8.0
Setting of courthouse square		
Parklike setting, lawn or trees	41 of 92	44.5
Modest parklike setting	41 of 92	44.5
Parking lots and street only	10 of 92	11.0
Monuments and memorials on the square		
Monuments/memorials	68 of 92	74.0
No major monuments/memorials	24 of 92	26.0

*Percentage of total surveyed.

squares, including seven with open plazas. These are located in Cotulla, New Braunfels, Ozona, Seguin, Uvalde, Victoria, and Zapata. Three other plazas, Fredericksburg, Gonzales, and Menard, are obscured to some degree by the addition of structures to the plaza. A more recent plaza, in Midland, altered what was originally a Shelbyville square. This small urban plaza and its recent civic center reinforce the central role of Midland's square, which suffers from enclosure by high-rise offices and hotels.

Following the plaza types, the next most popular block pattern for predominant squares is the two-block, which accounts for 11 percent of the sites. Several of these were not original, but came about as the result of reducing four-block plans or enlarging single blocks. Edinburg and Farwell both were former four-block squares. Angleton was previously a Shelbyville square. The two remaining four-block schemes also have lost ground. Eldorado's large square is home to numerous additional county buildings that compete with the courthouse. In the case of Weatherford, the square is given over to extensive parking lots and traffic controls.

All of the squares discussed above maintain the central focus of their communities. Squares with predominant roles display some telling correlations in terms of the nine major features used to interpret a square's role in the community.

One common feature associated with predominant squares is concentration of prominent buildings and land uses around the square. This usually involves the town's central business district. Ninety percent of the squares in this category are closely related with some form of CBD. The most typical arrangement is enclosure of the square by rows of prominent storefronts. Thirty-six or 39 percent of predominant squares were characterized by enclosed squares. Another thirty-four or 37 percent were nearly enclosed by both common-wall storefronts and free-standing structures. Only 24 percent of predominant squares could not be counted as enclosed. These are mostly in small towns with little development to rival the courthouse and are included with this group simply because the courthouse square dominates the surrounding townscape. However, not all small town squares manage that level of recognition, and the others are classified in the subordinate category.

Of the eight types of land use recorded, banks and retail uses appear to be good indicators of the square's centripetal influence. Hudson noted a similar relationship in many railroad towns where banks purchased prominent space near the town's square (Hudson 1985, 90). Of the squares surveyed, banks are found in 75 percent of those squares judged to exhibit a central role. This number declined to 35 percent of codominant sites with banks and only 23 percent of the subordinate squares. A definite pattern of greater frequency of banking institutions occurs in squares with a predominant role.

Another significant feature is the population of the community. None of the courthouses surveyed and judged to have predominant squares are found in towns exceeding a population of 100,000. Only two, in Midland and Victoria, could be found in towns with more than 50,000 people. Keep in mind that these figures refer only to those county seats surveyed. The majority of predominant squares are associated with towns that fall between 5,000 and 25,000 inhabitants (35 percent) and those between 1,000 and 5,000 (41 percent). This implies that cities over 25,000 are too large to be dominated by the courthouse square and those below a population of 1,000 find it difficult to manifest a central focus. The fourteen predominant squares below this threshold are included in this group because their courthouse squares are able to maintain a centripetal influence. The same is not true for all small towns, as shown below.

As noted above, the most common block pattern found at squares with a predominant role is the Shelbyville, as in Centerville (Figure 86). Much less in evidence are those block patterns that place the courthouse on an axis with a major street, such as the Harrisonburg and Lancaster squares. Such arrangements emphasize the prominence of the courthouse and might be expected to occur more often. There are four Harrisonburgs in this group, in Bellville, Goliad, Marfa, and Sonora. The squares in Marfa and Sonora are not fully developed, but anchor their respective townscapes.

The lone Lancaster in this category is in Anderson in Grimes County. Its hilltop location and prominent courthouse are visible for miles and loom large in a townscape of fewer than 350 persons. Yet, despite this dominance, the square remains underdeveloped in favor of the highway one block to the west. Another modest county seat, Throckmorton, is also counted among the predominant squares. In this case a quarter-block lot in a small town affords sufficient stature to the elegant courthouse (Figure 70).

Another related factor should be considered: structures sharing the

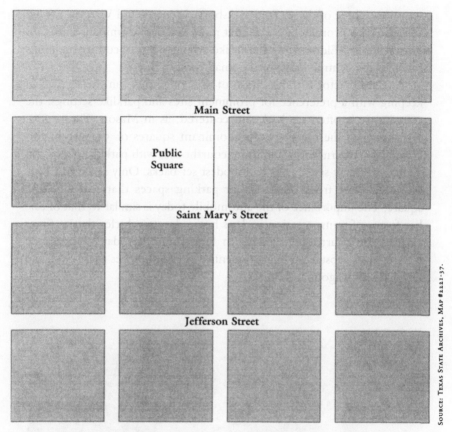

Main Street

Public
Square

Saint Mary's Street

Jefferson Street

Source: Texas State Archives, Map #2221-37.

Figure 86 Partial plan of Centerville in Leon County. The simple grid and square characteristic of the Shelbyville block pattern are typical of many predominant courthouse squares.

square with the courthouse. The traditional Anglo-American central courthouse square was characterized by a solitary courthouse on the square, but slightly less than half (46 percent) of the Texas predominant squares meet this definition. Of ninety-two surveyed predominant squares, fifty include at least one additional structure on the square. Most of these are jails or annexes that accompany the courthouse, which typically maintains the central location and architectural significance.

In some cases, the courthouse square has become a complex of government buildings. The county seats of Alpine, Angleton, Eldorado, Floresville, Fredericksburg, Karnes City, Menard, and Victoria fit this de-

The Centripetal Role of the Courthouse Square

scription. Three of these, Fredericksburg, Menard, and Victoria, are associated with prominent plazas that reinforce their dominant status. In Floresville and Eldorado a campuslike arrangement of county buildings provides the central focus for the small communities.

A related factor is the location of the courthouse on the square. In keeping with a preference for prominent sites and parklike settings, the courthouse is often set back and centered, as in Mason (Figure 87). Forty-nine of the ninety-two predominant squares or 53 percent followed this pattern, including those courthouses with parklike plazas. An additional thirty-six squares had modest set-backs. Only seven had little or no distance from the street or parking spaces that surround the square. The importance of the automobile today is similar to that of earlier forms of transportation such as horse-drawn vehicles that at times choked the courthouse square. In fact, some of today's landscaped squares are a substantial improvement over vast stretches of dust or sand left open for wagons and horses.

Figure 87 Mason County's courthouse square. In this case a two-block scheme provides a generous parklike setting and set-back for the courthouse, which is centered on the square.

THE COURTHOUSE SQUARE IN TEXAS

Parklike settings and set-backs are features typically associated with Anglo-American squares, as reflected in Price's definition for the classic central courthouse square. Often characterized by a lawn, shade trees, and other amenities, these spaces are costly in terms of maintenance and space, but are highly suggestive of the special and symbolic role of the square. All but 11 percent of the predominant squares maintained some form of set-back and lawn. More complete parklike settings were found in forty-one of the ninety-two county seats in this category. An equal number took a more modest approach. The degree and extent of such settings are highly dependent on block size, climate, and the amount of building on the square. In general, those county seats with relatively traditional courthouses maintain traditional settings as well.

Other notable features found on predominant squares are monuments and memorials. Most courthouse squares provide a space for these symbolic structures. Sixty-eight of the squares in this group display one or more markers or monuments, while twenty-four squares do not. The types of monuments and their social significance are discussed along with the symbolic role of courthouse architecture in the next chapter, on the social meaning of the square.

Most of the features held in common by those squares with a predominant role give a clear impression of the centripetal influence of the courthouse square. Together, these formal features are indicative of the civic importance of predominant squares.

CODOMINANT COURTHOUSE SQUARES: INFLUENCE AND ROLE

Seventeen county seats out of the 139 surveyed (Figure 84) share their civic role with other urban features or spaces. As might be expected, these codominant courthouse squares are often associated with large cities that include a number of significant urban spaces or towns with multiple plazas. Twelve of the seventeen county seats in this category have plaza or plaza-related block patterns (Table 22).

Four codominant courthouse squares are found in the state's largest cities: Austin, Dallas, Houston, and San Antonio. Mid-size cities in this category include Amarillo, Beaumont, Galveston, San Angelo, and Waco. However, smaller towns also have squares classified according to multiple

The Centripetal Role of the Courthouse Square

Table 22. Codominant Courthouse Squares by Block Pattern

COUNTY SEAT / COUNTY	COMPETING URBAN FEATURES
Plazas or Related Patterns: 12 of 17 (71.0%)	
Alice* / Jim Wells	City hall and CBD
Anahuac* / Chambers	Adjacent park with historic buildings
Austin*** / Travis	State capitol, UT Tower & parks
Crosbyton*** / Crosby	Adjacent park with historic buildings
Dallas* / Dallas	City hall and civic center
Houston* / Harris	City hall and plaza & other
Galveston*** / Galveston	Broadway, the Strand & other
Liberty / Liberty	City hall and historic plazas
Refugio*** / Refugio	Park with historic buildings
San Antonio*** / Bexar	Alamo Plaza, River Walk & other
San Diego** / Duval	City hall and main plaza
Waco*** / McLennan	City hall
Harrisonburgs or Related Patterns: 2 of 17 (12.0%)	
Kingsville*** / Kleberg	City hall and CBD
Rio Grande City* / Starr	Main plaza (nontraditional)
Shelbyvilles or Related Patterns: 1 of 17 (6.0%)	
Amarillo*** / Potter	City hall and civic center
Two-Blocks or Related Patterns: 1 of 17 (6.0%)	
Beaumont*** / Jefferson	City hall and civic center
Half-Block or Related Patterns: 1 of 17 (6.0%)	
San Angelo* / Tom Green	City hall

*Incomplete or inconsistent development around the square.
**Additional buildings on the courthouse square.
***Both incomplete development and additional buildings.

foci, as in Alice, Anahuac, Crosbyton, Kingsville, Liberty, Refugio, Rio Grande City, and San Diego. All of these small towns, except Alice and Kingsville, have plaza or plaza-related courthouses and share their prominent role in the community with a nearby park or another plaza. Many of those towns with codominant squares include another square or plaza with a city hall, a logical rival to the courthouse for the focus of the com-

SOURCE: TEXAS DEPARTMENT OF TRANSPORTATION, PHOTOGRAPH COLLECTION.

Figure 88 Aerial photo of Austin in the 1970s. Although the urban landscape was substantially altered in the eighties, Austin's capitol and square remain the dominant public space in the city. The county courthouse is placed on one of several public plazas in the city's grid.

munity. In Austin, the state capital, it is the capitol and its square that supersede the county courthouse in public prominence. Austin's urban landscape (Figure 88) presents a more complicated example, which is discussed below.

Data collected on county seats with codominant squares suggest a number of common features (Table 23). Unlike the predominant squares, this group is composed primarily of block patterns other than those of the Anglo-American tradition. This reflects the high percentage of plaza patterns (65 percent). There are fewer banks and retail uses and more high-rise buildings and office-only land use in the codominant group. The fact that high-rises are found at 53 percent of the codominant squares is a reflection of the high populations and high densities of those county seats. The state's three largest cities are counted in this category.

Codominant squares also accommodate more churches than the predominant group (35 percent compared to 29 percent), but less residen-

Table 23. Selected Features of Codominant Squares

SELECTED FEATURE	NUMBER	%*
Relationship of square to CBD		
Center of CBD (May be incomplete)	3 of 17	18.0
Adjacent to CBD	4 of 17	23.5
Removed from CBD (or no CBD)	10 of 17	59.0
Concentration of significant land use		
Enclosure by common-wall building	0 of 17	0.0
Near enclosure & free-standing building	11 of 17	65.0
Less enclosure & free-standing building	6 of 17	35.0
Population of the county seat		
100,000+	7 of 17	41.0
25,001 to 100,000	3 of 17	18.0
5,001 to 25,000	3 of 17	18.0
1,001 to 5,000	4 of 17	23.5
1,000 or less	0 of 17	0.0
Courthouse square tradition		
Traditional block patterns	5 of 17	29.5
Nontraditional block patterns	12 of 17	70.5
Urban morphology or block patterns		
Plazas and related patterns	11 of 17	65.0
All other block patterns	6 of 17	35.0
Structures on the square		
Courthouse only major structure	10 of 17	59.0
Additional building on square	7 of 17	41.0
Courthouse location at square		
Centered and /or set-back	8 of 17	47.0
Moderate set-back	4 of 17	23.5
Little or no set-back	5 of 17	29.5
Setting of courthouse square		
Parklike setting, lawn or trees	7 of 17	41.0
Modest parklike setting	7 of 17	41.0
Parking lots and street only	3 of 17	18.0
Monuments and memorials on the square		
Monuments/memorials	14 of 17	82.0
No major monuments/memorials	3 of 17	18.0

*Percentage of total surveyed.

tial use (35 percent compared to 45 percent). This is accounted for by the number of small towns in both groups. A more striking difference is the number of traditional enclosed squares in the predominant group (39 percent) compared to the codominant group, with no squares that fit that description. In towns that maintain much of their nineteenth-century fabric, the courthouse square remains the central focus. Where this pattern has been altered, the role of the square has changed too. Again, this may be related to differences in urban development. Yet codominant squares are found in both large and small towns, as supported by the fact that 41 percent of the county seats surveyed in this group exceed populations of 100,000 and 35 percent occur in towns numbering between 1,000 and 10,000 inhabitants.

All of the squares in the codominant group support some degree of additional governmental presence on the surrounding blocks. Again, this reflects, in part, the metropolitan nature of many of these county seats. With larger county populations and requirements for increased government services, several squares have witnessed a concentration of governmental agencies around the courthouse. This is a natural consequence of growth in the public sector and presents a special case of the courthouse square's centripetal influence on surrounding land use. By becoming a governmental center, some of these squares are able to retain or share many aspects of their role with other urban spaces.

Codominant squares generally favor parklike surroundings and setbacks for the courthouse, but exhibit features that occur less frequently among predominant squares. Almost 75 percent of the predominant squares include monuments, while 82 percent of the codominant squares include some type of monument, although the latter figure includes monuments on adjacent plazas as well. Together, these similarities and differences present a general view of the predominant square as the single focus for its community and the codominant square as one of multiple foci that accommodate many of the civic and social functions once reserved for the courthouse square alone.

Ten of the county seats in this group (59 percent) share their public role with a prominent city hall. Dallas and Houston are notable. Dallas' new municipal complex includes a dramatic city hall, designed by world-renowned architect I. M. Pei, convention center, library, reflecting pool, and public plaza. The courthouse and WPA-era Dealey Plaza have had to relinquish much of their former prestige and civic responsibility to the

Figure 89 Houston's city hall. As the role of city government and civic pride has increased, urban spaces such as these compete with the county courthouse and square, which often must share its public role.

city complex. Houston's city hall and reflecting pool (Figure 89) is also a WPA legacy. The civic presence of this space overshadows that of Houston's courthouse, which has become a county government center like that of Dallas.

Mid-size cities present a similar challenge to the courthouse square in Amarillo, Beaumont, San Angelo, and Waco. In all four the courthouses themselves are far more impressive than the city halls, but share their civic role with city hall, which typically assumes a greater responsibility for the public's well-being. In addition, many of the municipal complexes include a civic center and urban plaza that reinforce their ability to attract social activities once associated with the courthouse. Several courthouse precincts in the codominant category must divide their public "capital" with spaces that include a public park or plaza as well as other significant features in the urban landscape. Two of these, Austin and San Antonio, present exceptional circumstances. In both cases, multiple plazas provide opportunities for other public buildings.

Austin's courthouse square is overwhelmed by two urban landmarks—the state capitol and University of Texas tower. Oddly, there is little evidence of municipal government, in terms of the urban landscape, and Austin's courthouse complex (Figure 90) maintains a civic role by way of its siting on one of the city's original squares and association with other public buildings. San Antonio also shares a wealth of urban spaces and significant landmarks. The Main Plaza remains intact and affords the courthouse a major role alongside the historic but smaller cathedral. One block to the west, on the former Military Plaza, stands a stately city hall; but the greatest challenge to San Antonio's courthouse and Main Plaza is Alamo Plaza (Figure 91), which is larger and more often visited, especially by tourists.

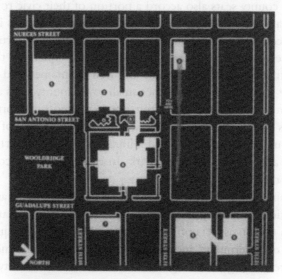

Figure 90 Plan of Travis County's courthouse complex and Wooldridge Park in Austin. This pattern is typical of many codominant squares that have become a center for county government.

Figure 91   Alamo Plaza in San Antonio. The Alamo's role in Texas history and myth has elevated the significance of this civic space in the minds of many Anglo-American visitors. The Main Plaza, cathedral, and county courthouse share a public role in an urban landscape rich in history and civic space.

Smaller county seats also accord a portion of their civic role to additional plazas. One of these, San Diego in Duval County, is interesting because it contains a Hispanic plaza surrounded by older structures, including the city hall and a separate courthouse square in the Anglo-American tradition. Each is parklike and well maintained and provides a dual legacy for the town. Two other small town county seats are worthy of comment. In Crosbyton the courthouse is sited on a corner diagonally across from a once open square, which is now the site of numerous historic structures, a museum, and a library. Anahuac's courthouse and square are also next to a historic park. In each case, the accompanying civic space rivals that of the courthouse.

Codominant courthouse squares represent something of an intermediary position between predominant squares and subordinate squares: they retain certain aspects of more traditional courthouse squares, such as the seat of government and use of symbolic features and monuments, but they are no longer the single civic focus in the community.

SUBORDINATE COURTHOUSE SQUARES:
INFLUENCE AND ROLE

The third category determined by field research is the subordinate courthouse square (Figure 84), which lacks the ability to focus the community's attention on the square. These spaces are peripheral to the life of the community—not necessarily in terms of location, but in terms of the role or function of the square within the context of its urban landscape, just as predominant squares were judged by their centripetal influence and not by their precise location in the city's grid. Centrality is also not simply a relationship to the CBD, but a reflection of numerous connections and affective ties to the community. These are reinforced by certain land uses, activities, and features associated with the square. Here, too, subordinate squares are lacking. Applying such measures, there are thirty county seats classified as subordinate squares (Table 24).

The features that characterize these squares are often in stark contrast to those of predominant squares. The most obvious difference is a limited association with the town's CBD. None of the subordinate squares anchor the central business district, and only one-fourth of them are adjacent. Twenty-two of the thirty (73 percent) county seats in this group are not associated with the CBD (Table 25), although in some smaller county seats there is little that might be defined as a CBD. Whatever the extent of development, the courthouse squares in these county seats are not an integral part of it.

Data collected on land use at subordinate squares indicate an association with fewer banks, more churches, and more vacant property. Residential land use also is typical of these courthouse squares. Again, this relationship depends on the extent of residential land use. Just as in the case of churches, the presence of a single residence near an otherwise established square does not necessarily diminish its traditional role as the central focus of the town. In some instances, these are historic homes of status; in other cases, their presence is a reflection of small-town land use. However, the high percentage (67 percent) of residences found around subordinate squares is very telling and accounts, in part, for the limited role of the courthouse square in the civic affairs of these towns.

The block patterns associated with most subordinate squares are Anglo-American prototypes. A majority (53 percent) of those surveyed rely on the Shelbyville pattern, although plaza patterns were found in 20

The Centripetal Role of the Courthouse Square

Table 24. Subordinate Courthouse Squares by Block Pattern

COUNTY SEAT / COUNTY

Shelbyvilles or Related Patterns: 16 of 30 (53.0%)

Bastrop*** / Bastrop	Mertzon*** / Irion
Belton* / Bell	Panhandle* / Carson
Corsicana* / Navarro	Port Lavaca* / Calhoun
Crystal City*** / Zavala	Rankin* / Upton
Cuero* / DeWitt	Rockport** / Aransas
Giddings* / Lee	Seymour* / Baylor
Kerrville*** / Kerr	Sinton* / San Patricio
Laredo*** / Webb	Stratford*** / Sherman

Plazas or Related Patterns: 6 of 30 (20.0%)

Boerne*** / Kendall	Fort Stockton*** / Pecos
Corpus Christi*** / Nueces	Hondo*** / Medina
Fort Davis* / Jeff Davis	Pearsall*** / Frio

Railroad-Influenced Patterns: 3 of 30 (10.0%)

Bryan* / Brazos	Kountze* / Hardin
Channing*** / Hartley	

Harrisonburgs or Related Patterns: 2 of 30 (7.0%)

Big Lake*** / Reagan
Hempstead*** / Waller

Lancasters or Related Patterns: 1 of 30 (3.0%)

Jourdanton* / Atascosa

Half-Block or Related Patterns: 1 of 30 (3.0%)

Nacogdoches* / Nacogdoches

Irregular-Block or Related Patterns: 1 of 30 (3.0%)

Guthrie*** / King

---

*Incomplete or inconsistent development around the square.
**Additional buildings on the courthouse square.
***Both incomplete development and additional buildings.

percent of the county seats. This indicates that block pattern alone is no guarantee of a central role for the courthouse square. Subordinate squares also have the lowest incidence of courthouses that are centered or set back (40 percent) and the highest rate of those with little or no

Table 25. Selected Features of Subordinate Squares

SELECTED FEATURE	NUMBER	%*
Relationship of square to CBD		
Center of CBD (May be incomplete)	0 of 30	0.0
Adjacent to CBD	8 of 30	27.0
Removed from CBD (or no CBD)	22 of 30	73.0
Concentration of significant land use		
Enclosure by common-wall building	0 of 30	0.0
Near enclosure & free-standing building	4 of 30	13.0
Less enclosure & free-standing building	26 of 30	87.0
Population of the county seat		
100,000+	3 of 30	10.0
25,001 to 100,000	1 of 30	3.0
5,001 to 25,000	10 of 30	33.0
1,001 to 5,000	13 of 30	44.0
1,000 or less	3 of 30	10.0
Courthouse square tradition		
Traditional block patterns	19 of 30	63.0
Nontraditional block patterns	11 of 30	37.0
Urban morphology or block patterns		
Shelbyvilles and related patterns	16 of 30	53.0
Plazas and related patterns	6 of 30	20.0
All other block patterns	8 of 30	27.0
Structures on the square		
Courthouse only major structure	14 of 30	47.0
Additional building on square	16 of 30	53.0
Courthouse location at square		
Centered and/or set-back	12 of 30	40.0
Modest set-back	8 of 30	27.0
Little or no set-back	10 of 30	33.0
Setting of courthouse square		
Parklike setting, lawn or trees	5 of 30	17.0
Modest parklike setting	11 of 30	37.0
Parking lots and street only	14 of 30	47.0
Monuments and memorials on the square		
Monuments/memorials	18 of 30	60.0
No major monuments/memorials	12 of 30	40.0

*Percentage of total surveyed.

set-back (33 percent). More indicative of a divergence from the usual patterns is lack of parklike settings. Subordinate squares exhibit such parklike settings in only 16 percent of the sites surveyed, and almost half (47 percent) were surrounded by parking lots, which often reduce a square's civic presence.

Related to this problem is the fact that twenty-six of the thirty squares in this group (87 percent) are not fully enclosed. This also reflects a limited association with the CBD and the fact that more than half (54 percent) of the subordinate squares surveyed occur in towns with populations below 5,000. Many of these small towns lack complete development around the square. This may reflect either a declining square or one that never matured. Land-use data further suggest that vacancy or lack of development is typical of subordinate squares. Indeed, if the centripetal role of the square is defined in part by its ability to attract significant land uses, vacant property (included in 43 percent of the subordinate squares) should be a clear indicator of the square's failure in this respect.

Figure 92 Courthouse square in Mertzon in Irion County. This vacant hilltop setting commands the landscape, but is removed from and peripheral to community life. The neighboring county seat, Rankin in Upton County, is similar.

Another problem with subordinate squares is accommodation of monuments or memorials. Compared to predominant squares, the squares in this group are much less likely to provide space for symbolic structures. Thus, the lack of monuments, parklike settings, and prominent locations for the courthouses contributes to a reduced civic role. This is not to suggest that all the courthouse squares in this group play no role at all. Rather, their function and social meaning in their communities are hampered and more limited. This is quite evident in towns like Mertzon (Figure 92) and Rankin in far west Texas, where the courthouse is situated on a lone hilltop, while most of the town's activities take place along the highway below.

Other squares in this group appear to be experiencing renewed interest on the part of their communities. Historic buildings are being restored on the squares in Bastrop and Giddings, and this may lead to renewal of the presence of the courthouse in the lives of these communities. A few county seats in this group maintain tidy squares with solitary, impressive courthouses, such as those at Corsicana, Cuero, Fort Davis, and Sinton. Yet their communities' attentions are focused elsewhere.

Future prospects for the civic role and centripetal influence of courthouse squares are uncertain at best if many of the trends suggested by the subordinate squares become the rule. However, the fact that only 30 of the 139 county seats surveyed were classified in this category is a positive indication that a greater urban presence for the courthouse square is preferred.

OBSERVATIONS ON THE COURTHOUSE SQUARE'S CENTRIPETAL ROLE

This comparison of the varied roles of predominant, codominant, and subordinate squares sheds light on the nature and the means of the courthouse square's centripetal influence on the community. This study also provides a means of assessing which squares perform certain functions and what morphological features support such roles. In addition, this comparative approach makes clearer the linkages between urban form and social meaning. Comparing the relative frequency of certain land uses and building types reveals much about the function and social meaning of the square.

Further comparisons between these categories also suggest which features may be diagnostic or at least characteristic of squares exhibiting a central role. There may be a tendency to dismiss such correlations as circular, but two factors argue for the usefulness of such indicators. One is that associations with specific building types, land uses, and locations reveal a great deal about the square's social and symbolic significance in the community. The second factor is that the data collected here indicate clear relationships between certain land uses and a square's civic role. Careful examination of these data supports a number of limited generalizations about the centripetal influence of the courthouse square.

First, many predominant courthouse squares were fully developed and completely enclosed by storefronts by the end of the nineteenth century. This suggests that towns that matured and stabilized during a time when squares were the central focus of social, economic, and political life were the most likely to maintain their roles—that is, if they did not continue to grow beyond all expectations and exceed the limits of the square. This is exactly what happened in metropolitan county seats, which are characterized by codominant or subordinate squares. No predominant squares are found in surveyed cities with populations over 100,000.

Comparing 1990 population figures of surveyed county seats (Table 26) reveals a number of trends. Predominant squares are less frequent (50 percent or less) in cities with 50,000 or more inhabitants. In surveyed county seats with populations between 50,000 and 1,000, predominant squares are found about 70 percent to 75 percent of the time. In towns below 1,000 persons, the courthouse square dominates in 78 percent to 87 percent of the cases. County seats with less than 100 persons were not surveyed. These data support two generalizations. First, in large metropolitan areas the courthouse square no longer dominates the urban landscape. Second, there is a remarkable consistency in the courthouse square's central role in county seats with populations between 50,000 and 5,000. This is less so in towns below 1,000 persons, where a fully developed square is less likely.

Most county seats planned in the nineteenth century called for traditional Anglo-American central courthouse squares, but not all were fully realized. In some cases, the squares never matured or declined quickly. In several instances, there were few or no public spaces to assume the function of the square. In other situations, the squares were revived, but

Table 26. Comparison of Population with Square's Centripetal Role

POPULATION	TOTAL NUMBER OF COUNTY SEATS	ROLE OF SQUARE	NUMBER	%*
100,000+	14 (10 surveyed)	Predominant	0 of 10	00.0
		Codominant	7 of 10	70.0
		Subordinate	3 of 10	30.0
50,000+	10 (4 surveyed)	Predominant	2 of 4	50.0
		Codominant	2 of 4	50.0
		Subordinate	0 of 4	00.0
25,000+	10 (8 surveyed)	Predominant	6 of 8	75.0
		Codominant	1 of 8	12.5
		Subordinate	1 of 8	12.5
10,000+	44 (18 surveyed)	Predominant	13 of 18	72.0
		Codominant	1 of 18	06.0
		Subordinate	4 of 18	22.0
5,000+	42 (27 surveyed)	Predominant	19 of 27	70.0
		Codominant	2 of 27	08.0
		Subordinate	6 of 27	22.0
2,500+	59 (32 surveyed)	Predominant	22 of 32	69.0
		Codominant	2 of 32	06.0
		Subordinate	8 of 32	25.0
1000+	46 (23 surveyed)	Predominant	16 of 23	69.0
		Codominant	2 of 23	09.0
		Subordinate	5 of 23	22.0
500+	14 (8 surveyed)	Predominant	7 of 8	87.5
		Codominant	0 of 8	00.0
		Subordinate	1 of 8	12.5
100+	13 (9 surveyed)	Predominate	7 of 9	78.0
		Codominant	0 of 9	00.0
		Subordinate	2 of 9	22.0
Below 100	2 (none surveyed)			

*Percentage of total surveyed.

The Centripetal Role of the Courthouse Square

173

their roles and associations were limited or shared with other significant urban spaces. Unlike these codominant squares, which retained certain aspects of their traditional role, the subordinate squares did not compete well with other features in the townscape. Such towns may have missed a critical phase of development at a time when the square might have become the center of the community. When the community prospered or resumed growth, the square was no longer an integral or viable space.

Fieldwork also revealed that a church or residence near the square did not preclude a central role, but did suggest a negative correlation between churches and the square's predominant role. Churches were counted in 29 percent of the predominant squares and 35 percent of the codominant squares. This ratio increased to 57 percent in the subordinate squares. This is contrary to most definitions of central courthouse squares and corrects previous assertions that churches are excluded from courthouse squares. Less surprisingly, field study found churches opposite the courthouse in thirteen of twenty-three (56 percent) county seats surveyed in the Spanish-Mexican culture area and in nine of nineteen (47 percent) surveyed sites in the Mixed culture area.

These observations suggest a number of interesting issues for future research. However, what is of immediate concern here is the relationship between the courthouse square and its community, particularly the square's centripetal influence. Today planners and inhabitants alike are attempting to restore a "sense of center" to their communities. Some reasons for this are pragmatic. Others are more psychological. Both reflect recognition of the value of social activities and symbols once attached to civic spaces such as the courthouse square and represented in the land use surrounding the square.

The question of which group of courthouse squares discussed above represents a direction for the future is uncertain. Centrifugal influences such as decentralization, suburbanization, commercial strip centers, and others place the role of the courthouse at risk. The loss of civic spaces capable of focusing and holding a community's identity is a complex issue. Part of the answer lies in a comparison of the architectural and symbolic features of the squares as well as their role in public ceremonies and events.

Chapter Eight

Symbolism and Social Activity
at the Courthouse Square

Beyond its role in shaping land use and the economic life of a community, the courthouse square also serves as a focus for symbols and rituals expressing shared values. These symbolic displays and events are typically expressed in parades, ceremonies, courthouse architecture, and monuments that commemorate persons or events important to the founding or well-being of the community. This analysis of the square's form and its role in the community relies on perceptions of courthouse architecture, types of monuments, and activities focusing on Texas squares. Previous studies of this nature have illuminated the connections between symbols and social meaning (Warner 1959; Rowntree and Conkey 1980; Goodsell 1988).

Interpretation of architectural and symbolic features involved data collected from field surveys on the monuments and architecture of the courthouse square. Information on social and ceremonial activities at the square was limited to sources on local history and did not include a systematic survey, as was the case with previous data. However, the results were equally revealing. All of the information collected on symbolic features and social activities is discussed in terms of a square's role in its townscape as predominant, codominant, or subordinate (Tables 27 and 28).

Symbolism and community can have many definitions and mean different things to different people. In this study there has been no attempt to address individual perceptions of the square except to recognize that, at times, events at the square represented contesting viewpoints on the definition of society. In the past the courthouse square could be the site

Table 27. Comparison of Courthouse Architecture at the Squares

ROLE OF SQUARE	ERA OF COURTHOUSE (Percentage of Sites Surveyed)			
	19th C.[a]	20th C.[b]	WPA Era[c]	Modern Era[d]
Predominant: (92)	55 (60.0%)	9 (10.0%)	9 (10.0%)	19 (20.0%)
Codominant: (17)	7 (41.0%)	1 (6.0%)	6 (35.0%)	3 (18.0%)
Subordinate: (30)	13 (43.0%)	4 (13.0%)	1 (3.0%)	12 (40.0%)

[a] Includes a range of styles built from 1860 to 1909, such as antebellum designs, Italianate forms, and neoclassical styles. These include asymmetrical and ornate elements as well as simpler symmetrical designs.

[b] Includes a range of styles built from 1910 TO 1933, with design elements of previous styles along with more symmetrical forms typical of neoclassical design.

[c] Depression-era deco styles built from 1933 TO 1941. Many of these designs employ symmetry and overt symbolism, but in a streamlined modern idiom.

[d] Includes a variety of contemporary styles built since 1945. These designs are simpler and more functional, with less use of detail and overt symbols. Some are indistinguishable from generic office buildings, including some high-rise designs.

Table 28. Comparison of Monuments, Markers, and Memorials

	ROLE OF SQUARE		
	Predominant (92)	Codominant (17)	Subordinate (30)
No. of Significant Monuments			
None/few	25 (27.0%)	2 (12.0%)	13 (43.0%)
Two or more	67 (73.0%)	15 (88.0%)	17 (57.0%)
Types of Monuments			
Founder	14 (15.0%)	8 (47.0%)	6 (20.0%)
Marker	27 (29.0%)	6 (35.0%)	3 (10.0%)
Veterans	36 (40.0%)	7 (41.0%)	11 (37.0%)
Other/local	44 (48.0%)	8 (47.0%)	11 (37.0%)

Note: Founders' monuments include local heroes or famous persons. Markers include local, county, or state events. Other/local includes miscellaneous local events, persons, or things.

for holiday celebrations or capital punishment. The days of public executions on the square are gone, but much of its symbolic role remains. One major aspect of the square's symbolism is expressed in courthouse architecture.

There were several major eras of courthouse building (Table 29). The first occurred during the 1880s and 1890s, when sixty-two of the current court buildings were completed; the second in the 1910s and 1920s, when forty-six and thirty-seven courthouses, respectively, were built. Another period of significant construction occurred as the result of the WPA. The last decade of substantial building activity came in the fifties, when twenty-two counties built new courthouses to replace older structures. Only one new building was constructed in the eighties. As testament to the enduring and generally conservative nature of the courthouse square, sixty-five current Texas courthouses (25 percent) were built before 1900. This figure refers only to those courthouses still in use in 1984 as photographed by J. L. Nance and those based on available sources (Welch and Nance 1971; Welch 1984) and site visits in 1991 and 1992.

Table 29. Dates of Construction of Current Courthouses by Decade

DECADE	CURRENT COURTHOUSES IN USE	% OF TOTAL
1860s	1	0.0
1870s	2	0.0
1880s	23	9.0
1890s	39	15.0
1900s	20	8.0
1910s	46	18.0
1920s	37	15.0
1930s	36	15.0
1940s	10	4.0
1950s	22	9.0
1960s	8	4.0
1970s	8	4.0
1980s	1	0.0
1990s*	1 (another under construction)	0.0
	254	(97.0)**

Note: Based on courthouses extant in 1984. Compiled by author from Welch 1984.
　　*Based on site visit.
　　**Percentages reflect figures rounded to whole numbers.

Additional aspects of the links between built form, symbolism, and the centripetal role of the courthouse square are represented in various monuments and memorials. These decidedly symbolic features commemorate elements of the community's past and consecrate the spaces they occupy. In most cases, such spaces are thought to be held in common for perpetuity and in this sense express the community's hope for the future.

Examining placement and types of monuments and memorials associated with the square also provides insight on the connections between the square's role and its social meaning. Field surveys noted major monuments found on or near the square (Table 28). The types of monuments recorded include stone or bronze forms to commemorate founders or other noteworthy persons, past events, or historical sites as well as memorials to veterans. In addition, objects of special affection or significance are placed on the square, such as local mascots or other memorabilia.

In broad terms, the predominant and codominant squares exhibit monuments more often than subordinate squares do. Specifically, the predominant and codominant squares contain a greater percentage (48 percent and 47 percent) of monuments specific to the community or county than those in the subordinate group (37 percent). The codominant squares are the most consistent in use of monuments, indicating that such symbolic displays remain a valuable function of this group.

Social activities and ceremonies are also crucial to the square's continued viability as the town's central focus. Like monuments, these events renew common beliefs and values. Such activities are, perhaps, a more ephemeral aspect of the square's centripetal influence, but they provide a living demonstration of the square's significance. Ceremonies and public events that are reenacted at the square attempt to maintain connections to past traditions and to reify the symbols associated with those traditions. In this way social meaning is transferred from generation to generation and reaffirmed among members of the community.

Information collected on social activities and public events is limited, but reflective of many events that take place at squares around the state, including celebrations of state independence, local events, or visits by notable persons. In many cases, the locations of fairs or routes of parades include the courthouse square, which in many ways functions as the community's "front yard."

Social gatherings, church meetings, and dances that once commonly took place on the square are not detailed, except to mention that they were a regular part of the life of the community in the nineteenth and early twentieth centuries. Equally significant, but not discussed, are activities associated with everyday commerce around the square, which were analyzed in terms of land use in the previous chapter. The focus here is on those events and symbols with the highest profile in terms of community involvement and their relationship to the square's role.

SYMBOLIC FEATURES AND SOCIAL ACTIVITIES OF PREDOMINANT SQUARES

In keeping with the centripetal role of predominant courthouse squares, most of the county seats in this group employ traditionally styled courthouses, offer a setting for significant monuments, and provide a place for public celebrations. In terms of architecture, 60 percent of the squares classified as predominant exhibit nineteenth-century edifices, and only 20 percent are postwar-era courthouses. Monuments are found in 74 percent of the squares in this group, and many are the scene for major public events.

Courthouse architecture plays an important part on most predominant squares, but that alone does not assure the square a central focus. The fact that fifty-five of ninety-two of these squares retain nineteenth-century courthouses reflects well on their contribution to the community and their enduring place in the townscape. Only nineteen of ninety-two predominant squares have courthouses built after 1945; thus, 80 percent exhibit courthouses that employ traditional styles and symbols. This indicates the relationship between symbolic features and predominant squares. Numerous examples of highly styled and symbolic structures on these courthouse squares can be found. James Riely Gordon's exuberant courthouses in Denton, Gonzales (Figure 93), La Grange, Stephenville, and Waxahachie all illustrate the point.

Also typical of predominant courthouse squares are founders' and veterans' monuments, which often follow certain conventions for their respective eras. Many markers rely on realistic likenesses, such as that for the founder of Fredericksburg, J. O. Meusebach (Figure 94). Veterans' memorials are likely to observe styles consistent with their time of dedication. Many memorials to the Confederacy take the form of upright stone obelisks on the square, while those dedicated to the memory of veterans of World War I often use vintage cannon or bronze statues. Memorials for World War II typically resemble cemetery headstones with the names of the fallen. More recent memorials, including those for

Figure 93 Gonzales County Courthouse designed by James Riely Gordon, one of Texas' foremost courthouse architects. This example typifies many of the features of his exuberant Romanesque style, such as round arches, turrets, and towers. Courthouses such as these became the focal point of many predominant squares.

Figure 94 Fredericksburg's monument to John O. Meusebach, the town's founder. This recent but traditionally styled memorial is placed in a central location, opposite the former courthouse, on what remains of the original plaza.

Vietnam veterans, adopt more abstract forms, such as Wharton County's memorial on the square (Figure 95). A few far-sighted designers of recent memorials provide space in their schemes for future veterans. This can be seen in Hillsboro, where a row of memorial benches, including one for Vietnam veterans, includes a conspicuous opening for two additional benches to commemorate future sacrifices.

Installation of these recent memorials on predominant squares reflects two related processes: belated recognition and reconciliation of the Vietnam experience and the renewal of a symbolic role for the courthouse square. For many county seats these are the first significant monuments erected on their squares in a generation. This renewal of ties to a common history and place is fundamental to the social meaning of the courthouse square as the center of the community.

Symbolism and Social Activity at the Courthouse Square

Figure 95 Veterans' Memorial in Wharton County. The dark, enigmatic form of this memorial is in stark contrast to the traditional symbolism employed by earlier monuments.

Other monuments found on the square recall a town's identity or claims to fame, such as Brady's boast to be the geographic center and the "Heart of Texas" (Figure 96). Some are attempts at civic booster-ism, such as the pump-jack touting the "billionth barrel" of oil pumped in Andrews County (Figure 97) or a bronze sculpture celebrating the "Cowboy Champions" of Bandera County. Other fanciful features recorded were a giant "goober" or peanut on Seguin's square, "Moola" the milk cow next to Stephenville's courthouse, and a stuffed longhorn steer in its own mausoleum in George West. More serious items seen on the squares were a navy jet in Beeville, a reduced replica of the Statue of Liberty in Midland, and a memorial kiosk in Kingsville. Although many of these objects represent a stereotypic or mythic view of the past, their presence on the square reflects a belief that it is the appropriate place for symbols that speak for the community at large.

Another related function for the courthouse square is to serve as the town "bulletin board." These efforts can be as simple as a hand-painted banner draped across the lawn of the square announcing a high-school football game or a portable signboard stationed at the square. Llano has

Figure 96 "Heart of Texas" marker
in Brady in McCulloch County.
Reminders like these at the square serve
to reinforce community identity.

Figure 97 Pump-jack on the Andrews County Courthouse square. Although the
juxtaposition of this object and the courthouse is atypical, such examples of civic
boosterism are not. This "monument" to the town's major industry proclaims the
county's "billionth barrel" of oil.

a permanent marquee at the front of the courthouse to announce local
events. In recalling past events, several east Texas squares erected ce-
ramic tile murals emblazoned with photographic images recounting
local histories. What these "signs" share is recognition of the square's
central location and the fact that most townspeople pass by in the regular course of events.

Symbolism and Social Activity at the Courthouse Square

Figure 98 Christmas fair in Fredericksburg. This photo showing the replica of the octagonal meeting house and fairgrounds was taken from the balcony of the second courthouse and present history museum. Scenes such as these are typical of predominant courthouse squares, in this case associated with a public plaza.

Major public events that take place on predominant squares typically involve parades or fairs. These often mark significant dates such as those associated with the town's founding or an Independence Day celebration. One of the earliest celebrations of this type occurred in Fredericksburg to mark the town's fiftieth anniversary in 1896. The central focus of that event was the main plaza and old octagonal meeting hall. Other events, such as a recent Christmas fair (Figure 98), still take place on Fredericksburg's plaza opposite the courthouse and next to a replica of the old meeting house.

To mark the Texas Centennial in 1936, numerous county seats staged parades at their squares. Gonzales, site of an early skirmish that initiated the struggle for Texas independence, witnessed a crowd of 25,000 and a parade of state dignitaries and locals (Figure 99) on the 100th anniversary of its famous battle in 1835.

Predominant courthouse squares in smaller cities and towns are the setting for less formal public gatherings. Recent field excursions hap-

SOURCE: SAN ANTONIO EXPRESS-NEWS, NOVEMBER 6, 1935.

Figure 99 Centennial parade in Gonzales. Gonzales staged two events to celebrate the 100th anniversary of Texas Independence. The first was the largest and attracted 25,000 spectators. That event marked the date of Gonzales' first battle in November 1835.

pened upon two open-air markets on courthouse plazas in Uvalde (Figure 100) and New Braunfels. Predominant plazas like these attract frequent activities for obvious reasons, in addition to offering open space. The central location and parklike atmosphere are conducive to such public activities. These are attributes of the compact, pedestrian city, which many predominant squares still offer. These uses are also a function of preservation of nineteenth-century townscapes that are associated with many predominant squares.

A related activity that takes place on many courthouse squares is display of Christmas decorations. This is not a trivial observation, and it reinforces the role of the square as the community "front yard." This symbolic use of the square was noted by coincidence, since many site visits took place between Thanksgiving and Christmas. Several of these local efforts are quite elaborate, such as decorations for courthouses in Marshall and Johnson City (Figure 101). Most holiday adornments are more modest, but few predominant squares are without these seasonal decora-

Symbolism and Social Activity at the Courthouse Square

Figure 100 Weekend market fair opposite the courthouse in Uvalde. The open plaza in the center of town is still used for both informal and formal public events. Such uses are typical of predominant squares.

Figure 101 Christmas decorations on the Blanco County Courthouse in Johnson City. This spectacular display of lights demonstrates the community's pride in the courthouse and the symbolic role of the square as a communal "front yard." An older similar display takes place in Marshall. More modest efforts are common in many Texas towns.

tions. One indicator of the community's perceived center is the location of the community Christmas tree or the setting for the town's most elaborate decorations.

Casual observation suggests that a correlation does exist between predominant squares and these displays. Many observers accept them as seasonal and not religious objects. Others challenge the placement of such iconography, citing the doctrine of separation of church and state. Yet the presence of these decorations on the square and the dialogue on its proper role are indicative of the square's importance.

The use of traditional courthouse architecture, the placement of major monuments, and the scheduling of formal and informal public activities characterize predominant squares. These features in combination reinforce the centripetal influence of the courthouse squares and set them apart from squares that are less consistent in the use of such symbolism.

SYMBOLIC FEATURES AND SOCIAL ACTIVITIES OF CODOMINANT SQUARES

In terms of symbolic features and social activities, codominant squares share many of the relationships associated with predominant squares. This is to be expected, since codominant spaces maintain similar elements, such as expressive architecture and significant monuments. Many codominant squares are found in larger cities, where there are more civic spaces, particularly city halls, to compete with the courthouse square. Another trend shared by many codominant squares is the clustering of public buildings and agencies at the courthouse, which is a natural nucleus for such structures. This is indicative of a trend to "zone" land use and presents an interesting irony, as building types tend to become indistinguishable and land use more distinctive.

The data on architecture (Table 27) indicate that codominant squares are similar to predominant squares, with only 18 percent post-1945 buildings. Interestingly, codominant squares have the highest ratio (35 percent) of WPA-era courthouses of the three groups. This is probably the result of the association of WPA courthouses with plazas, which are well represented in this group. These courthouses make use of symbolism and symmetry typically associated with public buildings, such as Austin's courthouse (Figure 102). Together these data indicate that

Symbolism and Social Activity at the Courthouse Square

Figure 102 Drawing of the "new" Travis County Courthouse in Austin. This postcard image from the thirties illustrates many of the features associated with WPA-era architecture. The caption on the card reads: "Travis County Court House one of the most complete structures of its kind in the country. Cost $1,000,000. Built of beautiful Travertine stone from Travis and adjoining counties. Houses all county government offices, with jail on top. Seven stories."

many codominant squares retain traditional elements and occupy an intermediate position with respect to the square's role.

Codominant squares favor monuments dedicated to founders. These types of markers occur in 47 percent of these squares, compared to 15 percent and 20 percent in predominant and subordinate squares, respectively (Table 28). This fact may reflect an early focus on the courthouse square in these county seats; this role was reduced over time as other civic spaces became sites for monuments. It also indicates a special role for codominant squares as a place for monuments: 82 percent of these spaces are associated with markers or memorials. This exceeds the ratio for both predominant and subordinate squares (74 percent and 60 percent, respectively).

The shared civic role characteristic of codominant squares is especially apparent in the social activities that occur at the square. Many of these events formerly focused exclusively on the courthouse. Today additional civic spaces witness such public events. In Dallas, for example, the courthouse square and Dealey Plaza were the scene of a Texas Centennial parade highlighted by a visit from President Franklin D. Roosevelt. That parade (Figure 103), like many in Dallas, included the main business street and courthouse. A similar route was followed by President John F. Kennedy's fateful motorcade in Dallas. Today a new city hall and civic center are the main staging areas for public celebrations, which may also pass by the courthouse. Dallas' Fair Park also has its share of major public events.

In Austin the capitol grounds (Figure 104) and Congress Avenue preempt the civic role of the courthouse square and Wooldridge Park, which is the site of smaller affairs. Austin's rich endowment of public spaces serves to diminish the courthouse square's role, but Wooldridge Park, located next to the courthouse, provides an intimate scene for outdoor gatherings and occasional weddings. The natural bowl-like form of the park and its central gazebo create an amphitheater effect that attracts

SOURCE: DALLAS PUBLIC LIBRARY HISTORIC PHOTOGRAPHIC COLLECTION, HAYES COLLECTION, NEG. #76-1/14028.9 DATED 6-12-36.

Figure 103 Crowd awaiting the arrival of FDR in Dallas. This was one of many parade routes that passed by the courthouse, which is silhouetted in the background.

Symbolism and Social Activity at the Courthouse Square

Figure 104 Celebrants on the capitol grounds in Austin. The state's capital city is well endowed with public spaces for major civic events. The courthouse square is one of four original satellite squares, which share their civic role with the larger, more central Capitol Square. Most parades take place on Congress Avenue and terminate at the capitol, such as this inaugural celebration for Governor Ann Richards in 1990.

small entertainment events as well. These affairs contrast markedly with more formal celebrations that take place at the capitol, although both can become the scene of demonstrations challenging public policies.

While the codominant squares maintain many of the traditional trappings associated with predominant squares, the former must share their civic role and symbolic functions with other urban spaces. One aspect of the codominant square that is not eclipsed is its use as the setting for major monuments and memorials. This fact along with the concentration of government services at many codominant squares argues for a specialized role for the squares in this group. This is consistent with larger county seats that witness increased land development and multiple foci for specific land uses. In many ways, then, the codominant squares perform some of the same functions as predominant spaces, but present a more limited and particularized version of a square's centripetal influence—in this case on public institutions and symbols.

SYMBOLIC FEATURES AND SOCIAL
ACTIVITIES OF SUBORDINATE SQUARES

Unlike the predominant or codominant squares, county seats with subordinate courthouse squares do not serve as foci of their communities and play a peripheral role in terms of symbolic features and social activities. In comparison with other groups, the subordinate squares have fewer traditional courthouses and monuments.

As a group, the subordinate squares exhibit the highest ratio (40 percent) of contemporary courthouse styles, which are not as supportive of a strong civic role as more traditional styles. Courthouses of this type are found in Bryan (Figure 105), Corpus Christi, Crystal City, Guthrie, Kerrville, Laredo, Nacogdoches, Port Lavaca, Rockport, and Seymour. The shortcomings of these structures are more symptomatic than causal—that is, the loss of civic importance at some squares predates construction of modern courthouses.

Figure 105   Contemporary courthouse in Bryan in Brazos County. Like many recent designs, this courthouse presents a functional facade that is largely indistinct from contemporary office buildings. Not pictured in this photo, an entry courtyard makes a gesture to past courthouses with a modest patch of lawn and walks with benches. Unfortunately, the other three sides are blank and make little connection to the community. Contemporary structures such as these are frequently found on subordinate squares.

Symbolism and Social Activity at the Courthouse Square

In addition, many other squares in this group are the sites for modern annexes that typically offer less by way of presence and connection to the community. While it is unfair simply to blame the square's lack of focus on the courthouse architect, this is an issue that points to the general dilution of a square's role. Not all such designs are associated with subordinate squares. In some cases, construction of modern courthouses represents a revival of civic pride or the practical need for better accommodations.

Perhaps one attempt to reconcile the pragmatic needs of the courthouse and its public presence in a modern city is Corpus Christi's courthouse complex, which adopts the form of a skyscraper. However, for all its bravado, the structure is marooned in a sea of parking lots and disconnected from the community by siting it well away from the city's waterfront and downtown. A modest urban plaza is the only pedestrian link from the street to the courthouse. Despite its high-rise profile and proximity to a new city hall, the courthouse remains peripheral to the community and subordinate to other civic spaces, particularly those along the waterfront that offer the most public amenities.

Figure 106 Foreclosure sale on the courthouse steps in Austin. Events such as this reflect a more mundane role for the square that is typical of subordinate squares.

In terms of monuments and memorials, subordinate squares were without significant markers in 40 percent of the squares surveyed. This is the highest ratio recorded. This group also has the smallest percentage (60 percent) of squares with significant markers. Only 23 percent have two or more major monuments. The types of monuments located on subordinate squares parallel those of the other two categories, but with lower percentages. The one exception is the type of monuments dedicated to local founders, which were noted in fewer predominant squares.

Assessment of social activities at subordinate squares presents something of a dilemma. Some of these squares may be the setting for public events, but their peripheral nature and lack of connection to a CBD or other features in the townscape argue for a diminished role.

One type of gathering at courthouse squares, which is common to all counties, is the legal ritual of public sales of foreclosed property. As stipulated by custom, these sales must take place once a month on the courthouse steps, which are considered to be the most public spaces. During the economic bust of the late eighties in Texas, foreclosure sales attracted record numbers, such as those in Austin in 1987 (Figure 106). Routine scenes like these may be more typical of subordinate squares, which probably witness more mundane governmental functions compared to community-wide celebrations found at more active squares.

Several of the problems associated with subordinate squares, in terms of their diminished centripetal role, may be related to the fact that many of the squares are in small towns with little development. This lack of connection to daily commerce and the life of the community is characteristic of subordinate squares, which is reflected in the absence of symbolic features compared to either predominant or codominant squares.

OBSERVATIONS ON THE SYMBOLIC ROLE
AND ARCHITECTURE OF
THE COURTHOUSE SQUARE

Analysis of the information above suggests certain relationships between the square's form and centripetal role in terms of symbolic features such as courthouse architecture, types of monuments, and social activities. While the data indicate an association between such symbolic features and the role of the square, they do not indicate cause and effect. The fact that a relationship between symbols and social values exists is rarely questioned, but the extent and impact of this relationship are often a matter of debate.

In another study of civic space that is relevant to this analysis, C. T. Goodsell surveyed municipal council chambers and noted three periods of architectural settings that reflected changing attitudes to the role of government. A "traditional" model that held sway from 1865 to 1920 was characterized by "formal" and "ceremonial" settings. A "mid-century" pattern was preferred from 1920 to 1960, but was more "pedestrian" and "utilitarian" in nature. A final category was a "contemporary" form that occurred after 1960. It was similar to the mid-century type in the utilitarian sense, but placed more emphasis on egalitarian arrangements (Goodsell 1988, 193–196). Goodsell focused on interior civic spaces, but his broad categories are loosely analogous to courthouse styles as well and reinforce the notion of linkages between architecture and social meaning.

The architectural historian P. K. Goeldner reflected on a number of issues specific to courthouse architecture, such as the significance of the courthouse as a building type in its own right and its revered location and role in the community. He also made more subtle reference to the public's perception of the building. Speaking specifically of the importance of nineteenth-century courthouses to their communities, as well as their architects, Goeldner remarked:

> To a high degree the nineteenth century courthouses of the Midwest and Texas represent the architectural aspirations of their builders, insofar as those aspirations were attainable. Because they belonged to the public it was hoped that they would please every citizen. If permanence of construction, generous expenditure and preferential siting are valid criteria, courthouses are the buildings by which the nineteenth century wished to be judged. (Goeldner 1970, 10)

It may be reasonable today to question such architectural expressions as elitist or exclusionary, but more relevant here is the fact that the courthouse and its square were often the focal point of the community in social, economic, and political terms. As such these civic spaces were also the scene of struggle for redefinition of society and the place of redress for inequalities. Depending on time and circumstance, the courthouse could represent either self-interest or the best ideals of self-government. It was usually the latter notion that inspired architects and builders, despite occasional attempts to flatter themselves or officials with opulent structures.

A common intent of much nineteenth- and early-twentieth-century architecture was to express in explicit fashion the civic role of the courthouse and to a lesser extent its mundane function as a hall of records. The first task was accomplished through architectural stature and symbolism; the second, through fireproof construction. Arson was an all too common way for scoundrels to escape pending prosecution as incriminating evidence was targeted for destruction. Many squares witnessed a series of succeeding courthouses as age, fire, and the desire for prestige led to the building of newer, safer, and grander structures.

For much of its history the courthouse was the dominant feature in the urban landscape as depicted in a number of architectural styles and periods. James Riely Gordon earned a national reputation for his eclectic use of the Romanesque, first popularized by H. H. Richardson. The Romanesque courthouse (Figure 93) and its variations were the most popular nineteenth-century styles in Texas (Goeldner 1971, 110). These buildings are identified by arches, towers, and turrets, polychromatic themes, and rusticated masonry. Another familiar and highly symbolic style is that of the "county capitol," which is characterized by templelike facades and a prominent dome patterned after the national capitol and later statehouses. Goeldner determined that this style was second only to the Romanesque, but of "little influence" outside of Texas and the Midwest (Goeldner 1971, 110).

During the early twentieth century, courthouse architecture was typified by the symmetry and composure of "Beaux-Arts classicism," which employed many of the same features as the county capitol, but with more Renaissance elements (Figure 107). This style came into national favor after the Columbian Exposition in Chicago in 1893 and later made its way to Texas (Goeldner 1971, 110).

There are other early courthouse styles recognized by architectural historians, but what is significant is their common intent to provide a focus for the urban landscape in keeping with the prevalent role for public buildings. These edifices remained unchallenged and in many cases are still the tallest structure in the county seat, if not the county. Courthouse rivalries for height and opulence came to an end during the Great

Figure 107 Courthouse in Waco in McLennan County, representing the neoclassical symmetry and Beaux-Arts style of many county capitols. Courthouses in this style provide a prominent setting and symbol for the whole community.

Figure 108 Courthouse in Edna in Jackson County. This example lacks some of the symbols and ornaments common to traditional designs, but retains the lawn, monuments, and generous set-back of the typical courthouse square. This sort of suburban plan was very popular in the 1950s.

Depression, however, and courthouse architecture reflected a more somber role.

During the thirties and early forties, most public building was the result of WPA-funded projects. Courthouses designed during this period were more modest in scale, but also hoped to project a public presence. They accomplished this by retaining symmetrical facades, formal siting, and attention to symbols and detail, but all in the idiom of modernism at the time, which featured streamlined design and art deco motifs. Travis County's courthouse in Austin is representative of this style (Figure 102), which still serves its community. The courthouse has undergone major renovations, but with little alteration of its architectural features.

Courthouses built after 1945 also relied on modern architecture, but with less desirable results when judged from the standpoint of the traditional public building, particularly as it relates to the courthouse. During the fifties and sixties, many courthouse designs favored a suburban look, much like a school campus, such as the one in Edna in Jackson County (Figure 108). Later courthouse architects, for reasons of economy and function, reduced set-backs, windows, and entrances to the street, which resulted in a loss of connection to the square and the community. There is little decoration or symbolic ornament or detail. An example of this kind of design is found in Bryan (Figure 105) and demonstrates a contemporary preoccupation with functional aspects of courthouses. This courthouse style approximates the appearance, and possibly the role, of a filing cabinet.

The relationships between built form, social activities, and symbols are deeply intertwined and difficult to assess. The point of including such a discussion in this analysis of the links between urban form and the centripetal role of the square is obvious: most of these features have been shown to focus attention on the square. The use of symbolic architecture, placement of monuments, and enactment of social rituals are not casual, unconnected events. They reflect long-held beliefs and traditions about the relationship of the individual to the community and the manifestation of those connections in the urban landscape.

Unlike earlier categories describing the urban morphology of the courthouse square, which are some of the most enduring patterns in the urban landscape, the categories presented here—predominant, codominant, and subordinate—are mutable. That is, although some county seats did alter their block pattern at the square and thereby change morphological categories, the role of the square as interpreted in this analysis changes more easily. Given time and renewed emphasis, a subordinate square might become a predominant feature in its townscape, or a former predominant square might be challenged by other civic spaces in the community to become a codominant space. This ongoing, dynamic process represents a complex interaction that shapes the future role for the courthouse square, which in turn shapes its surrounding landscape, often resulting in the creation of one of the most conservative and durable features of the urban landscape.

Chapter Nine

Afterword

The traditional image of the courthouse square portrays an imposing, multistoried masonry structure set amid a tree-shaded lawn punctuated by bronze figures, granite markers, a comfortable gazebo, and a flagpole or two. This nostalgic vision is a reality in many county seats and traces its immediate roots to the nineteenth century, when so many counties and county seats were formed in Texas. The assumed timeless character of many squares, however, masks a process of tentative beginnings, maturation, decline, and transformation. Yet for all this change, the courthouse and its square remain one of the most enduring civic spaces in the urban landscape of Texas.

Casual observers of courthouse squares are likely to notice consistencies of plan and recognize that the square is often the central focus of the town. More recent observers would no doubt perceive the decline of some squares and revitalization of others. This study bears out many of these observations. However, it also reveals that there is great diversity represented in the form and role of Texas courthouse squares. No single factor assures the square a central role. Rather, the specific combinations of urban features may reinforce or retard the square's centripetal influence.

This study makes more explicit the connections between urban form and social meaning, specifically the form and function of civic space manifest in Texas courthouse squares. The square's centripetal role is defined as the ability to attract certain land uses, activities, and meanings. This centripetal influence is a primary characteristic of the traditional courthouse square. In general, a square that demonstrates and maintains this function or property becomes the central focus of its community and performs a predominant role. Squares that share aspects of their civic function are classified as codominant and those that perform a more peripheral part as subordinate. This analysis of the role and evolution of courthouse squares in the urban landscape of Texas has been documented in a number of specific contexts (Table 30).

Table 30. Influences on the Form and Role of the Courthouse Square

INFLUENCE	EFFECTS ON THE SQUARE
Spanish	Established use of grid pattern and open plaza. Established plaza's central location and public role. Placed major public buildings/activities at plaza.
Mexican	Opened Texas to increased foreign settlement. Reinforced use of grid and role of main plaza. Continued use of plaza for public buildings and activities.
Central European	Used grid-pattern plan for frontier settlements. Reinforced traditions of open main plaza with major public buildings and activities.
Anglo-American	Settled and established urban landscape of Texas. Introduced central courthouse square based on models developed in colonial America that focused major buildings and activities at square. Placed courthouse on central square. Prescribed central location and role of county seats.
Urban form	Traditional courthouse squares used block patterns focused on central square reserved for courthouse. Nontraditional patterns often placed courthouse at main plaza or other prominent locations, such as railroad depot.
Land use	Central business district focused land use at courthouse square, such as banks, commercial establishments, and mixed land uses.
Social activities	Early use of courthouse as community center. Public ceremonies and events held on square. Reinforced social meaning and civic role of square.
Architecture	Reinforced public role and prominence of square. Provided focus and symbolic center of community.

Several conclusions can be drawn from this research. The first is the remarkable endurance of the courthouse square and its influence on the surrounding urban landscape. Many of the town planners and surveyors who laid out Texas county seats came upon an undeveloped landscape. Just as importantly, they came equipped with mental templates as to the nature and design of the city. Town planning traditions in Texas, as in much of the frontier West, emphasized a reliance on the grid-pattern plan and prominent square. Hispanic, Anglo-American, and Central European traditions favored a special role for the public square or open plaza. With the coming of the courthouse, both the open plaza and central square became the focus of the county seat. In addition, each of these traditions had long-standing associations with the civic role of the square in terms of specific land use, activities, and symbols.

The urban forms of most Texas towns were based on the block patterns that many Anglo-Americans preferred. These featured central squares for the courthouse. The simplest and most prolific of these was the Shelbyville. However, given the complexity and diversity of the urban landscape in Texas, this study has proposed a number of new prototype squares. Foremost among these are courthouses positioned on a plaza and those influenced by the railroad. Again, the common element was a prominent location for the courthouse; but some of these schemes were more successful than others in providing a focus on the courthouse.

Courthouse squares shape land use and symbolic features. Comparisons of eight different land uses reveal specific relationships with the civic role and centripetal influence of the square. Based on site visits to 139 county seats, three categories of squares have been developed here: predominant, codominant, and subordinate. This analysis includes a number of factors in the evolution of the county seat, such as population, the role of the city hall, and the proliferation of government services and agencies clustered around the courthouse square.

The combination of such factors over time led to variations in the influence of many courthouse squares (Table 31). Many maintained their traditional form and role; others were modified in some degree, but retained aspects of their original function. Nontraditional patterns could also be supportive of a predominant role for the courthouse square. In other instances, the square developed specialized functions as a government, cultural, or civic center or became associated with churches or

Table 31. Aspects of the Square's Centripetal Influence

CHARACTER OF SQUARE	CENTRIPETAL INFLUENCE
Traditional Square	Characterized by traditional nineteenth-century land use with prominent courthouse and parklike square surrounded by community's central business district.
Modified Square	Exhibits many of same features and role as traditional square, but may include additional buildings on square, incomplete CBD, or modified block pattern.
Nontraditional Square	Maintains central role in community, but is based on block patterns evolved from other planning traditions, such as those with open plaza or railroad-influenced plan.
Government Center	Characterized by concentration of public buildings and functions, which may include city hall, post office, or state agencies, but typically dominated by other county offices. Reduced connnection to CBD.
Cultural or Civic Center	Characterized by concentration of public buildings such as library, local history museum, or civic center. May include church. Reduced connection to CBD.
Educational or Recreational Center	Associated with churches, schools, parks, and less intensive public or quasi-public spaces. Little relation to CBD.

schools. All of these represent a variation on the square's civic role in the community.

Land policies and county formation that occurred as the result of settlement and independence also formalized and codified the role of the courthouse square in Texas. There were legal requirements for centralized locations and an implicit recognition of the assumed dominance of the county seat in the urban hierarchy. More importantly, the institutionalizing of the county as the primary arm of government placed the courthouse in an unrivaled position in the community—a fact that was immediately recognized and acknowledged by siting the courthouse on the town's central square.

Another set of indicators of the courthouse square's centripetal influence and social meaning reveals intimate relationships between social activities and symbols at the square. Particularly relevant are the design of the courthouse itself and the placement of monuments and memorials. Past and present public events also raise awareness or strengthen ties to the square and its place in the life of the community. Analysis of these features has confirmed those symbols associated with traditional courthouse squares and described a process of redefinition for others in the context of today's urban landscape. Many of the patterns, features, and activities of traditional squares remain viable, as demonstrated by the large number that retain a predominant role in their communities, although changes in the urban landscape often challenge that role. A number of features reinforce a square's centripetal influence or, conversely, set in motion certain centrifugal forces (Table 32).

Table 32. Factors Associated with the Square's Influence

CENTRIPETAL INFLUENCE	CENTRIFUGAL INFLUENCE
Favors traditional block patterns	Block patterns vary
Close relationship to CBD	Removed from CBD
Typified by enclosure of storefronts	Little enclosure
Relationship to financial institutions	Little relationship
Relationship to mixed-use retail	Reduced relationship
Reduced relationship to churches	Increased relationship
Reduced relationship to residences	Increased relationship
Typified by parklike setting	Reduced parklike setting
Favors courthouse centered on square	Greater variance in siting
Favors courthouse set back on square	Greater variance in siting
Relationship to monuments	Reduced relationship
Relationship to traditional styles	More modern architecture
Population threshold of 100,000	100,000+ or below 1,000
More stable population	Rapid growth or decline
Concentric growth	Irregular growth
Connection to public spaces	More isolated

Afterword

In spite of the remarkable endurance of many courthouse squares, change in the urban landscape was inevitable. The move over the last century from central city cores, the rise of suburbia, and the advent of "edge" cities pose numerous threats to the continued influence of many courthouse squares. In small towns the effects of population decline, the abandonment of the square by local businesses in favor of the highway bypass, and the loss of community symbols are factors that diminish the influence of the courthouse square (Francaviglia 1996).

One of the more common sights on the outskirts of small-town America is the local mall. On most weekends the parking lots of these stores are full, while the square's older businesses remain quiet. Recognizing this trend toward decentralization and peripheral developments, some town leaders now offer incentives to national chains to locate downtown near the square (Daniels and Keller 1991).

Centrifugal forces in larger cities are similar, but aggravated by scale. Squares in these settings no longer accommodate all the needs of the community in terms of commerce or civic space. In most cases, towns with populations over 100,000 witness an erosion of the traditional functions of the square, which must share or limit aspects of its civic role. Many of these spaces develop special functions related to county government or other related public agencies. Interestingly, a square's symbolic function in terms of architectural presence or placement of monuments may be enhanced in these instances.

A deeper question posed by this study goes beyond whether or not civic space and architectural symbolism can make a community whole again: why are such solutions often no longer sought? The failure of today's city to engender a sense of community is in part because many no longer believe it is possible to achieve such community in real or symbolic terms. This cynicism, born out of justified concerns for the future, sees only a divisive pluralism with little common ground, both literally and figuratively.

The courthouse square, when it functions as intended, provides such common ground. The parklike square, its imposing courthouse, and surrounding streets and businesses serve as a gathering place and symbol of the community. Although such spaces may be regarded by many as either parochial or paternalistic in terms of their intent and impact, the lesson to be learned from these squares is their ability to create civic spaces with the potential for focusing the dominant values of the community.

The courthouse square was designed to inspire and reinforce traditions that reflect a common bond. While today's society must be more inclusive than in the past, the ability of civic space and architecture to represent values supportive of a sense of community remains worthy of study. However, this book is not a call to return to the past. Rather, there is very good reason to examine previously successful and familiar urban forms in light of present challenges and to apply their virtues for the benefit of future urban landscapes capable of renewing community.

Texts Counties

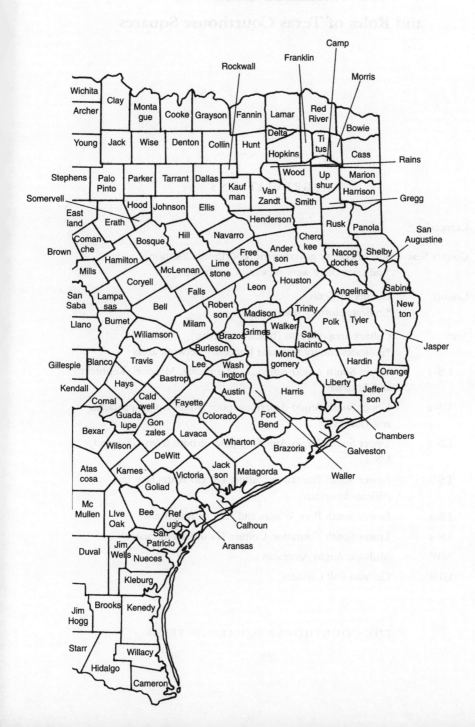

Appendix 2

Block Patterns, Features,
and Roles of Texas Courthouse Squares

ABBREVIATIONS

Categories

County Seat — Seat of county government (courthouse location)
*indicates there were previous county seats

County — County of Texas
*indicates former *municipio*

Area — Culture area of Texas (based on Jordan)
*indicates county seat near boundary between areas

US-1 — Upper South Anglo-American (Tennessee, Missouri, Kentucky, and Arkansas)

US-2 — Upper South Anglo-American (poor whites from Appalachia and Ozarks)

US-3 — Upper South Anglo-American (later groups from US-1 and US-2)

LS-1 — Lower South Plantation Culture (Anglo aristocracy and African-American)

LS-2 — Lower South Poor Whites and African-Americans

LS-3 — Lower South Plantation Culture (Louisiana influence)

MW — Midwest Anglo-American

GHC — German Hill Country

MIX	Mixed (Germans, Czechs, Wends, Poles, and LS-1, US-1, and SM)
SM	Spanish-Mexican
CH Square	Courthouse square typology *indicates special feature or change
CH Style	Courthouse architectural style *indicates more than one courthouse exists
Neo-1	Symmetrical without portico or columns
Neo-2	Symmetrical with portico and columns, without dome or tower
Neo-3	Symmetrical with portico, columns, and dome or tower
Ecl-1	Neoclassical elements dominant, combined with others
Ecl-2	Victorian or Romanesque elements dominant, combined with others
Ecl-3	Combination of elements, none dominant
Mod-1	Symmetrical, built 1900–1920s, sometimes similar in appearance to Neo-1
Mod-2	Depression-era buildings, 1930s–1940s
Mod-3	Contemporary, 1950s to present
Land Use	Special features adjacent to square or courthouse
B	Banking/financial institution
C	Church
F	Funeral home
G	Government building (federal, state, county, or city)
GS	Gas station
GZ	Gazebo (typically on square)
H	Historical district or traditional square and storefronts
HR	High-rise building (five or more stories)
HT	Hilltop (prominent)
L	Library or historical museum (may be on square)
M	Marker, monument, or memorial (typically on square)
O	Office (only)
P	Public park or space
PK	Parking lot

Block Patterns, Features, and Roles of Texas Courthouse Squares

R	Residential
RO	Retail and office
RR	Railroad
S	School (private or public)
V	Vacant land
X	Other
Role	Role of courthouse square
Pre	Predominant role (central focus of community)
Cod	Codominant role (shares focus of community)
Sub	Subordinate role (not central focus of community)
?	Unknown role (unvisited or no current data available)

Typological Classifications (Patterns)

S	Shelbyville (includes classic pattern and variants)
H	Harrisonburg (includes classic pattern and variants)
L	Lancaster (includes classic pattern and variants)
2B	Two-Block (includes classic pattern and variants)
4B	Four-Block (includes classic pattern and variants)
HB	Half-Block (courthouse site occupies one-half of a block)
QB	Quarter-Block (courthouse site occupies one-quarter of a block)
IB	Irregular-Block (courthouse sited on or next to irregular block)
P	Plaza (courthouse next to open plaza or square)
RR	Railroad (courthouse square influenced by railroad)
R	Related Pattern (block pattern closely related to a prototype)
UNC	Unclassified (not classified by previous researchers)

Typological Classifications (Suffixes)

A	Additional buildings/annexes associated with courthouse
I	Incomplete, undeveloped, or relocated CBD at courthouse
M	Modified plan either in street pattern or in building location
*	Indicates significant feature

COUNTY SEAT	COUNTY	AREA	CH SQUARE	CH STYLE	LAND USE	ROLE
Abilene*	Taylor	US-2	S (M) (?)	Mod-3	?	?
Albany	Shackelford	US-2	S (I)*(?)	Ecl-2	?	?
Alice	Jim Wells	SM	S (I)	Ecl-3	C,G,PK,R, RO,V	Cod
Alpine	Brewster	SM	S (A,I,M)	Ecl-3	C,F,G,L,R,RO	Pre
Amarillo	Potter	US-3	S (A,I,M)	Mod-2	B,G,HR,O,PK	Cod
Anahuac*	Chambers	LS-3	P-R (I)	Mod-2	G,P,O,R,V	Cod
Anderson	Grimes	LS-1	L (I,M)	Ecl-3*	G,HT,RO,V	Pre
Andrews	Andrews	US-3	S (A,I,M)	Mod-2	B,G,M,PK,R, RO	Pre
Angleton*	Brazoria*	LS-3	S/2B (A,I,M*)	Mod-2,3*	C,G,PK,RO,S	Pre
Anson	Jones	US-3	H (?)	Neo-3	?	?
Archer City	Archer	US-3	S (Other) (?)	Ecl-2	?	?
Aspermont*	Stonewall	US-3	P (?)	Mod-3	?	?
Athens*	Henderson	LS-1	S	Neo-3	?	?
Austin	Travis	MIX	P (A,I,M*)	Mod-2	B,G,GZ,HR, L,P,O,R	Cod
Baird*	Callahan	US-2	H (A,I,M*) (?)	Mod-1	?	?
Ballinger	Runnels	US-2	2B (A,I)	Neo-1	C,P,R,RO	Pre
Bandera	Bandera	US-2	S (A,I)	Neo-3	C,G,HT,L,M, R,RO,V	Pre
Bastrop	Bastrop	MIX	S (A,I,M*)	Neo-3	C,O,R,V	Sub
Bay City*	Matagorda*	LS-3	S	Mod-3	B,G,RO	Pre
Beaumont*	Jefferson*	LS-3	2B-R (A,I,M*)	Mod-2*	G,HR,PK,X	Cod
Beeville	Bee	LS-3	S (I)	Neo-3	B,GZ,M,PK, R,RO,V	Pre
Bellville*	Austin	MIX	H (M)	Mod-3	B,C,G,HT,L, PK,RO	Pre
Belton	Bell	MIX	S (I)	Neo-2	C,G,HR,O	Sub
Benjamin	Knox	US-3	S (I)	Mod-2	G,GS,V,X	Pre
Big Lake*	Reagan	US-3	H (A,I)	Mod-1	G,L,O,R	Sub
Big Spring	Howard	US-3	S (?)	Mod-3	?	?

Block Patterns, Features, and Roles of Texas Courthouse Squares

COUNTY SEAT	COUNTY	AREA	CH SQUARE	CH STYLE	LAND USE	ROLE
Boerne	Kendall	GHC	P (Other) (A,I,M)	Ecl-2	G,GS,L,O, PK,R	Sub
Bonham*	Fannin	US-1	S (A) (?)	Mod-2,3	?	?
Boston*	Bowie	US-1	S-R (A,I) (?)	Ecl-2	?	?
Brackettville	Kinney	SM	IB (A,I) (?)	Neo-3	?	?
Brady	McCulloch	US-2	2B (M)	Ecl-2	B,G,M,PK,RO	Pre
Breckenridge	Stephens	US-2	S (?)	Neo-2	?	?
Brenham*	Washington	MIX	S	Mod-2	B,G,RO	Pre
Brownfield	Terry	US-3	S (?)	Mod-1	?	?
Brownsville*	Cameron	SM	S (I) (?)	Neo-2	?	?
Brownwood	Brown	US-2	S (Other) (?)	Neo-2	?	?
Bryan*	Brazos	LS-1	RR-R (I,M)	Mod-3	G,GS,O,PK, RO	Sub
Burnet	Burnet	US-2	S (I) (?)	Mod-2	?	?
Caldwell	Burleson	MIX	S	Mod-1	B,G,HT,RO	Pre
Cameron*	Milam*	MIX	S (?)	Neo-2	?	?
Canadian	Hemphill	MW	S (A,I) (?)	Ecl-3	?	?
Canton*	Van Zandt	US-1	S-R (I) (?)	Mod-2	?	?
Canyon	Randall	US-3	S-R (A,I,M*)	Neo-1/ Mod-3*	B,P,PK,R, RO,V	Pre
Carrizo Springs	Dimmitt	SM	S	Mod-1	B,G,GS,R,RO	Pre
Carthage*	Panola	LS-1	S-R (M) (?)	Mod-3	?	?
Center	Shelby	LS-1	S (M) (?)	Ecl-2	?	?
Centerville*	Leon	LS-1	S (A,I)	Neo-1	G,GS,GZ,RO	Pre
Channing	Hartley	US-3	RR (A,I,M)	Neo-2	R,RR,V	Sub
Childress	Childress	US-3	S (?)	Mod-2	?	?
Clarendon*	Donley	US-3	S (?)	Ecl-2	?	?
Clarksville*	Red River	US-1	S (?)	Ecl-3	?	?
Claude	Armstrong	US-3	S (I)	Neo-2	B,G,PK,RO,V	Pre
Cleburne*	Johnson	US-1	S (Other) (?)	Ecl-3*	?	?
Coldspring	San Jacinto	LS-1	S (I)	Neo-2	B,GZ,PK,R, RO,V	Pre

COUNTY SEAT	COUNTY	AREA	CH SQUARE	CH STYLE	LAND USE	ROLE
Coleman*	Coleman	US-2	H-R (?)	Mod-3	?	?
Colorado City	Mitchell	US-3	RR-R (?)	Neo-2	?	?
Columbus	Colorado	MIX	S (I)	Neo-3	B,H,M,R,RO	Pre
Comanche*	Comanche	US-2	S (?)	Mod-2	?	?
Conroe	Montgomery	LS-1	S (A)	Mod-3	B,RO	Pre
Cooper	Delta	US-1	S (?)	Mod-2	?	?
Corpus Christi	Nueces	SM	S/P-R (A,I,M)	Neo-2/ Mod-3*	G,HR,O,P,PK	Sub
Corsicana	Navarro	US-1	S (I)	Neo-3	C,F,G,O,PK,R	Sub
Cotulla*	La Salle	SM	P (I,M)	Mod-2	C,G,GS,HT,L, P,R,RO,V	Pre
Crane	Crane	US-3	S-R (A,I) (?)	Mod-3	?	?
Crockett	Houston	LS-1	S (?)	Mod-2	?	?
Crosbyton*	Crosby	US-3	P-R (A,I,M*)	Neo-2*	B,G,GZ,L,P	Cod
Crowell	Foard	US-3	S (A) (?)	Mod-1	?	?
Crystal City*	Zavala	SM	S (A,I)	Mod-3	C,G,R,RO,S	Sub
Cuero*	DeWitt	MIX	S (I,M)	Ecl-2	B,C,F,G,O,R	Sub
Daingerfield	Morris	LS-1	RR (?)	Mod-3	?	?
Dalhart*	Dallam	MW	RR-R (I)	Mod-1	B,G,L,RO	Pre
Dallas	Dallas	US-1	S/P (I,M*)	Ecl-2/ Mod-3*	G,HR,M,O, P,PK	Cod
Decatur	Wise	US-2	S (?)	Ecl-2	?	?
Del Rio	Val Verde	SM	IB (A,I) (?)	Neo-2	?	?
Denton*	Denton	US-2	S (Other) (?)	Neo-3	?	?
Dickens	Dickens	US-3	S (A,I)	Neo-1	G,L,P,R,V	Pre
Dimmit	Castro	US-3	S*(?)	Mod-2	?	?
Dumas	Moore	US-3	S (?)	Mod-2	?	?
Eagle Pass	Maverick	SM	RR-R (?)	Ecl-3/ Mod-3*	?	?
Eastland*	Eastland	US-2	S (I) (?)	Mod-1	?	?
Edinburg	Hidalgo	SM	4B/2B (M*)	Mod-3	B,C,G,GS, M,P,PK,RO	Pre

Block Patterns, Features, and Roles of Texas Courthouse Squares

213

COUNTY SEAT	COUNTY	AREA	CH SQUARE	CH STYLE	LAND USE	ROLE
Edna*	Jackson*	LS-3	RR (A,I,M)	Mod-3	B,GS,RO,RR	Pre
Eldorado	Schleicher	US-3	4B (A,I,M)	Neo-2	B,C,G,GS,L, R,RO,X	Pre
El Paso*	El Paso	SM	IB (?)	Mod-1	?	?
Emory	Rains	US-1	S*(?)	Neo-3	?	?
Fairfield	Freestone	LS-1	S (A)	Neo-2	B,G,M,RO	Pre
Falfurrias	Brooks	SM	RR-R (I) (?)	Neo-2	?	?
Farwell	Parmer	US-3	4B/2B (A,I,M*)	Mod-1	C,O,P,PK,R, S,V	Pre
Floresville*	Wilson	MIX	S (A,I,M)	Neo-3	B,G,GS,PK,R, RO,V	Pre
Floydada	Floyd	US-3	S (A)	Mod-3	B,GZ,L,RO	Pre
Fort Davis	Jeff Davis	SM	P-R (I)	Neo-3	B,C,G,GS, P,R,V	Sub
Fort Stockton	Pecos	SM	P (A,I,M)	Neo-2	C,G,L,M,O, PK,V	Sub
Fort Worth*	Tarrant	US-1	2B/P (I,M*) (?)	Neo-3	?	?
Franklin*	Robertson	LS-1	H (?)	Ecl-1	?	?
Fredericksburg	Gillespie	GHC	P-R (A,I,M*)	Ecl-2/ Mod-2*	B,F,G,L,P, PK,R,RO	Pre
Gail	Borden	US-3	S (A,I) (?)	Mod-2	?	?
Gainesville	Cooke	US-1	S (?)	Neo-3	?	?
Galveston	Galveston	LS-3	P (A,I,M*)	Mod-3	C,G,HR,M, O,P,PK	Cod
Garden City	Glasscock	US-3	S (A,I)	Neo-2	C,GS,P,R,V	Pre
Gatesville	Coryell	US-2	S (?)	Neo-3	?	?
George West*	Live Oak	LS-3	RR-R (A,I)	Neo-2	B,G,M,PK, R,RO	Pre
Georgetown	Williamson	US-2	S	Neo-3	B,G,H,L,RO	Pre
Giddings	Lee	MIX	S (I)	Ecl-2	B,C,G,GS,O, R,RO	Sub
Gilmer	Upshur	LS-1	2B-R (?)	Mod-2	?	?
Glen Rose	Somervell	US-2	S*(?)	Ecl-3	?	?
Goldthwaite	Mills	US-2	S (?)	Neo-2	?	?

COUNTY SEAT	COUNTY	AREA	CH SQUARE	CH STYLE	LAND USE	ROLE
Goliad	Goliad*	MIX	H (I)	Ecl-2	B,G,H,L,RO	Pre
Gonzales	Gonzales	MIX	P (A,I,M*)	Ecl-2	B,C,G,GS,M, P,PK,RO	Pre
Graham*	Young	US-2	2B-R (A,M*)	Neo-2	B,C,F,G,M, PK,RO	Pre
Granbury	Hood	US-2	S	Ecl-3	B,C,GZ,H,L, PK,RO	Pre
Greenville	Hunt	US-1	S (I) (?)	Mod-1	?	?
Groesbeck*	Limestone	LS-1	S-R (I,M*) (?)	Neo-2	?	?
Groveton*	Trinity	LS-1	2B (A,I,M)	Neo-2	B,C,G,GS,R, RO,V	Pre
Guthrie	King	US-3	IB (A,I,M)	Ecl-1/ Mod-3*	GS,R,V,X	Sub
Hallettsville*	Lavaca	MIX	S	Ecl-2	B,G,PK,RO	Pre
Hamilton	Hamilton	US-2	S	Neo-3	B,G,GS,L,RO	Pre
Haskell	Haskell	US-3	S (M) (?)	Neo-2	?	?
Hebbronville	Jim Hogg	SM	S (A,I) (?)	Mod-1	?	?
Hemphill*	Sabine	LS-1	S (A)	Neo-2	B,G,RO	Pre
Hempstead	Waller	LS-1	H (A,I,M*)	Mod-3	G,R,RO,X	Sub
Henderson	Rusk	LS-1	L (Other) (?)	Mod-1	?	?
Henrietta*	Clay	US-3	S (?)	Neo-3	?	?
Hereford*	Deaf Smith	US-3	S (A,I,M)	Neo-2	B,L,PK,RO	Pre
Hillsboro	Hill	US-1	S	Ecl-3	B,G,H,HT, PK,RO	Pre
Hondo*	Medina	GHC*	P-R (A,I,M*)	Neo-2	B,C,G,PK,RO	Sub
Houston	Harris	LS-3	S/P-R (I)	Neo-3/ Mod-3*	G,HR,O,P,PK	Cod
Huntsville	Walker	LS-1	S (M)	Mod-3	B,C,G,PK,RO	Pre
Jacksboro	Jack	US-2	S-R (I,M) (?)	Mod-2	?	?
Jasper	Jasper*	LS-2	S (A)	Ecl-3	B,G,GZ,RO	Pre
Jayton	Kent	US-3	4B (?)	Mod-3	?	?
Jefferson	Marion	LS-1	S-R (A,I,M*) (?)	Neo-2	?	?
Johnson City*	Blanco	US-2	S (I)	Neo-3	B,G,PK,R,RO	Pre

Block Patterns, Features, and Roles of Texas Courthouse Squares

COUNTY SEAT	COUNTY	AREA	CH SQUARE	CH STYLE	LAND USE	ROLE
Jourdanton*	Atascosa	SM	L (I,M)	Ecl-3*	O,PK,V	Sub
Junction	Kimble	US-2	S (I)	Mod-1	B,G,R,RO,V	Pre
Karnes City*	Karnes	MIX	2B-R (A,I,M*)	Ecl-2	C,G,GS,H,M, PK,R,RO,V	Pre
Kaufman*	Kaufman	US-1	S-R (M) (?)	Mod-3	?	?
Kermit	Winkler	US-3	S (I) (?)	Neo-2	?	?
Kerrville	Kerr	US-2	S (A,I)	Mod-1	B,C,F,G,GS, HR,PK,V,X	Sub
Kingsville	Kleberg	SM	2B/H (A,I,M*)	Neo-2	G,M,O,P,R,V	Cod
Kountze*	Hardin	LS-2	RR-R (I)	Mod-3	G,O,PK,R,V	Sub
La Grange	Fayette	MIX	S	Ecl-2	B,M,RO	Pre
Lamesa	Dawson	US-3	S (?)	Mod-1	?	?
Lampasas	Lampasas	US-2	S	Ecl-2	B,G,GZ,H, PK,RO	Pre
Laredo	Webb	SM	S (A,I,M*)	Ecl-3	B,G,O,P,PK	Sub
Leakey	Real	US-2	S (A,I,M)	Neo-1	R,RO,V	Pre
Levelland	Hockley	US-3	S (I) (?)	Neo-2	?	?
Liberty	Liberty*	LS-3	P-R (A,I,M*)	Mod-2	B,G,PK,RO	Cod
Linden*	Cass	LS-1	S*(?)	Neo-2	?	?
Lipscomb	Lipscomb	MW	RR-R (?)	Neo-2	?	?
Littlefield*	Lamb	US-3	RR-R (A,I,M*)(?)	Mod-3	?	?
Livingston	Polk	LS-1	RR (A,I,M)	Neo-2	G,R,RO,RR,V	Pre
Llano	Llano	US-2	S (A,M)	Ecl-2	B,G,L,PK,R, RO,V	Pre
Lockhart	Caldwell	MIX	S	Ecl-2	B,G,PK,RO	Pre
Longview	Gregg	LS-1	S-R (I)*(?)	Mod-2	?	?
Lubbock	Lubbock	US-3	2B (?)	Mod-3	?	?
Lufkin*	Angelina	LS-1	S (A)	Mod-3	G,PK,RO	Pre
Madisonville	Madison	LS-1	S	Mod-3	B,C,G,RO	Pre
Marfa*	Presidio	SM	H (I)	Ecl-2	C,G,R,RO	Pre
Marlin	Falls	MIX	S (?)	Mod-2	?	?

COUNTY SEAT	COUNTY	AREA	CH SQUARE	CH STYLE	LAND USE	ROLE
Marshall	Harrison	LS-1	L (Other) (?)	Ecl-2/ Mod-3*	?	?
Mason*	Mason	GHC*	2B (A,M)	Neo-3	B,G,M,PK,RO	Pre
Matador	Motley	US-3	S (I)*(?)	Mod-2	?	?
McKinney*	Collin	US-1	S (?)	Neo-2/ Mod-3*	?	?
Memphis	Hall	US-3	RR-R (?)	Neo-2	?	?
Menard	Menard	US-2	P-R (A,I,M*)	Mod-2	C,P,PK,R, RO,V	Pre
Mentone*	Loving	US-3	S (I) (?)	Mod-2	?	?
Meridian	Bosque	MIX	S (?)	Ecl-3	?	?
Mertzon*	Irion	US-3	S (A,I)	Mod-2	C,G,HT,R,V	Sub
Miami*	Roberts	US-3	RR-R (?)	Neo-2	?	?
Midland	Midland	US-3	P-R (I)	Mod-2,3	B,HR,M,O, P,PK,X	Pre
Monahans*	Ward	US-3	QB (?)	Mod-2	?	?
Montague	Montague	US-2	S*(?)	Neo-2	?	?
Morton	Cochran	US-3	S (I)	Mod-3	B,G,RO	Pre
Mount Pleasant	Titus	US-1	S (M) (?)	Mod-3	?	?
Mount Vernon	Franklin	US-1	P (A,I) (?)	Neo-3	?	?
Muleshoe	Bailey	US-3	S (A,I)	Mod-1	B,G,L,PK, R,RO	Pre
Nacogdoches	Nacogdoches	LS-1	P/HB (I)	Mod-3	C,GS,PK,RO	Sub
New Braunfels	Comal	GHC	P (A,M)	Ecl-2	B,G,GZ,P,RO	Pre
Newton*	Newton	LS-2	S (A,I)	Ecl-2	B,GS,GZ, M,RO	Pre
Odessa	Ector	US-3	S (?)	Mod-3	?	?
Orange	Orange	LS-3	RR (A,I) (?)	Mod-2	?	?
Ozona	Crockett	US-3	P (A)	Ecl-3	B,C,F,G,HT, L,PK,RO	Pre
Paducah	Cottle	US-3	S (?)	Mod-2	?	?
Paint Rock	Concho	US-2	S (I,M)	Ecl-2	GS,R,RO,V	Pre
Palestine*	Anderson	LS-1	S-R (?)	Neo-3	?	?

Block Patterns, Features, and Roles of Texas Courthouse Squares

217

COUNTY SEAT	COUNTY	AREA	CH SQUARE	CH STYLE	LAND USE	ROLE
Palo Pinto	Palo Pinto	US-2	S (I)*(?)	Mod-2	?	?
Pampa	Gray	US-3	P-R (M*) (?)	Mod-1	?	?
Panhandle	Carson	US-3	S (I,M)	Mod-3	C,M,P,R	Sub
Paris	Lamar	US-1	S (A,I) (?)	Neo-2	?	?
Pearsall	Frio	SM	P-R (A,I,M*)	Mod-1	C,G,L,P,R,S,V	Sub
Pecos	Reeves	US-3	S (?)	Ecl-1	?	?
Perryton*	Ochiltree	MW	S (I,M) (?)	Mod-1	?	?
Pittsburg	Camp	LS-1	HB (A,I) (?)	Mod-1	?	?
Plains	Yoakum	US-3	2B-R (A,I,M)	Mod-3	B,L,P,R,RO,S,V	Pre
Plainview	Hale	US-3	S (A,I) (?)	Ecl-3	?	?
Port Lavaca*	Calhoun	LS-3	S (I)	Mod-3	G,O,R,RO,V	Sub
Post	Garza	US-3	H-R (A,I,M) (?)	Mod-1	?	?
Quanah*	Hardeman	US-3	S (M) (?)	Ecl-3	?	?
Quitman	Wood	LS-1	2B-R (?)	Neo-2	?	?
Rankin*	Upton	US-3	S (I,M)	Mod-3	HT,O,PK,R,V	Sub
Raymondville*	Willacy	SM	S (A,I,M)	Neo-2	C,F,G,O,PK,R,V	Pre
Refugio	Refugio	SM	P (A,I,M*)	Mod-1	G,L,M,O,P,R,V	Cod
Richmond	Fort Bend	LS-3	S (A,I,M)	Neo-3	G,HR,L,R	Pre
Rio Grande City	Starr	SM	H (I,M*)	Mod-2	C,G,HT,M,P,PK,R,S	Cod
Robert Lee*	Coke	US-3	S (A,I)	Mod-3	B,G,P,R,RO	Pre
Roby	Fisher	US-3	S (A,I) (?)	Mod-3	?	?
Rockport	Aransas	LS-3	S (A,I,M)	Mod-3	C,G,O,R,RO,V	Sub
Rocksprings*	Edwards	US-2	S-R (A,I,M) (?)	Neo-1	?	?
Rockwall	Rockwall	US-1	S (?)	Mod-2	?	?
Rusk	Cherokee	LS-1	S (?)	Mod-2	?	?
San Angelo*	Tom Green	US-3	HB (I)	Neo-2	B,C,G,HR,O,RO	Cod
San Antonio	Bexar*	SM	P (A,I,M*)	Ecl-2	C,G,HR,P,PK,RO,X	Cod

COUNTY SEAT	COUNTY	AREA	CH SQUARE	CH STYLE	LAND USE	ROLE
San Augustine	San Augustine*	LS-1	S (A)	Neo-2	B,G,GZ,RO	Pre
San Diego	Duval	SM	P-R (A,I)	Ecl-3	F,G,GS,P,PK, R,RO	Cod
San Marcos	Hays	MIX	S	Neo-3	B,G,RO	Pre
San Saba	San Saba	US-2	S (?)	Neo-3	?	?
Sanderson	Terrell	SM	S (A,I,M) (?)	Ecl-3	?	?
Sarita	Kenedy	SM	RR (I,M)	Mod-1	G,P,R,RR,V	Pre
Seguin	Guadalupe	MIX	P	Mod-2	B,C,G,HR,M, P,RO	Pre
Seminole	Gaines	US-3	S (A)	Mod-1,3	B,G,GS,RO	Pre
Seymour	Baylor	US-3	S (I)	Mod-3	B,RO	Sub
Sherman	Grayson	US-1	S (?)	Mod-2	?	?
Sierra Blanca	Hudspeth	SM	RR (A,I) (?)	Ecl-3	?	?
Silverton	Briscoe	US-3	S (A,I)	Mod-1	B,G,GS,GZ, M,PK,RO,V	Pre
Sinton*	San Patricio*	SM	RR/S (I,M)	Mod-1	C,GS,O,R,X	Sub
Snyder	Scurry	US-3	S (A,I) (?)	Mod-3	?	?
Sonora	Sutton	US-3	H-R (A,I,M)	Ecl-2	C,G,HT,R, RO,V	Pre
Spearman*	Hansford	MW	RR-R (A,I,M)	Mod-2	B,C,G,PK,RO	Pre
Stanton	Martin	US-3	S (A,I) (?)	Mod-3	?	?
Stephenville	Erath	US-2	S	Ecl-2	B,G,H,M,RO	Pre
Sterling City	Sterling	US-3	S (A,I)	Mod-2	B,G,GS,L,R, RO,V	Pre
Stinnett	Hutchinson	US-3	S (A,I)	Mod-1	B,C,G,GS,HT, R,RO,V	Pre
Stratford*	Sherman	MW	S (A,I)	Neo-2	C,R	Sub
Sulphur Springs	Hopkins	US-1	P (A,M) (?)	Ecl-2	?	?
Sweetwater	Nolan	US-3	S (?)	Mod-3	?	?
Tahoka	Lynn	US-3	H-R (?)	Neo-2	?	?
Throckmorton	Throck- morton	US-3	QB (I)	Ecl-3	G,GS,R,RO	Pre

Block Patterns, Features, and Roles of Texas Courthouse Squares

COUNTY SEAT	COUNTY	AREA	CH SQUARE	CH STYLE	LAND USE	ROLE
Tilden	McMullen	LS-3	S (A,I,M)	Ecl-3	B,G,GS,R, RO,V	Pre
Tulia	Swisher	US-3	S (A,I) (?)	Mod-3	?	?
Tyler	Smith	LS-1	2B (?)	Mod-3	?	?
Uvalde	Uvalde	SM	P (M*)	Neo-2	B,G,P,PK,RO	Pre
Van Horn	Culberson	SM	S (A,I,M) (?)	Mod-3	?	?
Vega*	Oldham	US-3	S (A,I)	Mod-1	B,G,R,RO,V	Pre
Vernon	Wilbarger	US-3	S (?)	Neo-2	?	?
Victoria	Victoria*	LS-3	P (A,I)	Ecl-2/ Mod-3*	B,C,G,HR,M, O,P,PK,RO	Pre
Waco	McLennan	MIX	P-R (A,I,M*)	Neo-3	B,C,G,HR,O, P,PK,RO	Cod
Waxahachie	Ellis	US-1	S	Ecl-2	B,G,H,L,RO	Pre
Weatherford	Parker	US-2	4B (M)	Ecl-2	B,G,PK,RO	Pre
Wellington	Collings- worth	US-3	S (?)	Mod-2	?	?
Wharton	Wharton	LS-3	S	Ecl-3	B,G,M,RO	Pre
Wheeler*	Wheeler	US-3	S (I)*(?)	Neo-2	?	?
Wichita Falls	Wichita	US-3	S (A,I,M) (?)	Mod-3	?	?
Woodville	Tyler	LS-2	S (A,I,M)	Ecl-3	B,C,GS,L,R, RO	Pre
Zapata	Zapata	SM	P (I,M*)	Mod-3	B,G,GZ,HT, P,R,V	Pre

A Note on Sources and Methods

Many sources had to be consulted to complete the morphological classification of Texas' courthouse squares. No single archival source holds this information. As a result, information had to be gathered from large statewide archival collections, state government agencies, local historical collections, local government agencies, and field surveys.

A major source of documentation was the collection of Sanborn Insurance Company Maps housed at the Center for American History located in Austin on the University of Texas campus. Previous research also depended upon these primary source materials, as they provide detailed information on block patterns, land uses, and buildings for many nineteenth- and twentieth-century communities. The Sanborn maps offer varying degrees of coverage for more than two hundred Texas county seats. These maps were updated periodically by Sanborn's agents, enabling today's researcher to chart changes in a community building by building and block by block. This elaborate recordkeeping, some of which dates to the 1880s, provided valuable data on the urban morphology of courthouse squares as well as the evolution and transformation of specific squares. Yet, for all their detail, the Sanborn Company's maps are only two-dimensional representations and are incomplete. Most mapping ended in the 1950s, and by that time revisions were not recorded with the same detail as in earlier versions. Since some fifty or more county seats in Texas were never mapped by the Sanborn Company, additional sources and methods of data collection were necessary to complete classification for all county seats.

Additional archival sources involved the State of Texas Archives and Library, Texas Historical Commission, and General Land Office of

Texas. Information gathered included maps, original town plats, photographs of the courthouses and squares, and county histories. Other material found in the Eugene C. Barker Texas History Collections of the Center for American History included documents in vertical files on Texas towns and newspaper collections. These data provided a record of social events and celebrations associated with the squares as well as documentation of changes in the built form of the square.

Fieldwork was necessary to supplement the archival coverage and to describe sites never before classified. This work took place over a two-year period, but was concentrated in the months of December 1990 and January, February, and March 1991. The fieldwork documented 139 county seats. Over 7,500 miles of travel was divided into ten separate excursions that totaled more than thirty days in the field. Photographic documentation of selected sites included more than 2,000 slides and print images.

Field surveys were used to note ground plans and important adjoining urban spaces; to photograph the courthouse, square, and other significant buildings; and to collect archival materials, such as county maps and town plats. Note was made of each square's street patterns, land use, building types, and significant monuments. On-site inspection recorded additional features, such as gazebos, courthouse architecture, monuments and memorials, and community bulletin boards. Also noted were the location of the central business district and the vitality of the square and surrounding properties. Visits to local archival collections yielded original town plats in county clerks' files. In some instances, additional materials were collected that documented social activities, both formal and informal, focused on the squares. These data on street patterns, land use, and activities were necessary to determine those elements that either reinforce or undermine the centripetal role of the square. This resulted in the compilation of a database for all 254 county seats (Appendix 2).

Bibliography

Agnew, J. A., J. Mercer, and D. E. Sopher, eds. 1984. *The city in cultural context*. Winchester, Mass.: Allen and Unwin.

Aikins, D. B., et al. 1971. *The square: Descriptive and predictive modeling of central courthouse square towns in the South Central United States*. National Science Foundation Student Originated Studies, No. GY-9142. University of Oklahoma College of Environmental Design.

Anderson, G. S., Jr. 1968. The courthouse square: Six case studies in Texas: Evolution, analysis, and projections. Master's thesis, School of Architecture, University of Texas at Austin.

Arbingast, S. A., et al. 1976. *Atlas of Texas*. Austin: Bureau of Business Research, University of Texas at Austin.

Arreola, D. D. 1992. Plaza towns of south Texas. *Geographical Review* 82: 56–73.

Baker, T. L. 1979. *The first Polish Americans: Silesian settlements in Texas*. College Station: Texas A&M University Press.

Balfours, A. 1990. *Berlin: The politics of order, 1737–1989*. New York: Rizzoli.

Benevolo, L. 1981. *The history of the city*. Translated by G. Culverwell. Cambridge, Mass.: MIT Press.

Benjamin, G. G. 1974. *The Germans in Texas*. Austin, Tex.: Jenkins Publishing Co., 1910. Reprint by the author (page references are to reprint edition).

Biesele, R. L. 1928. The history of the German settlements in Texas, 1831–1861. Ph.D. dissertation, University of Texas at Austin.

Brasseaux, C., G. R. Conrad, and R. W. Robinson. 1977. *Courthouses of Louisiana*. University of Southwestern Louisiana Architecture Series, No. 1. LaFayette: Center for Louisiana Studies.

Braunfels, W. 1988. *Urban design in western Europe: Regime and architecture, 900–1900*. Translated by K. J. Northcott. Chicago: University of Chicago Press.

223

Broadbent, G., ed. 1980. *Meaning and behavior in the built environment*. New York: Wiley Interscience.

Burns, R. S. 1978. *100 courthouses: A report on North Carolina judicial facilities*. Raleigh: School of Design, North Carolina State University.

Buttimer, A., and D. Seamon, eds. 1980. *The human experience of space and place*. New York: St. Martin's Press.

Carroll, H. B. 1943. *Texas county histories: A bibliography*. Austin: Texas State Historical Association.

Carter, H. 1983. *An introduction to urban historical geography*. London: Edward Arnold Publishers.

Chipley, S. K. 1985. Plazas and squares of Texas: An analysis of the design evolution of the Texas courthouse square and its urban context. Master's thesis, University of Texas at Arlington, Department of Landscape Architecture.

Clay, G. 1980. *Close-up: How to read the American city*. Chicago: University of Chicago Press.

Conger, R. N. 1945. *Highlights of Waco history*. Waco, Tex.: Hill Printing and Stationery Co.

Connor, S. V. 1951. The evolution of county government in the Republic of Texas. *Southwestern Historical Quarterly* 55: 163–199.

Conzen, M. P. 1977. The maturing urban system in the United States: 1840–1910. *Annals of the Association of American Geographers* 67: 88–108.

Conzen, M. R. G. 1981. *The urban landscape: Historical development and management*. London: Academic Press.

———. 1988. Morphogenesis, morphological regions and secular human agency in the historic townscape, as exemplified by Ludlow. In *Urban historical geography: Recent progress in Britain and Germany*, edited by D. Denecke and G. Shaw, 253–272. New York: Cambridge University Press.

Cosgrove, D. 1984. *Social formation and symbolic landscape*. London: Croom Helm.

Cotner, R. C. 1973. *Texas cities and the Great Depression*. Austin: Texas Memorial Museum.

Coursey, C. 1962. *Courthouses of Texas*. Brownwood, Tex.: Banner Print.

Craig, L., and the Staff of the Federal Architecture Project. 1977. *The federal presence: Architecture, politics, and symbols in United States government building*. Cambridge, Mass.: MIT Press.

Creighton, J. A. 1975. *A narrative history of Brazoria County*. Angleton, Tex.: Brazoria County Historical Commission.

Crouch, D. P., D. J. Garr, and A. I. Mundigo. 1982. *Spanish city planning in North America*. Cambridge, Mass.: MIT Press.

Cruz, G. R. 1988. *Let there be towns: Spanish municipal origins in the American Southwest, 1610–1810*. College Station: Texas A&M University Press.

Cummins, L. T., and A. R. Bailey, Jr., eds. 1988. *A guide to the history of Texas*. New York: Greenwood Press.

Cutrer, T. W. 1985. *The English Texans*. San Antonio: University of Texas Institute of Texas Cultures at San Antonio.

Daniels, T. L., and J. W. Keller. 1991. What do you do when Wal-Mart comes to town? *Small Town* 22, no. 2: 14–18.

Davies, C. S. 1986. Life at the edge: Urban and industrial evolution of Texas, frontier wilderness—frontier space, 1836–1986. *Southwestern Historical Quarterly* 89 (April): 443–554.

Day, J. M. 1964. *Maps of Texas 1527–1900: The map collection of the Texas State Archives*. Austin, Tex.: Pemberton Press.

Demangeon, A. 1962. The origins and causes of settlement types. In *Readings in cultural geography*, edited by P. Wagner and M. Mikesell, 506–516. Chicago: University of Chicago Press.

Domosh, M. 1987. Imagining New York's first skyscrapers, 1875–1910. *Journal of Historical Geography* 13: 233–248.

Doxiades, C. A. 1968. *Ekistics: An introduction to the science of human settlements*. New York: Oxford University Press.

Duncan, J. S. 1976. Landscape and the communication of social identity. In *The mutual interaction of people and their built environment*, edited by A. Rapoport, 391–401. The Hague: Mouton.

Dupree, H. 1968. The pace of measurement from Rome to America. *Smithsonian Journal of History* 3, no. 3: 19–40.

Flannery, J. B. 1980. *The Irish Texans*. San Antonio: University of Texas Institute of Texas Cultures at San Antonio.

Francaviglia, R. V. 1973. County seat centrality as a regional trait. *Geographical Survey* 2, no. 2: 1–21.

———. 1996. *Main street revisited: Time, space, and image building in small-town America*. Iowa City: University of Iowa Press.

Frantz, J. B., and M. Cox. 1988. *Lure of the land: Texas county maps and the history of settlement*. College Station: Texas A&M University Press.

Fulmore, Z. T. 1915. *The history of geography of Texas: As told in county names*. Austin, Tex.: Steck Publishing Co.

Galvez, Bernardo de. 1951. *Instructions for governing the interior provinces of New Spain*. Translated by D. E. Worcester. Berkeley, Calif.: Quivira Society.

Gammel, H. P. N. 1898. *The laws of Texas, 1822–1897*. Vol. 6. Austin, Tex.: Gammel Book Company.

Georgetown Heritage Society. 1987. *Georgetown*. Georgetown, Tex.: Georgetown Heritage Society.

Glazer, N., and M. Lilla, eds. 1987. *The public face of architecture: Civic culture and public spaces*. New York: Free Press.

Goeldner, P. K. 1970. Temples of justice: Nineteenth century county courthouses in the Midwest and Texas. Ph.D. dissertation, Columbia University.

Goodsell, C. T. 1988. *The social meaning of civic space: Studying political authority through architecture.* Lawrence: University Press of Kansas.

Gregory, D., and J. Urry, eds. 1985. *Social relations and spatial structures.* New York: St. Martin's Press.

Gutheim, F. 1981. *The federal city: Plans and realities.* Washington, D.C.: Smithsonian Institution Press.

Handler, A. B. 1983. *The American courthouse: Planning and design for the judicial process.* Chicago: American Bar Association. Original ed., Ann Arbor, Mich.: Institute of Continuing Legal Education, 1973.

Hardoy, J. E. 1978. European urban forms in the fifteenth to seventeenth centuries and their utilization in Latin America. In *Urbanization in the Americas from its beginnings to the present,* edited by Sol Tax, 215–248. The Hague and Paris: Mouton Publishers; Chicago: Aldine.

Harris, J. B. 1972. *Urban Texas: Past—present—future.* A report prepared for the Texas Urban Development Commission, Arlington.

Harris, M. 1953. *Origin of the land tenure system in the United States.* Ames: Iowa State College Press.

Harvey, D. 1985. *Consciousness and the urban experience.* Oxford: Basil Blackwell.

Hatcher, M. A. 1927. *The opening of Texas to foreign settlement, 1801–1821.* Bulletin No. 2714: April 8, 1927. Austin: University of Texas.

Hines, R. M. 1986. Arkansas courthouses: Architectural style and tradition. Master's thesis, School of Architecture, North Texas State University.

Hitchcock, H., and W. Seale. 1976. *Temples of democracy: The state capitols of the USA.* New York: Harcourt Brace Jovanovich.

Hudson, J. C. 1982. Towns of the western railroad. *Great Plains Quarterly* 2, no. 1: 41–54.

———. 1985. *Plains country towns.* Minneapolis: University of Minnesota Press.

Jackson, C. C. 1996. Where is your county seat? A study of how Texas county seats were located. Master's thesis, University of Texas at Arlington, Department of History.

Jackson, J. B. 1980. *The southern landscape tradition in Texas.* Fort Worth, Tex.: Amon Carter Museum.

Jenkins, J. H. 1965. *Cracker barrel chronicles: A bibliography of town and county histories.* Austin, Tex.: Pemberton Press.

Johnson, H. A., and R. K. Andrist. 1977. *Historic courthouses of New York State: Eighteenth and nineteenth century halls of justice across the Empire State.* New York: Columbia University Press.

Jones, O. L., Jr. 1979. *Los paisanos: Spanish settlers on the northern frontier of New Spain.* Norman: University of Oklahoma Press.

Jordan, R. H., and J. G. Puster. 1984. *Courthouses in Georgia 1825–1983*. Norris, Ga.: Norcross.

Jordan, T. G. 1966. *German seed in Texas soil: Immigrant farmers in nineteenth-century Texas*. Austin: University of Texas Press.

———. 1967. The imprint of the upper and lower south on mid-nineteenth-century Texas. *Annals of the Association of American Geographers* 57 (December): 667–690.

———. 1970. The Texan Appalachia. *Annals of the Association of American Geographers* 60 (September): 409–427.

———. 1986. A century and a half of ethnic change in Texas, 1836–1986. *Southwestern Historical Quarterly* 89 (April): 385–422.

Jordan, T. G., J. L. Bean, Jr., and W. M. Holmes. 1984. *Texas: A geography*. Boulder, Colo.: Westview Press.

King, A. D. 1980. *Buildings and society: Essays on the social development of the built environment*. London: Routledge and Kegan Paul.

King, I. M. 1967. *John O. Meusebach, German colonizer in Texas*. Austin: University of Texas Press.

Kniffen, F. B. 1965. Folk-housing: Key to diffusion. *Annals of the Association of American Geographers* 55: 549–577.

Knox, J. 1991. Dealing with a volume chain store: Carroll, Iowa, guides development and protects its downtown. *Small Town* 22, no. 2: 19–23.

Knox, P. 1984. Symbolism, styles, and settings. *Architecture and Behavior* 2: 107–122.

Krampen, M. 1979. *Meaning in the urban environment*. London: Pion.

Kubler, G. 1978. Open-grid town plans in Europe and America. In *Urbanization in the Americas from its beginnings to the present*, edited by Sol Tax, 327–342. The Hague and Paris: Mouton Publishers; Chicago: Aldine.

Lich, G. E. 1981. *The German Texans*. San Antonio: University of Texas, Institute of Texan Cultures.

McKitrick, R. 1918. The public land system of Texas, 1823–1910. *Bulletin of the University of Wisconsin No. 905, Economics and Political Science Series 9*, no. 1: 1–172.

Machor, J. L. 1987. *Pastoral cities: Urban ideals and the symbolic landscape of America*. Madison: University of Wisconsin.

Mayo, J. 1988. *War memorials as political landscape: The American experience and beyond*. New York: Praeger.

Meinig, D. W. 1969. *Imperial Texas: An interpretive essay in cultural geography*. Austin: University of Texas Press.

———. 1986. *The shaping of America: A geographical perspective on 500 years of history: Vol. 1, Atlantic America, 1492–1800*. New Haven: Yale University Press.

Miller, T. L. 1972. *The public lands of Texas, 1519–1970*. Norman: University of Oklahoma Press.

Millon, R. 1967. Teotihuacán. In *Readings from Scientific American: Cities: Their origin, growth, and human impact*, edited by K. Davis, 82–92. San Francisco: W. H. Freeman and Co.

Nance, J. M. 1963. *After San Jacinto: The Texas-Mexican frontier, 1836–1841*. Austin: University of Texas Press.

Norton, P. F. 1977. *Latrobe, Jefferson and the National Capitol*. New York: Garland Publishing.

Ohman, M. M. 1982. Diffusion of foursquare courthouses to the Midwest 1785–1885. *Geographical Review* 72: 171–189.

Pare, R. 1978. *Courthouse: A photographic document*. New York: Horizon Press.

Pearce-Moses, R. 1987. *Photographic collections in Texas: A union guide*. College Station: Texas A&M University Press.

Peet, G., G. Keller, and R. J. Brink. 1984. *Courthouses of the commonwealth: Photographs*. Amherst: University of Massachusetts Press.

Perry, G. 1984. *Texas heritage series 1984 collection featuring nineteenth century courthouses*. Boerne, Tex.: Perry Enterprises.

Peveto, C. W. 1984. *Texas courthouses past and present: A bibliography*. Monticello, Ill.: Vance Bibliographies.

Pillsbury, R. R. 1968. The urban street patterns of Pennsylvania before 1815: A study in cultural geography. Ph.D. dissertation, Pennsylvania State University.

Price, E. T. 1968. The central courthouse square in the American county seat. *Geographical Review* 58: 29–60.

Radoff, M. L. 1960. *County courthouses and records of Maryland. Part One: The courthouse*. Publication No. 12. Annapolis: Maryland Hall of Records Commission.

Ragsdale, K. B. 1987. *The year America discovered Texas: Centennial '36*. College Station: Texas A&M University Press.

Rather, E. Z. 1904. De Witt's colony. *Texas State Historical Association Quarterly* 8, no. 2: 95–196.

Reed, St. Clair G. 1941. *A history of the Texas railroads and of transportation conditions under Spain and Mexico and the Republic and the State*. Houston: St. Clair Publishing Co.

Relph, E. 1987. *The modern urban landscape*. London: Croom Helm.

Reps, J. W. 1965. *The making of urban America: A history of town planning in the United States*. Princeton, N.J.: Princeton University Press.

———. 1969. *Town planning in frontier America*. Princeton, N.J.: Princeton University Press.

———. 1979. *Cities of the American West: A history of frontier urban planning*. Princeton, N.J.: Princeton University Press.

————. 1981. *The forgotten frontier: Urban planning in the American West before 1890.* Columbia: University of Missouri Press.

Riché, P. 1978. *Daily life in the world of Charlemagne.* Translated by J. A. McNamara. Philadelphia: University of Pennsylvania Press.

Robinson, W. B. 1972. The public square as a determinant of courthouse form in Texas. *Southwestern Historical Quarterly* 75: 339–372.

————. 1983. *The people's architecture: Texas courthouses, jails, and municipal buildings.* Austin: Texas State Historical Association.

Roemer, F. 1935. *Texas, with particular reference to German immigration and the physical appearance of the country.* San Antonio: Standard Printing Company.

Rowntree, L. B., and N. W. Conkey. 1980. Symbolism and the cultural landscape. *Annals of the Association of American Geographers* 70: 459–474.

Rykwert, J. 1976. *The idea of a town: The anthropology of urban form in Rome, Italy and the ancient world.* Princeton, N.J.: Princeton University Press.

Santos, S. A. 1979. *Courthouses of Bexar County, 1731–1978.* San Antonio, Tex.: Bexar County Historical Commission.

Schellenberg, J. A. 1987. *Conflict between communities: American county seat wars.* New York: Paragon House.

Schuyler, D. 1986. *The new urban landscape: The redefinition of city form in nineteenth-century America.* Baltimore: Johns Hopkins University Press.

Short, C. W., and R. S. Brown. 1939. *Public buildings: A survey of architecture of projects constructed by federal and other governmental bodies between the years 1933 and 1939 with the assistance of the Public Works Administration.* Washington, D.C.: Government Printing Office.

Speck, L. W. 1985. The hut, the temple, and the tower: Toward an American urbanism. In *Architecture for the emerging city,* edited by L. W. Speck, 6–25. New York: Rizzoli International.

Stanislawski, D. 1946. The origin and spread of the grid-pattern town. *Geographical Review* 36: 105–120.

————. 1947. Early Spanish town planning in the New World. *Geographical Review* 37: 94–105.

Stilgoe, J. R. 1982. *Common landscape of America, 1580–1845.* New Haven, Conn.: Yale University Press.

Taylor, V. H. 1969. *The Franco-Texan Land Company.* Austin: University of Texas Press.

Tyler, P. A., and R. Tyler. 1983. *Texas museums: A guidebook.* Austin: University of Texas Press.

Wagner, P. L., and M. W. Mikesell, eds. 1962. *Readings in cultural geography.* Chicago: University of Chicago Press.

Ward, D., ed. 1979. *Geographic perspectives on America's past: Readings on the* historical geography of the United States. New York: Oxford University Press.

Ward-Perkins, J. B. 1974. *Cities of ancient Greece and Italy: Planning in classical antiquity.* New York: George Braziller.

Warner, W. L. 1959. *The living and the dead: A study of the symbolic life of Americans.* New Haven, Conn.: Yale University Press.

Welch, J. R. 1984. *The Texas courthouse revisited.* Dallas: GLA Press.

Welch, J. R., and J. L. Nance. 1971. *The Texas courthouse.* Dallas: GLA Press.

Wheeler, K. W. 1968. *To wear a city's crown: The beginnings of urban growth in Texas, 1836–1865.* Cambridge, Mass.: Harvard University Press.

Whisenhunt, D. W. 1979. *New Mexico courthouses.* El Paso: Texas Western Press.

Whitehand, J. W. R. 1981. *The urban landscape: Historical development and management.* London: Academic Press.

———. 1987. *The changing face of cities: A study of development cycles and urban form.* Oxford: Basil Blackwell.

Wisseman, C. L., trans. 1971. *Festival edition for the fiftieth anniversary jubilee of the founding of the city of Fredericksburg.* Fredericksburg, Tex.: Fredericksburg Publishing Co.

Wood, J. S. 1991. "Build, therefore, your own world": The New England village as settlement ideal. *Annals of the Association of American Geographers* 81: 32–50.

Yoakum, H. 1935. *History of Texas from its first settlement in 1685 to its annexation to the United States in 1846.* 2 vols. Austin, Tex.: Steck Co., 1855. Reprint, New York: Redfield (a facsimile reproduction of the original 1855 ed.; page references are to reprint edition).

Zelinsky, W. 1951. Where the South begins: The northern limit of the cis-Appalachian South in terms of settlement landscape. *Social Forces* 30: 172–178.

———. 1990. The imprint of central authority. In *The making of the American landscape,* edited by M. P. Conzen, 311–334. Boston: Unwin Hyman.

Zucker, P. 1959. *Town and square: From the agora to the village green.* New York: Columbia University Press.

Index

Aachen, Germany, 140
Abbey of Saint Gall, 64–65
Abilene (Taylor County), 38, 142
Achteck, 140
Adelsverein, 135, 137, 138. *See also*
  Society for the Protection of
  German Immigrants in Texas
African-American subculture, 6, 7, 9.
  See also Lower Southern
  subculture
Aikins, D. B., 20, 21
Alamo, 125
Albany (Shackelford County), 38
Alberti, Leon Battista, 67
Albuquerque, New Mexico, 124
Alexandria, Virginia, 77
Alice (Jim Wells County), 38, 105,
  142, 160
Alpine (Brewster County), 38, 132,
  152, 157
Amarillo (Potter County), 38, 159,
  160, 164
Anahuac (Chambers County), 82,
  130; plaza square of, 83, 92–93,
  160, 166
Anderson (Grimes County), 58–59,
  153, 156

Anderson County, 44, 45
Andrews (Andrews County), 38, 152
Andrews County, 38, 152, 182, 183
Angelina County, 39, 142, 152
Angleton (Brazoria County), 46, 51,
  153, 155, 157
Anglo-American courthouse squares,
  123; compared to others, 80–81;
  features of, 84, 159; precedents of,
  63, 70–71, 75, 77–79; significance
  of, 61–62; types of, 18–23, 26,
  31, 151, 157, 167. *See also* four-
  block squares; Harrisonburg
  squares; Lancaster squares;
  Shelbyville squares; two-block
  squares
Anglo-American subculture, 6, 7, 10,
  13; influence of, 200, 201. *See also*
  Anglo-American courthouse
  squares
Annapolis, Maryland, 75
Anson (Jones County), 55
Appomattox Court House, Virginia,
  77
Aransas County, 39, 168
Archer City (Archer County), 43, 44
Archer County, 44

231

Arles, Frances, 66
Armstrong County, 39, 40, 152
Aspermont (Stonewall County), 83, 92
Atascosa County, 58, 60, 142, 168
Athens (Henderson County), 35
Austin, Moses, 130
Austin, Stephen F., 74–75, 132
Austin (Travis County), 16, 75; archi-
  tecture of, 188, 197; codominant
  square of, 159, 160, 161, 165;
  plaza square of, 83, 90; role of,
  187–190, 192, 193
Austin County, 55, 56, 153

Bahía, 6. *See also* Goliad
Bailey County, 39, 152
Baird (Callahan County), 55
Ballinger (Runnels County), 46, 142, 153
Bandera (Bandera County), 38, 152
Bandera County, 38, 152, 182
Bastrop (Bastrop County), 38, 130, 168, 171
Bastrop County, 38, 168
Bay City (Matagorda County), 35, 152, 153
Baylor County, 39, 168
Beaumont (Jefferson County), 46, 51, 159, 160, 164
Bee County, 38, 152
Beeville (Bee County), 38, 152, 182
Bell County, 38, 168
Bellville (Austin County), 55, 56, 57, 153, 156
Belton (Bell County), 38, 168
Benjamin (Knox County), 38, 152
Berlin, Germany, 134, 140
Bern, Switzerland, 134
Bevil (municipality), 16
Béxar, 6, 16. *See also* Bexar County; San Antonio

Bexar County, 83, 86, 160
Big Lake (Reagan County), 55, 142, 168
Big Spring (Howard County), 35
Blanco County, 39, 152, 186
Boerne (Kendall County), 168; plaza
  square of, 82, 83, 84, 97, 98
Bonham (Fannin County), 38
Borden County, 39
Bosque County, 35
Boston (Bowie County), 44
Bowie County, 18, 44
Brackettville (Kinney County), 117, 118–119
Brady (McCulloch County), 46, 153, 182, 183
Braunfels, Wolfgang, 64, 66, 67
Brazoria County, 46, 153
Brazos County, 18, 103, 106; two-
  block square in, 51, 168, 191
Breckenridge (Stephens County), 35
Brenham (Washington County), 35, 152, 153
Brewster County, 38, 142, 152
Briscoe County, 39, 152
Brooks County, 103, 106, 108
Brown County, 44
Brownfield (Terry County), 35
Brownsville (Cameron County), 38
Brownwood (Brown County), 43, 44
Bryan (Brazos County), 197; rail-
  road-influenced square of, 103,
  106, 107, 168, 191
Burleson County, 35, 152
Burnet (Burnet County), 38
Burnet County, 38

Caldwell (Burleson County), 35, 152, 153
Caldwell County, 35, 152
Calhoun County, 39, 168

Index

233

Index

235

square of, 118, 120, 121, 168,
191
Nacogdoches County, 82, 118, 120,
168
Navarro County, 39, 168
New Bern, North Carolina, 76
New Braunfels (Comal County),
136–138, 185; plaza square of,
82, 83, 84, 88–90, 137–138, 152,
155
Newcourt, Richard, 72–73, 75
New England, 77
New Spain, 124
Newton (Newton County), 39, 152
Newton County, 39, 152
New York, New York, 71
Nolan County, 35, 142
Nueces County, 83, 99, 168
Nuestra Señora de Guadalupe del
Paso, 125
Nuestra Señora de los Dolores de los
Ais, 125

Ochiltree County, 39
Odessa (Ector County), 35, 142
Oglethorpe, James, 70, 76
Oldham County, 39, 142, 152
Old Panama City, 128
Orange (Orange County), 103, 106,
111–113
Orange County, 103, 106, 111–112
"Ordenanzas de Descubrimiento,
Nueva Población y Pacificación de
las Indias, Dadas por Felipe II en
1573," 128
orthogonal plan, 143. See also rail-
road-influenced square
Ozona (Crockett County), 83, 84,
152, 155

Paducah (Cottle County), 35
Paint Rock (Concho County), 39,
41, 152
Palatine Chapel, Charlemagne's, 140
Palestine (Anderson County), 44, 45
Palo Pinto (Palo Pinto County), 39
Palo Pinto County, 39
Pampa (Gray County), 83, 93, 97,
142
Panhandle (Carson County), 39, 41,
142, 168
Panola County, 44
Paris (Lamar County), 39
Parker County, 46, 51, 53, 153
Parmer County, 46, 51, 52
Pearsall (Frio County), 142, 168;
plaza square of, 83, 97, 98
Pecos (Reeves County), 35, 142
Pecos County, 83, 168
Penn, William, 71–72, 75, 82
Perryton (Ochiltree County), 39
Philadelphia, Pennsylvania, 71–75,
132
Pittsburg (Camp County), 118, 120,
121–122
Plains (Yoakum County), 46, 153
Plainview (Hale County), 39
plantation culture, 9, 75. See also
Lower Southern subculture;
Upper Southern subculture
plaza squares: codominant, 160, 161,
165, 166; discussed, 23, 81–101,
137, 143, 201; examples of,
136–139, 165, 166; illustrated,
22; influences on, 82, 85, 89; list
of, 152; modified, 92–97; number
of, 24, 26–28, 30, 80; predominant, 153–154; related, 97–101;
role of, 101, 122, 128–133; subordinate, 168

San Augustine County, 39, 152
Sanderson (Terrell County), 39
San Diego (Duval County), 83, 97, 160, 166
San Diego, California, 124
San Felipe de Austin, 11, 55, 74–75, 130–132
San Francisco, California, 124
San Francisco de los Neches, 125
San Francisco de los Tejas, 125
San Jacinto County, 39, 152
San José de Nazones, 125
San Juan Bautista, 125
San Marcos (Hays County), 35, 152, 153
San Miguel de Linares de los Adaes, 125
San Patricio (municipality), 16
San Patricio County, 39, 142, 168
San Patricio de Hibernia, 130
San Saba (San Saba County), 35
San Saba County, 35
Santa Barbara, California, 124
Santa Fe, New Mexico, 124
Santa Fe de Granada, Spain, 127
Sarita (Kenedy County), 103, 106, 108–109, 153
Savannah, Georgia, 70, 76
Scamozzi, Vincenzo, 69
Schleicher County, 46, 51, 153
Schubert, Friedrich A., 139
Scurry County, 39
Seguin (Guadalupe County), 83, 84–85, 152, 155, 182
Seminole (Gaines County), 39, 152
Seymour (Baylor County), 39, 168, 191
Sforzinda, Italy, 69
Shackelford County, 38
Shelby County, 39

Shelbyville squares: codominant, 160; discussed, 20, 23, 32–46, 75, 201; illustrated, 19; lists of, 35, 152; number of, 24, 26–29; predominant, 151, 152, 153, 156; subordinate, 168
Sherman (Grayson County), 35, 168
Sherman County, 39
Sierra Blanca (Hudspeth County), 103, 106, 111, 113, 142
Silverton (Briscoe County), 39, 152
single-block squares, 155
Sinton (San Patricio County), 39, 105, 142, 168, 171
six-block squares, 20, 21, 24
Smith County, 46
Snyder (Scurry County), 39
Society for the Protection of German Immigrants in Texas, 135–138, 141
Socorro (mission), 125
Somervell County, 35
Sonora (Sutton County), 55, 57, 153, 156
Spain, 126, 127; and Texas immigration, 6, 77, 130. *See also* Spanish culture
Spanish culture: and courthouse squares, 77, 123–130, 200; compared to German, 135, 137. *See also* Spanish-Mexican subculture
Spanish-Mexican subculture, 10; courthouse patterns of, 26, 28, 55, 82, 85, 174. *See also* Hispanic subculture; Mexican subculture; Spanish culture
Spearman (Hansford County), 103, 104, 106, 111, 113, 115, 116, 142, 153
Stanton (Martin County), 39, 142
Starr County, 55, 160

Index

243

Victoria (Victoria County), 16, 82, 86–87, 130, 157; plaza square of, 83, 152, 155, 156, 157–158
Victoria County, 83, 152
Viesca (municipality), 16

Waco (McLennan County), 83, 84, 97, 99, 159, 160, 164, 196
Walker County, 39, 152
Waller, Edwin, 75, 90
Waller County, 55, 142, 168
Ward County, 118, 120, 142
Washington (municipality), 16
Washington County, 38, 152
Waxahachie (Ellis County), 35, 152, 153, 179
Weatherford (Parker County), 46, 51, 53, 153, 155
Webb County, 39, 168
Wellington (Collingsworth County), 35
Wharton (Wharton County), 35, 152, 153
Wharton County, 35, 152, 181, 182

Wheeler (Wheeler County), 39
Wheeler County, 39
Wichita County, 39
Wichita Falls (Wichita County), 39
Wilbarger County, 35
Willacy County, 39, 142, 152
Williamsburg, 75
Williamson County, 35, 36, 37, 150, 151, 152
Wilson County, 39, 142, 152
Winkler County, 39
Wise County, 35
Wood County, 46
Woodville (Tyler County), 39, 152
Wooldridge Park (Austin), 189–190

Yoakum County, 46, 153
Young County, 46, 51, 153

Zapata (Zapata County), 82, 86–87, 152, 155
Zapata County, 152
Zavala County, 39, 168
Zucker, Paul, 67–69